GW00689538

Voices
of
Independence

Voices
of
Independence

New Black Writing from Papua New Guinea

Edited by Ulli Beier

St. Martin's Press
New York

© University of Queensland Press, St Lucia, Queensland, 1980

St. Martin's Press, Inc., 175 Fifth Avenue, New York, N.Y. 10010
Printed in Australia
First published in the United States of America in 1980

Library of Congress Catalog Card Number 80- 10818

ISBN 0 312 85084 0

Contents

ix   Acknowledgements
xi   Papua New Guinea: The Voices of Independence
      by Ulli Beier

Autobiography

 3 Michael Somare
       Initiation
15 Somu Sigob
       The Story of My Life

Poetry

27 John Kasaipwalova and Ulli Beier (translators)
       Yaulabuta
34 Kama Kerpi
       Five Poems from *Call of Midnight Bird*
39 Hengenike Riyong
       Five Poems from *Nema Namba*
44 Russell Soaba
       Seven Poems from *Naked Thoughts*

Fiction

49 Iriye Diaya
       A Successful Marriage at Last!

54 Kama Kerpi
      Cargo
63 John Kasaipwalova
      Bomana Kalabus O Sori O!
79 Russell Soaba
      From *Wanpis*
93 John Kolia
      A Memo on Missionaries

Plays

113 Arthur Jawodimbari
       The Sun
129 Kumalau Tawali
       Chauka
147 Nora-Vagi Brash
       Which Way, Big Man?
165 John Kolia
       A Pair of Locks

165   1. The Locked-up Library
173   2. The Library of Locks

180 Albert Toro
       The Massacre
189 John Kasaipwalova
       The Naked Jazz

Essays

207 Kundapen Talyaga
       Should We Revive Initiation Rites in
       Enga Society?
215 Jacob Simet
       From a Letter to the Editor of *Gigibori*
218 Bernard M. Narokobi
       Art and Nationalism
224 John Waiko
       Komge Oro: Land and Culture or Nothing
230 Bernard M. Narokobi
       Towards a Melanesian Church
236 John Kasaipwalova
       Sopi

247 Glossary
249 Notes on Contributors

Acknowledgements

Thanks are due to *Kovave, Gigabori,* and to Jacaranda Wiley Ltd for permission to use the materials in this anthology as acknowledged on each opening page.

The drawings which appear at the beginning of each contribution were originally published in *Kovave Special: Modern Images from Nuigini.* The artists are: Taita Aihi (pages ix, 15, 27, 113), Marie Aihi (page 34), Akis (pages 93, 165, 189, 207), Georgina Beier (pages 54, 79, 215), Kavage (pages 3, 49, 63, 129, 147, 173, 180, 218), Kamban Lamang (pages 224, 230), and John Man (pages 39, 44, 236). For further information about these artists see *Modern Images from Niugini, Kovave Special Issue,* Jacaranda Press, 1974.

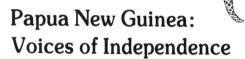

Papua New Guinea:
Voices of Independence

Black Writing from Papua New Guinea, which appeared in this series in 1973, documented the first phase of Papua New Guinean writing, beginning in 1968 with Albert Maori Kiki's autobiography and leading up to self-government in 1973. Those five years were a period of great optimism. Everybody sensed that the colonial period had come to an end. Papua New Guineans were at long last being heard. After a century of silent acceptance, the voice of protest rang out clear and hard, and the young writers — mostly students at the university and other tertiary institutions — felt that with their writing they were contributing towards political awareness and to the creation of a national identity. *Kovae, The Papua Pocket Poets* series and *New Guinea Writing* provided good outlets for the writers, and their work was also successful abroad. Jacaranda Press initiated a Pacific Writers series; Canberra's Prompt Theatre produced several PNG plays in Canberra and Sydney, and Kiki's autobiography was translated into German.

Since self-government, both the political and the literary climate have changed considerably. To the superficial observer it seemed at first that during the years between self-government and independence (which finally came in 1975) the writers "movement" had lost momentum and the writers, after their turbulent university years, were settling back into comfortable careers and had lost their literary ambitions. Such an assessment of the situation was made by several people at the Writers Conference organized by the Literature Department of UPNG in 1976.

However, this interpretation laid too much emphasis on the fact that some writers who had been prominent around 1970 had since ceased to write (only temporarily in many cases, as we learned later), and it ignored the fact that new young writers were springing up everywhere and that there was merely a change of emphasis and of outlets.

The 1968-73 generation of writers had used writing mainly as a political weapon. The achievement of self-government and, above all, independence meant not only that their immediate aim had been accomplished but that there was now, for the first time, an opportunity to go into action. And what young nationalist would not seize such an opportunity, be it on the national or on the village level? So we soon found John Kasaipwalova and John Waiko absorbed in village politics and village movements; Leo Hannett became absorbed in the Bougainville controversy. Others, like Vincent Eri and Rabbie Namaleu accepted major government positions and have simply become too busy to write. However, writers like Russell Soaba and Kumalau Tawali never ceased writing; Waiko and Kasaipwalova have started to write again, and completely new writers like Nora-Vagi Brash, Benjamin Umba, and John Kolia have appeared since independence.

Because the original emergence of writing was centred on the University of Papua New Guinea, many observers have erroneously concluded that because the university has produced very few writers in recent years, there has in fact been a decline of writing in Papua New Guinea. However, the scene has merely shifted from the university to other institutions — for example, the National Broadcasting Commission, the National Theatre Company, the Raun Raun Theatre, and the Institure of Papua New Guinea Studies.

The decline of the university's role is tragic, particularly in view of the fact that the Literature Department contained such brilliant staff as the Ugandan poet Taban lo Lyong, Dr Prithvindra Chakravarthi, and Elton Brash, and, more recently, three Papua New Guinean teaching fellows, including the poet Kumalau Tawali. However, morale in the university *as a whole* has been low. The university has been ruled with a heavy hand by the Ministry of Education. The secretary of education refers to the university as "our chief manpower training institution". Accordingly, most students are channelled into education courses. Subjects like economics are also considered respectable and — for some obscure reason — even "useful". The sciences are obviously encouraged, but subjects like literature, history, and political science are being regarded as both superfluous and potentially "dangerous". Staff have been reduced in all these subjects and student intake severely restricted (Only one student took creative writing during the first semester of 1978). There is even talk in the University Council and the Ministry of Education of abolishing the Arts Faculty altogether. In the meantime, the number of students who are allowed to take arts subjects is determined from outside the university (the total enrolment in the Arts Faculty in 1978 was only thirty-seven). Students can also be forced to change their course in midstream. Thus students who have been studying history or literature can be ordered to switch to education.

The government has also been extremely harsh on the students' desire to express political opinions. Some students lost their scholarships because they led demonstrations. After a relatively harmless demonstration protesting against the Indonesian invasion of East Timor, student leaders were forced to apologize to the Indonesian ambassador. Ironically, the colonial government had been more sympathetic to student political action.

Thus over the last two years the university has in fact degenerated from a university to a "manpower training institution" which has little room for or tolerance of creative activity. Not even the most gifted and enthusiastic staff have been able to counteract this trend.

Against difficult odds, publication of the Papua Pocket Poets series was kept going by Dr Chakravarthi all these years, though *Kovave* was allowed to collapse. With *Kovave* gone, and Don Maynard's *New Guinea Writing* being geared mainly towards schools by his successors, there were few outlets left for Papua New Guinean writers in the crucial years after self-government. Jacaranda Press, which had been so helpful in the early years, also lost its interest.

In these critical years it was the National Broadcasting Commission (or rather Peter Manau and Peter Trist in its production unit) who stepped into the breach and provided the major outlet for writers. The NBC, though grossly understaffed in its production department, has produced close to eighty radio plays by Papua New Guinea writers. It has provided encouragement, editing, and payment for writers. It has publicized writing and writers, and several new authors have emerged solely in response to the NBC. The NBC has also broadcast short stories, serialized novels, and provided work for readers and actors. During the last few years its contribution has been of the utmost importance, and if only it could be persuaded to pay professional fees to writers it could continue to play a leading role.

The National Theatre Company of Papua New Guinea, though extremely slow to get off the ground, has nevertheless stimulated people to write for it. In particular, the emergence of Nora-Vagi Brash and Albert Toro must be considered an important success of the company. By contrast the Raun Raun Theatre in Goroka uses no scripts at all. The company plays exclusively in Pidgin, addresses itself to village audiences and uses markets, "singsing" grounds, and schools as venues. While songs and dances are rehearsed, dialogue is largely improvised. This important group is continuing the tradition of oral literature in a modern context. It fulfils an important function in Papua New Guinea today and reminds us of the fact (as does the NBC) that the importance of the written word in Papua New Guinea should not be overestimated.

The Literature Bureau of the Department of Education has held annual writing competitions. These have also channelled modest sums of money into the hands of writers. On the whole, however, they have not produced new writers, prizes tending to be distributed among the established writers.

In recent years the Institute of Papua New Guinea Studies has emerged as a kind of publishing house for new Papua New Guinea writing. In this the institute has — deliberately — overstepped its brief. The institute is a research institute that records and analyses art, music, folklore, and oral history. It has been the main publisher of oral literature and history in recent years. But because of the absence of other publishers and because some leading writers (Russell Soaba and John Kolia) actually work there, the Institute has recently begun to publish fiction, poetry, and drama. Its current list includes two volumes of poetry, three novels, and fifteen radio plays.

Since independence there has been some change in the subject matter of Papua New Guinea writing and a shift towards different forms. The major concern with the question of cultural identity is still with us; but the simple act of self-assertion through auto-biography has become less necessary since independence. In fact, Michael Somare's *Sana,* published on Independence Day itself, has been the last autobiographical work of real importance. Questions of cultural identity have been explored in recent years through a number of essays, in which writers like Bernard Narokobi, Kundapen Talyaga, Jacob Simet, and John Kasaipwalova try to arrive at a firmer philosophical basis for the poetic emotions expressed in the late sixties. The sober examination of cultural issues by these writers since self-government has been a major contribution. There have been far fewer re-evaluations of the past. No work has been created in the mood of Arthur Jawodimbari's *The Sun* (the only work included here that dates from the period before self-government), though Albert Toro has embarked on a kind of Melanesian *Roots* in his *Sugar Cane Days* serial, and the poets Kama Kerpi and Hengenike Riyong have given us two very exciting interpretations of Chimbu culture and religion.

Political events have obviously made a critical examination of colonialism rather less relevant. Instead, there is already disillusionment with the national government; its conservatism, its easy acceptance of foreign business, its timid stand towards Indonesia, and the resultant "betrayal" of the West Irian freedom fighters. Above all there is disillusionment with the power-hungry bureaucracy and the increasing pompousness and Westernization of the so-called elite. Papua New Guinean writers have not been slow to take up these causes: John Kasaipwalova looks at the inability of the central government to communicate at a village level; Nora-Vagi Brash takes a critical look at the new elite and its mannerisms; John Kolia takes us away for the first time from the romantic presentation of village society (still somewhat evident in Tawali's *Chauka*) and introduces us to its violence and male chauvinism. So far the West Irianese cause has remained a taboo subject, partly because writers have little first-hand knowledge of the issues. John Kolia, the only writer who has visited Jayapura, came back with the startling discovery that in some cases the Irianese have been rather well integrated into the Indonesian structure. His collection of short stories on Jayapura will be published in a volume entitled *Traditionally Told.*

Only John Kasaipwalora has produced a play ("My Brother my Enemy") that is an outright attack on the Government's action against the West Irianese Freedom movement. The National Theatre Company has courageously toured PNG with that play.

The writers position has become more difficult and more ambiguous since independence. In the late sixties the young angry writers were seen as natural allies by Papua New Guinea's politicians. The writers then helped to form public opinion and politicl consciousness and exercised some influence on the stance of leading politicians. But now the government is sensitive to criticism, and many politicians fail to distinguish between issues and personalities. Writers on the whole have been tolerated rather than encouraged. There are few intellectuals in parliament, and the leaders of the nation are pragmatic men not given to ideologies. Many of the younger people have found the government un-inspiring and mildly unsympathetic to their own aims and ambitions, but they have themselves not espoused alternative political ideologies. Mostly the writers have seen themselves as social critics rather than political rebels. During the years since self-government many of them have taken an unsentimental look at their own communities, both rural and urban. The unflinching way in which many have learned to look at themselves is one of the healthiest symptoms of Papua New Guinean society today.

Ulli Beier

Autobiography

Michael Somare

INITIATION

Shortly after the Japanese had left Karau, the boys of my age group were brought together for our first initiation. This was a kind of qualifying test in which our courage and endurance were tried. No boy who failed the test would have been allowed to proceed to the real initiation.

The ordeal started with a day of fasting. We were given no food or drink all day. At about five o'clock in the afternoon we were taken down to the beach to be severely beaten. Ten of our elders formed a line. They stood with their legs wide apart about two yards from each other. They were dressed up in their feathers, and they were holding their lime gourds. We were made to crawl through their legs, and as we were passing through, the men lashed out at us with their lime sticks. Some, who were smoking, burnt us with glowing tobacco. Our mothers' brothers waited for us at the end of the line. They wanted to see how strong we were. They were singing:

When you live under your mother's leg
you do what you like,
you have what you want.
You ask for food,
you receive it.
You ask for water,
you receive it.

A chapter from *Sana; An Autobiography of Michael Somare* (Port Moresby: Niugini Press, 1975, distributed in Australia by Jacaranda Press, Brisbane).

You come and cry,
you want to eat a big fish,
your mother cooks it for you.
But now,
now, you come under your father's leg.
Now you pay
for being treated softly at home.
A new time begins for you
when you must know
that you will be a man.

We crawled through the legs as quickly as we would. We wanted to reach our uncles, who were there to save us. But our ordeal was not yet over. The worst was yet to come. The men had built a long, low beach shelter with leaves. This shelter had been filled with bees, ants, beetles — anything that bites. We were asked to crawl through the shelter. The most courageous boys went first and our uncles were there to receive us again. They grabbed us and threw us into the salt water. This made our wounds and bites sting even more. Our uncles wiped us down with *tapa* cloth. They pretended to cry and spoke to us with slight mockery:

Sorry my nephew,
sorry.
I wish you were in your mother's house.
What made you come here?
What made you come and suffer here?
Sorry my nephew,
sorry.

Then they took us to the *haus tambaran* where we were told about future initiations. They frightened us, but at the same time they instilled us with courage.

The next day we were taken into a specially fenced off place on the beach. We were each given a shield and five light spears cut from the branches of coconut trees. So that the impact would be slightly reduced, the sharpened point of the spear was wrapped with a pink flower that grows on the beach. We were made to throw spears against each other. All day long the fight went on. Most of us received some minor injuries.

On the evening of that day our parents had to feast those who beat us and those who protected us. The feasts were to thank them for helping their children through the first ordeal of initiation. My foster father, Saub, killed two pigs on that day.

My second test came some eighteen months later. I had spent a whole year in Wewak where I received some private instruction to prepare me for school. But when the time came for the important second initiation. I was sent home to participate.

Again we were made to fast. We were brought into the *haus tambaran*. It was the first time we had entered the secret meeting place of men. We had no water at all — only dry food and dry sago. Our throats were so parched that it became more and more difficult to eat this dry food. Only once a day would an old man bring down a coconut from a tree. We were to share the juice of only one nut between us. But this was not an ordinary drink. For a tiny bit of dirt was scraped from one of the most important *kakars* and mixed with the coconut juice. That drink was then called *ngaser*. It was a power drink — a drink that created a magic link between us and our ancestors. It was a drink that marked the beginning of a relationship with the ancestral spirits — a relationship that would grow closer and more intense the older we became.

We were now ready to confront the first important *brag,* or spirit ancestor, in the *haus tambaran.* The spirit of this initiation was known as *kairaba.* The spirit was represented by a dancing mask and was mounted on a frame of sticks. The long bamboo flutes were blown in the house, and the *timit* songs again prepared us for the hardships that would follow:

This is a big day for you.
You pleased yourself in your parent's house,
you did what you liked
But today is different,
today you will suffer.
Your ribs and stomach will suffer.

Then the real ordeal began. One by one we were dragged off and thrown across a large *garamut* drum. The men beat us with heavy, flat fighting sticks. They started beating our legs near the ankles and gradually worked their way up across our backs and up to our shoulders. Blood flowed freely. Our maternal uncles again acted as our defenders. They sang:

He is very close to me,
close to me,
and to my sister.
Don't be too harsh on him.
Have pity.
We are watching.
Remember
your turn is coming soon!

With these words they tried to restrain the men beating us. They reminded them that in another initiation it would be *their* nephews who would be beaten, and if they overdid things people might take their revenge then. My parents presented the uncles with two baskets of *galip* nuts for this service.

The following day we were taken to the beach. Our uncles washed us in sea water. They rubbed us with leaves and spoke incantations over us. Finally we were taken into a palm leaf enclosure to be circumcised.

Some days later, when we had somewhat recovered from the operation, we were painted, decorated, and dressed in new *tapa* cloths. Then we were taken in procession through the town. The women were excited: "Our boys are coming back!" they shouted. The mothers particularly were waiting proudly to see their sons. Again the parents presented food to those who had carried the responsibility for the initiation.

During the days of waiting in the *haus tambaran* we learned many things. We were told about our next initiation when we would meet *aram brag,* the water spirit, and would have to endure further ordeals with fire and water. We learned the names of the various *brags* who were dancing in the *haus tambaran*. We learned to recognize the tunes of the flutes. These were the tunes belonging to the various clans, the tunes for happiness, the tunes for sadness, and the tunes for fight. We learned how each important *kakar* had its own flute and each important man had his own flute. We learned to recognize the *garamut* rhythms identifying happiness, mourning and war. We learned that regular contact with the *brags,* our collective ancestors, gave a man strength and courage. The *brags* gave a man power to fight, power to make peace, power to change people's minds, and power to attract women. They would weaken one's enemy, confuse his mind and make him vulnerable.

We learned about our food taboos. No man was permitted to eat the animal of his canoe. My own canoe is the pig, and I still do not eat pork, though in ceremonies I can kill pigs for others to eat. We were given and taught our designs — the designs that, when we grew up, we were to use on canoe prows, spears, paddles, house posts and eating dishes. We were told legends and myths about the origins of animals and plants and about the origins of many of our customs. We learned the sacred songs that we were to sing for the *brags*. We were told that a strong man abstained from women. He who indulged in women and lived with his wives all the time would become weak, would be a poor fighter and vulnerable to his enemies. We were told that in marriage there was an exchange system that obliged us to give one of our sisters to the man whose sister we had married.

All these ordeals, the new knowledge that we had gained, and the ritual preparations had made us ready for manhood. We were now able to marry. We could marry girls who had been initiated and had received the sacred tattoo marks between their breasts.

I should have gone through my third big initiation a few years later, but at that stage of my life I was busy fighting my way through school, and my studies could not be interrupted. Nevertheless, I remained determined that some day I would perform the full rites.

For the time being I saw less and less of my village and my elders. I made sure, however, that I remained in contact; and whenever I got a chance to go home, I showed my respect to the elders, the keepers of tradition. I tried to show them that, wherever my career took me, I would still identify with them. I obeyed many old rules that my new way of life encouraged me to disrespect.

Only once did I break an important village rule, and even then I broke it with the consent of the elders. That was in 1971, when I became the first young man to be shown the sacred *kakar* images. Since I had become chairman of the museum board of trustees in 1969 my interest in these objects had grown. The more dealings I had with the national museum, the more I became aware that our country was being systematically plundered by artefact dealers. The best collections of Papua New Guinean art were to be found in Switzerland, Germany and America! Our own collection was relatively poor. As we discussed ways and means of protecting our artistic heritage, I became more and more anxious to be shown the *kakars*. I knew that some had already been stolen and there was a danger that more would disappear. I also had reason to fear that ,when the present *gapars* (priests) died, their successors might care less about the preservation of the sacred objects. I felt that it might be best to persuade the *gapars* to break an ancient rule and to let me see and photograph the objects. If that were done, there was at least a chance of keeping track of the objects and a hope that a stolen object might be traced.

I negotiated with the senior priests, Wino and Karok, for several months. Many other elders had to be consulted on the matter. I was helped by the fact that I proposed to make the trip with Ulli Beier, who, although an outsider, was at least of the right age group and therefore a little more acceptable. Nevertheless, there was long and severe argument. Some of the old men felt that the very structure of society would be destroyed by such an act. Others, including Wino himself, were more pragmatic. They argued that the system had already been disrupted and disturbed in numerous ways. They knew that the younger generation might never again become *gapars* and doubted whether in thirty years time anybody would be prepared to take on such an office. Wino thought that there was now a justification for showing the *kakars* to a younger man so that they could be photographed and their story preserved in writing.

We were finally given the date when a group of men from Darapap would come in a motor canoe to collect us in Wewak. They were going to travel all night and then pick us up in Wewak at seven o'clock in the morning. However, when we went down to meet them they had not arrived. We waited till midday, but there was no canoe. We thought they might have changed their minds or that maybe something was wrong with their engine. We became impatient with waiting and decided to rent a small motor boat. It took me several hours to find a boat and an engine. We then went to pick up a cousin who would help us to navigate the boat to Darapap. We finally set out rather late. It was nearly five o'clock, and it was clear to us that we would have to make a night trip. When we were almost to Cape Moem the boat developed engine trouble. We managed to get it going again, but the trouble recurred several times; and when we were opposite the army camp at Moem the engine finally refused to start. We had to drift ashore, tie the boat up, and beg the army to lend us a Land Rover to take us home.

We reached Wewak after dark to find that the canoe from Darapap had arrived! The old men laughed and chided me: "And who are you to think that when *we* tell you that we are coming to fetch you, you can set out on your *own* and succeed?" They did not seem at all surprised at our failure, since we had gone against their instructions. They told us they would take us to the village the next day, but they could not promise us that we would see the images. The elders wanted to hold another meeting with us before coming to a final decision.

It was growing dark when we arrived in Darapap after a stormy nine-hour trip. We were led to the men's house where the discussion was resumed. But all the arguments were suddenly resolved with the dramatic arrival of Wino. Night had now fallen, and we could neither see nor hear the old man coming up the steps behind us. But he had such magical presence that we sensed him there and instinctively turned around. He assessed us immediately and resolved the issue without further arguments. He sat down and soon declared that he would ask the *kakars* to come down for us the following morning. It was a night of intense ritual preparation for Wino and Karok. We were instructed to provide a dish of food and a basket of *galip* nuts the following morning.

If we were to be shown the *kakars,* it was necessary for the next *orob,* or age group, to see them at the same time. These were senior men in the community who had not made the *gapar* stage and consequently had not seen the objects. Ulli Beier, who was approximately the right age, was assigned to this *orob* for the day. I was much too young, but I was given the role of Ulli Beier's interpreter to justify my presence. The step taken by Wino and Karok was so unusual that it had to be rationalized in such a way. Tension could be felt among the younger men who had not been equally favoured.

The next morning we walked to the beach with our *orob.* We had to wait at a special place for the signal to be given. A fighting spear had been placed on the beach to warn all strangers that they should keep away. After some time an old man appeared from the grove and received our food gifts. We waited until the *gapars* in the grove had eaten the food. Then, finally, we were allowed into the presence of the *kakars.* They were lined up ceremonially in a long line, and next to them on the right were several long bamboo flutes. Wino and Karok, both wearing the *doatakin* hair band and heavy shell decorations, squatted on either side of the line. The atmosphere was indeed awe inspiring. We remained in complete silence. At last we were told we could take photographs. The flutes were blown. All the men were extremely serious, and the total impact of the scene in the grove was quite overpowering. When a slight rain began to fall we were told that the images had to be wrapped up and taken back to the *haus tambaran.*

I was aware of the seriousness of the occasion. Never before had this ancient rule been broken in the village. I could see that Wino and Karok were deeply moved by the event, but I did not, at the time, realize what a huge sacrifice the old men were making by allowing me to see the objects. Only later did they explain to me that these *kakars* were to be seen and handled only by the *gapars;* and whenever the time came for the next age group to be admitted into this rank the incumbent *gapars* had to retire. In order to show the images to us on this occasion, they had been forced to admit the whole age-group to which Ulli Beier had been temporarily attached, and this meant that they now had to go through with the entire ritual and initiate a new line of *gapars.* Wino and Karok handed all their power over to them. The day Wino and Karok showed us the images on the beach was the last day on which they handled the *kakars.*

Had we known the extent of the disruption we were to cause we could certainly not have proceeded with the ritual. We had not tried to pressure them in any way. Their willingness to go ahead with the unorthodox ritual betrayed a deep conviction that the world they represented was already lost. When the chief priest of such a powerful cult wants his secrets to be recorded, he has clearly lost confidence in its future. It is difficult to imagine how a man so disillusioned could be as powerful and as charged with magic and vision as Wino. But Wino had clearly understood that this might be the only way of creating some kind of link between the older and the younger generation.

It was not easy to imagine that Wino was no longer a *gapar,* that the *kakars* no longer spoke through him, and that he was no longer prophet, priest, and indeed ruler of the community. It was strange to think that he would have to say of himself: *"Mi stap nating".*

My third initiation should have taken place when I was sixteen or maybe seventeen years old. But it had to be postponed again and again because of my prolonged absence from the village. As I became more and more involved in politics — and particularly when I became the chief minister — many of the elders in my village began to doubt whether I would ever come home to complete my initiation. However, I was now, more than ever, determined to go through with the ceremony. As chief minister, it was particularly important that I should not separate myself from my people. It was now essential that I establish my identity at home and that I receive the wisdom and strength that my elders were willing to pass on to me from my forefathers.

At last, in December 1973, the initiation took place. The person in charge of the ceremony was my Uncle Saub. When my father, Ludwig Somare, was alive, he had specifically asked him to look after my initiation. Saub had three sons of his own: Akam, Abi and Maja. But it was to me and not to them that he passed on my grandfather's tile — Sana.

Saub had prepared eight pigs for the ceremony, and other uncles and aunts had contributed more. A total of sixteen pigs were killed for my initiation. As is the custom at Murik Lakes, the jawbones of these pigs were all tied on a string and hung up in the men's house. A pig's jawbones are a symbol of wealth and an historical record at the same time. After generations to come, people will still be reminded of the various initiations by the jawbones in the men's house.

It was not possible for me to carry out the ceremony exactly as it had been carried out some thirty or forty years ago. My other duties as chief minister made this impossible. It was impossible for me to go into isolation for three or four months before the ceremony. Instead, my isolation lasted only three days — a symbolic gesture rather than the real thing. During this period I was not allowed to see my family or friends. I was starved and given no water to drink. The only thing I was allowed to take was a little bit of very dry sago. I could see that in the old days the isolation period represented a considerable endurance test. Although I was not allowed to eat, I had to provide plenty of food for those who carried out the rituals. My relations brought this food to the men's house every day, and I had to watch my uncles eat their delicious meals. There were two other aspects in which the ceremony deviated from tradition. My ears and nose should have been pierced to hold the shell ornaments with which I was to be decorated. In the old days Veronica [Somare's wife] would also have had to take part in the ceremony. In a ritual re-enactment she would have symbolized the ancestral woman, Areke, who had given birth to the *kakar* images. Apart from these omissions the ritual was carried out faithfully and correctly in all aspects.

This was the first time in my life that I was admitted into the deepest part of the men's house where the images were kept. It was in that inner part of the house that I was given the history and ritual of the clan.

One of the first and most important ceremonies was called "the snake". I was surrounded by some ten or fifteen men holding a rope. The rope symbolized a snake — a large fighting snake. They were dancing around me, with the *orob* leading the way and representing the snake's head. Covered only with a small loincloth, I had to stand in the middle while the men tried to frighten me, beat me with sticks and burned my body with firebrands. It was an endurance test in which I had to prove that, as a leader of the clan, I would be brave, steadfast and willing to fight. My three little sons were brought into the house to watch this ritual. They stood watching outside the ring made by the snake. It was believed that some of the power of the fighting snake would also be transferred to them.

After the snake ceremony I was taught the *timit* songs. Only Saub knew these songs, and he had to repeat them ten times so that I could learn them. When the time for the *timit* songs had come Saub rose to his feet. There was silence. Then he ordered some of the floor boards to be taken out. During the singing we all sat around the hole in the floor spitting. It was believed that if we were to swallow our saliva during the singing of the *timit* songs we would forget them, or, even if we remembered them, they would not be effective. After the singing we had to wash our mouths with salt water to stop saliva from being produced for some time.

When we all sat round the hole, Saub said:

Now you have left your mother's womb.
You have come to this place to receive power.
With this power you must go out and lead—
lead in initiation, lead in fight, lead in peacemaking.
The strength now has been given to you.

After these words he began to sing. These songs were heard by all, but they were being passed on to me alone. Only I would be allowed to use them in the future. One of the *timit* songs goes as follows:

O ai oo ma moa gai oo
o cagao   ooo
ma moa gai o o.
Sh sh sh o o.
Ao o o makuma gao
o agai o o mokina gai o e e.
Ai o moana gai o agau o
mikuma gai o arao.

O I am in a pig's canoe,
I am in a canoe.
Sh sh sh o o.
I have become
a new spirit.
I am in a pig's canoe.

These incantations refer to the pig, which is my *canoe head* and the magic animal of my clan. The incantation is to enable the high-powered *gapar* spirit to enter the pig and act through it. The pig thus possessed becomes a symbol of the power of the clan.

When Saub had finished singing, I came out of the men's house and was taken home. Here I was made to sit on two bags of *galip* nut and was decorated with food — yams, coconuts, sweet potatoes and sago were hung on me like shells. Those of my uncles who were conducting the ritual of my initiation then came to pick that food off. It was another way of demonstrating my debt to them. By taking the food directly off my body they created another spiritual link between us. They then gave me a leaf containing lime, mustard and ginger to eat. It burnt my tongue severely. It was the last of the endurance tests.

At last I was dressed in all the magnificent ornaments of Sana. This beautiful decoration is known as *yamdar*. I wore a crown of bird-of-paradise feathers on my head, and on my fore head I wore the *doatakin* band. This was made of human hair and identified me as a senior *orob,* or ritual leader, of the community. Round my neck was a *tarer* — a band of dogs' teeth. A *numboag* covered my chest. This was *tapa* cloth studded with large mother-of-pearl shells. I wore armlets and wristlets covered with dogs' teeth. On my forehead and shoulders were *usigs* — pairs of pigs' tusks. These represent great wealth among my people. Perhaps the most spectacular ornament I wore was the *nemberan* — *a tapa* cloth apron on which a face had been embroidered with cowry shells. This face represented a *brag* — an ancestral spirit — and it symbolized the new power that was transferred to me in this ceremony. My insignia of office were a tall walking stick decorated with bird-of-paradise feathers, *usigs,* and a painted basket.

People now came to greet me and to celebrate my initiation with me. Some of my uncles jokingly stuck cockatoo feathers in my hair. These were called *kandapan.* Each feather was supposed to represent one adultery that they had committed. They joked and said, "Look, now that you are a chief and a clan leader you must show your strength in every way. If you are really a man you should be able to seduce four women, just as I have done."

The *yamdar* dress was not the only one I wore that day. I am not only the head of my family, I am also the head of Veronica's family. Because there was no senior man in her line, the important title of *onkau* was passed on to me. After wearing *yamdar* I was dressed up again with the regalia of *onkau.* This showed that I was the head of Veronica's family. *Onkau,* however, is not as important as *yamdar.*

Two days later I went to Wotam to be decorated by my mother's family. Here I was given the shells and decorations of *mindamot,* another important title. My mother's people felt that they wanted to have a part in the ceremony. They did not want it to be said that I was initiated and installed as chief but they had made no contribution. When I assumed the *mindamot* title, it strengthened the family link between us.

For me, the installation ceremony meant that I had again struck roots at home. Rather than remaining a floating city dweller I had been reintegrated with my clan, my family and my village. The wisdom of Sana, my grandfather, had been passed on to me together with his strength and his fighting spirit. Most important to me is the fact that Sana was the great peacemaker — the man who sat down to eat with his enemies before agreeing to fight them. He could not have passed on better wisdom to guide me in my job as chief minister of Papua New Guinea.

Somu Sigob

THE STORY OF MY LIFE

In 1933, when I was approximately sixteen years of age, I left home to attend a government school. There was only one government school then, and it was at Malaguna near Rabaul. So I arrived in 1933 and began school. I think I met two teachers from Manus. One was John Pusai and the other Piwen. They were the first two native teachers among other white teachers. I think the headmaster was Mr Gross. He became the director before retiring.

So I attended school until 1938, when I joined the New Guinea Police Force. I started as bandsman in the New Guinea Police Force Band with Mr Crawley. I was in the band from 1938 to 1940, when I was transferred to Wewak, for some white men there had formed a fighting group to fight against Germany. They were camped in Wewak, and I was transferred to that group of soldiers to be bugler in the camp. I was in Wewak until 1942, when Japan started bombing Rabaul. So I went with Mr Taylor to Aitape sub-district. I stayed in Aitape, and in 1942 Japan had already taken hold everywhere. I ran away with Mr Taylor.

I went through the bush to the middle of the Sepik, arrived at Angoram and stayed with a *kiap*, Mr Ellis. At that time Mr Ellis was a bit crazy and he got a group of policemen and fought against our group of policemen, including me, Mr Taylor and other Europeans

Recorded in Pidgin by students in the Department of History at the University of Papua New Guinea. Translated into English by Kakah Kais. Reprinted from *Gigibori* 2, no. 1 (April 1975): 32-36.

too. Perhaps he did not want us to leave the place and so created a big fight.

Some policemen ran away, and perhaps some Europeans too. I think a *kiap* from Maprik was shot and killed. Mr Taylor took me, and I came back to Wewak. I stayed in Wewak until Japan took it over, then I left Wewak and took to the bush, reached Maprik, came down the Sepik, then followed a tributary of the Sepik right up to Ramu. Following the Ramu I went up to Bundi, thence to Kundiawa in the Chimbu. That time we took the Catholic sisters and some Chinese and brought them all down to Bena Bena. Mr Taylor then told me to accompany the group down to Moresby. I accompanied them to Moresby and, I don't know, maybe they were sent to Australia.

I stayed in Moresby and joined. At that time there was no ANGAU [Australian New Guinea Administrative Unit] there was PAU or something like that. I stayed a short while and ANGAU was formed. So we brought groups of Hanuabadans who were leaving their village to a faraway place called Manu Manu, which was near Kairuku.

Oh yes, and I nearly forgot to tell about the time when I didn't have plenty of policemen with me and I looked after a group of Mekeos and Kikoris. I couldn't speak Motu, and I was scared because they were all big men and I was only a little policeman. They were all labourers, and, to make matters worse, I didn't know them too well. Still, I had to accompany them as they took the cargo to Bisiatabu while the trucks proceeded Kokoda way. Trucks transported food and ammunition forward, and when returning brought back the wounded soldiers.

We worked night and day. At one stage the Australian soldiers fired mortars, but they miscalculated the distance to the target, and, when the mortars exploded close to us, the labourers ran for their lives. It was real hard work. When they ran away they didn't head for Moresby but went through the bush until they reached their villages. Later the *kiaps* caught them, gave them some punishments and sent them back. I only stayed there for a month.

We had no water to drink, and making fire to cook was forbidden. Biscuits and canned meat were the only food we and all the soldiers had to eat. The soldiers looked after us very well. They worked hard to fight the Japanese as well as look after us, and we also toiled to carry the wounded, many of whom had broken arms, had lost their eyes or had intestines hanging out. We carried many of them, and some died on the way, while others managed to reach the hospital.

When we arrived at Kokoda rubber plantation, I went down with dysentery. During that time the labourers had to carry me as well as the soldiers. I couldn't walk. If I had walked, I could have died. I was about to die when I was sent to the native hospital on Gemo Island. So I was cured of the sickness. I didn't go back. While the fight went on I stopped at Hanuabada. I was really glad.

As for me, I didn't kill any Japanese. I saw the Japanese being shot and witnessed the Japanese shooting Australians, but for me, nothing. And I can say that during the war the Australian soldier was a very tough jungle fighter. I can criticize the Americans a little here. My judgment of the war is that the Americans were not good in the jungle. If some Japanese made a noise in the bush they wouldn't do like the Australians, who would scout until the Japanese were found and easily god rid of. No, they would pour ten thousand bullets into that area of the bush and destroy the surrounding vegetation. And then it would be discovered that there were only two Japanese. If the Americans were landing, they would fire at the landing area when they were still out at sea. After the area had been shelled clean out of vegetation they would then land. In the jungles of New Guinea — I don't know about other places — the Australian soldier was a real tough jungle fighter. I never saw an American who could equal him. Americans were only good at floating at sea, hammering their targets with big guns and causing devastation to places. That's my outlook on the war.

As for the Papua and New Guinea soldiers, they fought well, yes, but I am concerned about the fact that they were not well trained. They would just be shown how to use the trigger, align the foresight and the bull-sight, and, if they did everything right, they could hit the target on the bull's-eye, and oh! And so they could kill Japanese. That's all. I thought, well, never mind, just push out the enemy from our territory. Many won and many sold themselves as food to the Japanese. Luckily they did not know me.

Well, after moving around the fighting zones for a while, I came back and started a little training depot at Elevala to give some kind of training to policemen. After about only six months of its existence the Americans and Australians poured into the place. And they moved us out and we started a depot at an SDA [Seventh Day Adventist] rubber plantation at Bisiatabu. So we started the depot there, and I and two buglers from Manus — Kabui and Silibau — we three only were buglers. And we three buglers wanted to form a bugle band, but there was no drummer, so I just got the drums and played them anyway, even though no one had even taught me how to do it. There was no bass drum, only a side drum, but I had a go at it just to make the recruits happy to go on parades. And so we went on.

In 1943, I think, Mr Crawley arrived, and he saw me and said, "Oh, is it true that all your bandsmen have died and you are the only one living? I think we must get some young boys and train them as buglers." So we got some from Aroma and sent word to the *kiaps* in Rigo to get some young *mangi*, no not *mangi*, some young boys — *mangi* is a bad word. They arrived and we trained them in bugle. Later we started the band.

At this time I became a lance-corporal. I was a little happy now that I was *bosboi*. And so we started the band and I played a trumpet, but the trumpet mouthpiece was a little too small, and my neck was strained all the time. So, in the reshuffle, Master Crawley told me to play a trombone, and I played second trombone, but I reduced the length to naught as my hand was short. I was really good at putting the note straight, but sometimes, if it was a low note and I tried my best to reach the low sound, I could not return to the original note, for my arm was too short. So I quit this instrument, the trombone, and got another brass instrument. But I got tired of it because of too many solos.

The two brass instruments that I didn't like were the iphonom and solophonom [probably euphonium and, perhaps, solo euphonium]. I had to really carry the backbone of the music everytime. So I stayed on iphonom for a while before I became a drum major. This was really something. I was very happy because my eyes were not glued to music any more. I held the stick and led, chasing the flies while the rest of the band followed behind me. So I stayed as a drum major, and I was the best man at reading drum. And so the band master told me to conduct all drummers because I was the best drummer. I stayed just on drumming, and I wasn't on brass instruments any more.

So this band grew strong, and we went down to Australia and stayed in Brisbane. We did a kind of walk then, the meaning of which I don't really know. We used to play and march in the little towns in Victoria and New South Wales. In Victoria we stayed in a place for a week. And it was really bad. I nearly got cross with the bandmaster. He put us there for one week. That place was terribly cold. And we stayed in the zoo. We were each issued with nine blankets, and they were very heavy. So we played and marched to raise funds for the war. It was as if we were little pictures for putting money towards the war. We came back to Brisbane and stayed until the German war ended, then we returned to Moresby.

After returning to Moresby we built a big police training depot at Sogeri. We left Bisiatabu and went to Sogeri. By this time the war had ended, so the police force was divided. The Royal Papuan Police were stationed in Moresby, while the New Guinea Police Force was moved to New Guinea. The band was also divided, and I was made to act as bandmaster. So I got the New Guinea Police Force band in Lae, while Mr Crawley got the Papuan band and stayed in Sogeri.

I was stationed at Malahang Training Depot in Lae. We then moved to Rabaul and stayed at Tavui. Our depot used to be where the girls' secretarial school is now. We stayed there and they straightened everything. They said there was no Papua New Guinea; the two would have to be put together again. Too much hard work. The band moved to and fro, and I was tired already.

We left Rabaul and came back again to Moresby. But we did not join the Papuan band. My band was stationed at the headquarters in Konedobu. Mr Crawley's band was still stationed at Sogeri. At this time I was promoted to sergeant, second class. We stayed in Konedobu, and every afternoon we would exhaust ourselves marching up the hill to government house to lower the flag. I did not take much liking to this kind of fooling around.

Later, both bands were joined together again at Sogeri. So at this time I transferred to the depot as instructor and was promoted to sergeant, first class. I was instructor at the depot, and I was soon made regimental sergeant-major for the depot. I was a big man now and a little happy again. At this time I saw again the faces of all the old sergeants and corporals who used to give me something to think about. And I said, "This is my time now, your time has ended." I really taught them something. When they did not stand up straight I would put them in their right position, and some of them even shook under my anger, losing grip of their rifles. I was RSM at the Sogeri Police Training Depot for, I think, two years.

Then there was talk of setting up a new depot in Goroka. So I went up to Goroka with the now Superintendent Burns to set up the new depot. Sergeant-Major Christian Arek [later a sub-inspector], the brother of Paul Arek, took over my position and stayed in Sogeri. I went up to Goroka and stayed at the depot for two years before I was transferred to the town police and worked with Mr Holloway, who is now police commissioner in Konedobu. We set up the police station in Goroka. At that time Mr Downs was district commissioner at Goroka. I was transferred back to Moresby.

As I have said, I was getting tired of police work. You wouldn't be willing, but still they would send you like a mail bag here and there, and I had been in the police force about eighteen or almost twenty years and was beginning to get sick of the idea of transfer. Of course my time to finish was drawing near.

When I finished I didn't know anymore how to live differently. I went home and stayed there, doing nothing. I thought I would stay for a little while and then join the police force again. But a new council was started. So I was elected councillor and represented three villages in the Finschhafen council. I was later elected president of that council.

After I had spent a few years in the council there was talk of electing some people to the Legislative Council. So I thought, "I must try, whether I win or lose." I think the New Guinea coastal councils knew very well that I was a *maus wara* [a good talker], because every time there were combined meetings of representatives of all councils I dominated them. They believed in me, thinking "a good talker like him should get all our votes and win". I think this was what they thought. So I put in my name to stand for election to the Legislative Council. And I won.

So I represented three districts — Sepik, Madang, and Morobe. In Papua, John Guise represented the area extending from Milne Bay To Abau. A Daru man, Simoi Paradi, was elected to represent the area extending from Central to Daru. And Kondom represented New Britain. Nicholas Brokam represented Buka (Bougainville), Manus, and Kavieng (New Ireland). Some members were appointed by the government.

The time for us to talk was not like it is in the House of Assembly today. The government had the majority, and sometimes the appointed members did not believe anything. Sometimes, when we succeeded in swaying them, they would come on our side. But if we didn't succeed in swaying them they would side with the government, and we just wasted our breath without getting anything through. They defeated us almost every time. Sometimes, when I got very angry, I was the first one to talk out during the working session. Our speaker was Sir Donald Cleland. I think he got sick of my hot-headedness because whenever they talked about work I said, "It's no use, it's no use and who are we voting against? We are only six elected members, while you, the government, have the majority. We must just talk and let it die." I wasted my time for nothing, voting, so I used to leave my seat and go out. I knew we could not win. Maybe we were bad. During that time I was appointed a DO [district officer].

I later accompanied the Australian delegation to New York. It was thought that Papua should not go. New Guinea could go and sit at the back during the talks on New Guinea at the United Nations conference. So I was appointed. I was appointed the first time. And I went with a doctor — Dr Hessen Muas, the president of Nauru. Now he is president. Before that he wasn't president, he was Chief Commander Robert. We went together the first time and also the second time. The second time I was asked: "Who do you want to go with you?" And I talked Dr Gunther into letting my friend John Guise come with me. They all said he was a Papuan, but I said, "Oh, never mind. He is not coming for this conference. I am the one who is going to the conference. He is going as a young fellow for me to look after. I know he is a Papuan, but I want him to come with me." Dr Gunther took my word, and the government okayed everything. So John Guise came with me. When we were at the conference he was my young boy, but as soon as we came out he acted big and too hot-headed for me.

At the United Nations I was not given a chance to say much. I went as an observer and sat behind the Australian representative, Mr W. McCarthy. He was appointed from Canberra to talk on behalf of the Trust Territory of New Guinea. He talked on matters concerning New Guinea, while I sat behind him. Sometimes the hot-headed Russian representative would ask questions. And if they wanted to know whether the Australian representative was telling the truth or not they would point to me, and I would say, "It's true."

If Australia talked about the things that she had done, and it was true, I couldn't say no. When asked about the development trends in education, agriculture, and the general preparation by Australia, I would say: "Yes, it's true." Some Africans also wanted to know whether it was true or not. They knew it was true, but they were just hot-headed.

So we left New York at the end of the conference, and I think we spent a week in Washington before returning to join the United Nations delegates. They were going to straighten out some trouble and flare-ups between China and India over the border issue. During that time they appointed a group of people to look into the trouble. We went on their charter. And we went to Rome, across to England, then to Paris, Burma, and Berlin, thence across the continent to Pakistan, Calcutta, Palestine, Cairo, Bangkok, Arabia, Hong Kong, down to Singapore and, finally, to Australia.

Then, finally, I finished with all this *maus wara* politics and came to stay around at home. Oh, but I have cut half of my talk! There is one other story about what happened to me in London. But that was really something stupid. You know, there were so many things to see that you won't find here.

When I went I thought I was a man, but everything I saw appeared to me as if I was asleep and dreaming. And I drank plenty of whisky and got *spak* [drunk]. Once I went to a show, man! I saw it and was very surprised. There was dancing, and the girls were stripped to the waist, their breasts bare. They were dancing, and that time I wanted to watch, but I was not really drunk. I was far from the hotel where I was staying, and I didn't know where I was. The taxi drivers really confused me. The hotel where I was staying was called Walldock Hotel. As for the place where I was, I didn't know which way or what direction. And when I had finished watching that thing and made my way out the door I was too drunk already. I couldn't find anybody to help me; even the taxi driver confused me and wouldn't listen to me. He thought I was an African or a something nothing.

Since I couldn't find my way, I leaned against the wall of a big building and went to sleep. I was fast asleep. But I really praise the policemen in London. Perhaps if it had been New York or Australia, ah, I'd have been just a rubbish man in the deep sea!

The police came and found the hotel key with the name of the hotel on it, and they also found the United Nations card. I didn't know which way they took me. When they brought me to the hotel I didn't know. I only realized the next morning that my tie and shoes had been taken off, and I thought, "Oh, did I have trouble or how did I come back here to sleep? If I walked in the night, then maybe I was too drunk when I came back to the sisters here." Later, when I went down to have my meal, the young woman in the office said, "Did you know you had trouble last night?" I said I didn't know. "I think the policeman took you and brought you home. " I had nothing to say.

I said, "What kind of policemen brought me home?"

"If it had been in some other country the policemen wouldn't have brought you home, instead they would have brought you to the other house." And I was really glad.

From then on I never went for that kind of walkabout. Every afternoon I would go and watch the changing of the guards — real smart, the mounted guards. I forgot the night shows and pictures, I didn't want them. I just went to see the queen's guards and came straight back to the hotel, just so the policemen wouldn't lock me up. Maybe next time they wouldn't take me home but take me to the cell.

Well, finally, I have ended up here in Port Moresby as a security guard in the university library. You know what happened? It was like this. When we talked about the setting up of this university, John Guise and I fought strongly for Dr Gunther to leave his position as assistant administrator and become vice-chancellor, since he had a long-time resident in New Guinea, and all young New Guineans would look to him, as an old father, which was good. And so our points got through. I think Dr Gunther recalled my words from the Assembly and therefore, when he became the vice-chancellor, he sent word for me at home to come to the university. That is why I am here now. And now he has left me.

Poetry

YAULABUTA:
THE PASSION OF KAILAGA

A Free Adaptation

Canoe beautiful like rainbow,
vibrant like beautiful women!
We practise Yaulabuta at night
until dawn breaks open our hearts.
We have mastered the song:
our bodies are eager for action.
Our hearts feel happy. Like sailors
from distant islands sighting land.
O beautiful clouds on the horizon at daybreak,
soft and round like a woman's underbelly!
O Kailaga, beautiful like rainbow,
vibrant like beautiful women.

I walk on the beach in darkness.
Sandpipes flutter noisily.
I speak incantations over ginger:
I want to revive the memory of Kailaga.

"Yaulabuta" is a traditional poem whose central theme is the capture and tragic death
of the chief of Kumwageya village. It belongs to the category of poem known as
wositola. This version was recited by Kadamwana and Moluwai, "keepers of the
words" of this song in Yalumgwa village. Translated by John Kasaipwalova and Ulli
Beier.

I cast my words over the sea:
I want to recreate Kailaga.
Memories rise in the mind, like seagulls soaring high
from the horizon.
We are overcome by grief.
O tears of those who died.
The whole village goes into mourning.
We are crying on the beach of Tuma,
poised between the living and dead.
We are crying on the beach of Tuma,
the island of the dead.
I walk on the beach in darkness:
sandpipes flutter noisily.

The village of Kumwageya,
a place of fighting!
The village of Kumwageya,
a place of fighting!
Kailaga was the chief.
His canoe missed its course,
carried by currents from Misima.
They forced him to land at Kauloveka beach.
Kailaga, your seat was on fire.
When Kailaga was at war, his seat was on fire.

Kailaga clear as a pond,
his forehead bright as dawn!
Our chief's *silasila* leaf,
he washed his face with it.
Kailaga's Kula magic,
he washed his face with it.
O memories of past competitions!
Our newly born children
are mourned for by women.
Our children so fragile,
are mourned for by women.
Kailaga clear as a pond,
his forehead bright as dawn!

The canoe has been launched;
it skims the waves lightly.
The canoe has been launched;
it skims the waves lightly.

The Kumwageya sailors became restless,
their hearts became sad; they saw
that Kailaga had changed course.
Their hearts became sad.
Kailaga tied on his chiefly decorations;
they befit a chief.
His arms are beautifully adorned;
they befit a chief.
"Oh my husband has changed course!"
The canoe has been launched;
it skims the waves lightly.

The shocking news of our chief,
it ate our hearts.
The shocking news of our chief,
it ate our hearts.
He was tempted to change course,
he turned to the north.
He ventured into enemy waters.
He was lured by the promise of Kula wealth
from Chief Bugwabwaga.
Kailaga was misled by rumours
spread by his enemies.

His canoe speeds along,
the enemies are watching the ocean,
Kailaga's canoe speeds along,
the enemies are watching the ocean.
Tomawawa was watching carefully.
They suddenly came from the sea:
they pulled out the rudder of the canoe,
the canoe shuddered in agony.
They pulled out the rudder of the crew,
the crew shuddered in agony.
Sailing near the shore
they had chanted incantations
to help the sea,
but their canoe was captured.
They sang to help the sea,
but Kailaga was captured.
Mulimuli jumped into the canoe,
he donned Kailaga's famous cowrie belt.

Tomawawa pulled out the solava necklace,
he cut the boar's tusk necklace
from his chest — O Kailaga!

Mukwadea carried the news,
the news of their chief.
The sole survivor carried the news,
the news of their chief:
he drifted into the open sea.
His wives went into their houses,
they emptied their baskets.
They emptied their baskets,
they cried on the beach.
Canoe from Kumwageya,
your paddles were split at sea.
Canoe from Kumwageya,
your paddles were split at sea.

The married crew
stood speechless on the beach.
The married crew
stood speechless on the beach.
Kailaga too was a married man
and he was the most silent.
Our children will be scattered,
our blood will flow on the beach.
They sharpened their shell knives,
they split our heads.
Momyobikwa: burst with pride!
Decorate your arms with
the chief's armbands!
You wear the decorations of chief Kailaga.
They walk around the prisoners.
"I wear the armbands of a chief!"
The married crew
stood speechless on the beach.
Kailaga was the most silent.

"My friend, my co-wife,
restless on your mat.
My friend, my co-wife,
we are restless on our mats.
We are silenced in our house.

We are struck lifeless."
"Widow, what was your dream
of our husband's coming last night?"
"He gave me ripe betel-nuts to husk,
that's what I saw in my eyes.
He presented me with young betel-nuts.
I cried on my mat.
He gave me ripe betel-nuts to husk,
that's what I saw in my eyes."
"My friend, my co-wife,
we are restless on our mats."

"O my husband Kailaga,
they have toppled him from my breast.
I cry till daybreak,
calling for my husband."
"Your name Kailaga.
cornered and chased on the open sea.
O my husband Kailaga,
they have toppled you from my breast.
I cry till daybreak,
calling for my husband."

So brave was the woman,
she searched the beach.
So brave was the woman,
she searched the beach.
So brave was Bovayesa,
she was drawn to the enemy's village,
she looked for Tomawawa.
"They dragged you, Kailaga,
the chief who is my husband,
they drank your blood,
they tore out your eyelashes!
O chief Kailaga!"
Bovayesa was drawn
to the house of Lubabelu.
"The chief is my husband,
they drank his blood,
they tore out his eyelashes.
O chief Kailaga!"
So brave was the woman,
she searched the beach.

The abandoned canoe,
only our sons will paddle it!
Kailaga abandoned,
only our sons will avenge him!
My numerous *solava* necklaces
I will pay as ransom.
But alas: they trussed him up,
they used the boom of his canoe
as a carrying stick.
I am stunned into silence.
They burnt Kailaga,
they burnt him like a pig.
The women mourn,
they cry all their cries,
they mourn with tearful wailing.
Abandoned canoe:
only our sons will paddle it.

O memories of past competitions!
Even his captors are crying on the beach.
So outstanding was the dead man.
So outstanding was Kailaga.
Kailaga son of Gudibobiu,
your fleet lies on the beach.
The enemy paddled them ashore,
they had surrounded your canoe.
Kailaga, clear as a pond,
your forehead bright as dawn!
You plucked the leaves of *silalsila*
to cast magic over the entire beach.
So handsome was Kailaga!
He parted the sand
to wash in sacred water.
His forehead lit up and sparkled,
it shone in the centre of the villages.
So handsome was Kailaga.

O shocking news of our chief,
it ate our hearts.
Our eyes were stunned:
they massacred our chief
and all his people.

Our minds are stunned:
they massacred our chief
and all his people.
Shocking news of our chief,
it ate our hearts.
So handsome was Kailaga.

Kama Kerpi

HUT ON A RIDGE

So majestic
silhouetted against the grey unripe dawn.
Resting place of a weary soul
father and protector of the hillmen.

Raw winds
streaming softly and cautiously
through heavy clothed hills
collecting on the ridge
only to move on to another.
A hut stands solid
rooted on the laterite hill.

Down the valley
where a new day is beginning
a black child asks:
"Black mother, who lives up there?"
"Black son, your protector dwells up there.
Don't point or death will eat your hand!"

———

These five poems are from *Call of Midnight Bird* (Port Moresby: Papua Pocket Poets, 1973).

MOMENTS OF INITIATION

Vital moments come,
We, like Adam,
Adams banished
From paradise of childhood.

The solemn march,
To register for service.
Childhood life glows dimmer behind.
Before awaits,
I march to wear the heavy shell.

No longer
Will I hunt gamebirds,
But human heads,
No longer
Will I walk in the shade,
But bask and bathe in the open.

The farewell march,
Mother's midnight stories
A defeated bush fire.
I vomit formative years,
I walk for my share of the ginger.

The solemn march,
Only the winds
Whistling through giant trees
Accompany murmurs of encouragement
From dead fathers.

CALL OF MIDNIGHT BIRD

We all sit around him,
Eyes cast
On the victim of their magic.

Our minds running wild,
Mine crawling into formative years,
Moments I learned to follow his footsteps.

I race here and there,
Hunting the cream of childhood,
Yet he haunts me,
Because he is part of my history,
All around me,
I hear them helpless in the pool
Of bitterness and sorrow.

On approaching
the hour of the spirits
I feel very strange.

Far in the night
Over the hills or beyond
The call of the midnight bird,
Harbinger of Father's departure,
Welcome signal of the dead.

I grab his hand
To hear the last pulse.
Fraction late.
It is not the hand that showed me how to shoot.
It is not the face that blinded married women.
Yet this object was my father.

Father said only women cried.
Yet the moment my little brother lifts
The lifeless hand in tears,
Father forgive me.
I have to rain a few drops,
For I can hardly hold the outburst.

THE SIMPLE JOYS OF LIFE

We sat around the fire.
Doors barred to shield off
the cold mountain winds.
The flicker of firelight
leaping before our eyes.

And there under the cover of darkness
the old woman began
stories of long ago,
of her formative simple joys.
And there we followed her on an unused trek
passing through an old ruined kingdom.

Filing over the horizon were the days
of wars and hill-farming,
where feasting and hunting
became the simple joys of life,
a life that remains a scar in her.

Sorrow masked her wrinkled face.
It was a nightmare,
and only sleep awoke us from a
strange journey. .

FATHER, YOUR FACE

Father!
Why do you wear
This long haggard face,
The type mother wears
On melancholy occasions,
Like funerals beyond the ridges?

Why, Father?
Why these silent looks?

During the dead years
Were you known as Boma
Ruler of many wives?
Are you not the son of Umar?
A warlord who summoned warriors
To assemble for battles.
Did you not run ahead of them to battles?

Call me the ungrateful son
Who ran away from the front lines
In mother's midnight stories.
Do you not call me
"The stormy flashes"?
Have you not labelled me
"The seasonal homecomings
Of the kingfishers"?

Father!
Your black blood runs fresh
In my white veins,
So let me hear the voice
I once heard long ago
Unwrap this secret you keep.
For your face speaks many hateful words.

Hengenike Riyong

DEATH

My weak body rests.
A voice erupts
Shaking me up.
Eyes half closed I sit up:
The voice growls.
I depart quietly
Blackening my bed.
The fleas and bedbugs disperse.

Though the young people feel clumsy about it
Death really scares no one.
When the oinya leaves
He looks alien.

These five poems are from *Nema Namba* (Port Moresby: Papua Pocket Poets, 1974)

THE MOUNTAIN

On your forebody
Little twigs nourish.
On your unshaven face
Trees bury their roots.
On your breasts
The tallest peaks sprout.
On your resting feet
Your children play.
Shedding flood of tears
They laugh and cry.
Uprooting your hair
Emptying your stomach
They drift down the falls
Across the plains
And head for the blue ghost.
Everything is drained —
    the best soil gone,
    the rocks and tree stumps
    remaining exposed
    everywhere.
And you sleep
With your calm hands folded.

NOKONDI

The Helpless Creature

Moon moon,
Shout the excited children.
Stars stars, say older children.
The brighter children count
One to thirty
And say they have come to twenty ten.
And that is the end of the number system.
The sound of the children
The sound of the drum
All seem to make the great

Choir of the village.
Soon the little ones are away
Creeping in like little chickens
Into the warmth of the mother's wings
Pressing onto the mother's breasts
Like leeches clinging onto humans
Sucking the blood.
Mothers under their little temporary shelter
Laugh away.
As the child clings onto the breast
He rests under his mother's care
With no fear, nor danger
As his spirit travels to its distant land.
Weak body lies helplessly
With its nourisher
Both under one cover
All in peace.

CIVILIZATION

Standing, emptying
Myself to the endless flow of flies
Buzzing over my nose,
Under my feet
Countless noises
Like blue flies over a dead pig,
My eye refuses
But I keep myself
Head upright, looking and exploring.
Cats walk past,
Dogs bark as they pass,
Pigs squeak
And ducks wave me goodbye
All in a busy forest.
I stand with stripped
And naked mind
Tuning in doubtful thoughts
Blowing out bubbles of unused air.

Jungle home,
a busy forest.
A cat under the fern,
A crow among the branches,
All under jungle home.
Excreta passed onto
The wet floor of the forest,
The decayed leaves,
Bones that shine
Pollute the jungle home.
Snake on its body
Crawls with its dark evil eyes
Looking for the chicken eggs
All well kept
In brown hot shrubs,
Hawks hungry for
Helpless day-old chickens
Look down under thorns and shrubs.
O jungle home,
Your virginity is ruined.

THE DEATH OF MY GRANDFATHER

One dull cold night
He rested his broad back against his wooden bed
And slept and never woke again.

His old rusty bag beside his bed.
Under his bed most carefully tucked away
Was his smoking bamboo pipe
Wrapped in a black bark.
With green and purple mould there it lies
In the dark dungeon of the "haus man".
What a pity no one lives in it.

This might be called a lonely death.
The house had its own alien life beneath the sun
Yet both belong to the village and none are one.
The roots and bones lie close among the soil
And from his grave he ascends his gourd
Leaves towards the lonely sky.

Now the white ants make their home in his skull
His old friend the fire has walked across the "haus man"
And blackened the old house and the grave fence
Burying him half in ashes as he rests.

Sad news made its way to my ears.
The teacher released me.
I hurried across the rugged ranges
Down the valleys
Across the rivers
Longing to see my grandpapa
To the village that was full of music and drum
And did not discover a single life.
On the very soil I came into
Every second I spared
Sad memories rushed dominating my little cap
And there I stood
On the soil where my grandpapa was vomited into.

From a thousand feet I hang my heart
Not for all but the beats of his drum
Nothing precious to sacrifice
But my swaying heart.

Russell Soaba

SEVEN POEMS FROM "NAKED THOUGHTS"

A medley of tall wood distort
streaks of light into the floorbeds
of this vast virgin jungle.
Weak sunlight
dances lazily 'gainst the illusive downflow
of falling lianas. Birds of paradise
sing at brief intervals,
yet as time would destine
this to be, vanish into the depths of massy
green, into the depths of some dark ocean.
Somewhere a lonely
bird whistles. Or is it a bird, really?
A hunter perhaps, perhaps just the wind,
even a tune, and echoey. Or simply a call, a scream in fact?
Still, a sound
maybe some dialectical utterance—
a message

Reprinted from *Naked Thoughts* (Port Moresby: Institute of Papua New Guinea Studies, 1978).

Come to my village
one day
and you will see that . . .
No, what
you see are two eyes
stilled
and a smile falsified. Here,
let me
move an inch, and there,
right before you is the red curtain
falling
into streams of dreams.

Those men who are now completely lost
could command the wind to blow my house down.
Sure, the wind would come, these timber walls would fall
the iron roofing would fly, leaving only I
at this table, writing.

I was on my way down to the bottom
of an abandoned water well.
I've been crawling downwards for years
and I've known my movements well in the dark.
Some youngster trying to be funny, I think,
slipped and fell upon my shoulders.
Slipped again off my shoulders and
fell head first to the bottom.
(He should at least have asked for advice.)

heavy windows of mucous red
long tall storeys of orange buildings
fading yellow as the day wears on
would there be green parks below?

in the ice of this city
rainbows
are never complete

anxiety stares
waiting for the world
to define

happiness

is a rainbow
where waters leap
and fall red

what a pity
you have asked me to speak
at this time

I would rather sing

Fiction

Iriye Diaya

A SUCCESSFUL MARRIAGE AT LAST!

Once upon a time there lived a tiny dwarf. He was as filthy as a mudstone. His clothes were as ragged as a beggar's. It was not because he was poor or unemployed. He had a good job, earning good wages, because he was working for important people. But instead of drawing his pay, he always asked his employers to save it for him. Nobody knew why he wanted to save every penny he earned. Whenever his employers wanted to pay him, he would say: "Sir, I don't want the money now, but I wish to continue working for you." Thus he continued to work for years, without being paid.

One day he was sent to a different place to work. This was a bigger and more impressive place. Then he said to his boss: "Sir, you know that all this time I have been sacrificing all my time and life for my employers and I have never asked them for my pay. But now, master, I wish to have a ring on my finger. Will you please order one for me with the help of my previous employers." And sure enough, the boss sent away the order.

Years passed, but his appearance never improved. He was always the same and could almost make you vomit when you passed him.

Eventually the ring did arrive. To him, it was going to be a magic ring; one that was going to help him at any time. One day his ring

Told by Iriye Diaya of Koali Tomba village and translated by Frank Nimi. From *Kewa Stories*, collected by Stephen Rambi and Frank Nimi, edited by Ulli Beier (Port Moresby: Institute of Papua New Guinea Studies, 1977).

notified him that there was going to be a celebration for all races and people in the country. His ring told him that he must go and participate in it, for surely he was going to be the winner. That evening he went to bed very early. As usual his sleeping place was right by the fireplace, among the ashes, which kept him filthy all the time. When he got up the next morning, he brushed the dust off his clothes and went off on the back of the horse, which his master had lent him the day before. Soon he arrived at his destination.

He found himself a place in the corner of the field and sat among the multitudes, keeping his eyes wide open. He could see many people practising how to catch a ball, but he thought they were only entertaining themselves while they were waiting for the real event.

Eventually the queen took up her seat, in front, among the spectators. She took up her notes and read to the public: "Whoever will catch this ball, which I shall throw into the air personally, will marry my daughter."

He was still very uncertain of how he was going to win this event, because the other competitors were many times bigger than himself. He was as thin as an ant compared with these huge people. Even so, he never lost courage. He thought that he was another human being, and he would at least try.

When the queen released the ball, he jumped into the sky and caught the ball before it could make its curve. The crowd had lost the fortune, and they dispersed quickly. They were sad, because they had lost their opportunity. Angry people couldn't pull the ball away from him, because the queen had seen it clearly. It was time for the queen to give away her daughter to the winner. The queen appeared on the stage and announced: "With the authority of the royal family, I confirm the marriage between you and my daughter. May your future be bright and prosperous. It is your responsibility now to maintain her and her offspring and look after her best interest." But all these words were not spoken proudly, because she was not happy to give her daughter to a creature of stunted growth, unhygienic, and almost inhuman. The dwarf stood there feeling very important.

"Now," said the queen, "you two shall walk holding hands." But the dwarf replied: "No, I am not going to. I am not going to hold hands with the daughter of the highest." The magic ring told him that the princess would know what to do and that she would walk on her own and without his guidance.

Soon they were ready to go to the dwarf's house. "Jump in my car and we'll drive home," said the princess. "No thank you," said the dwarf, "I shall walk and you may drive ahead." He told her how to find his house. But the princess was very annoyed with the fellow's behaviour. However, she had no choice but to drive alone. To her surprise, the dwarf arrived at the same time. No one really knew how he had done it. The dwarf went straight to lie down by the fireplace. All the princess could find to settle on was a dirty, ragged bed.

That evening the meal was cooked by the princess and she called her husband to come and eat with her. But the dwarf refused to eat with her. This made the princess feel sick deep inside. "I wish I hadn't come with this ignorant and arrogant dwarf," she thought. "But who is to be blamed for it? My mother, the queen, is the source of all my problems."

Later that evening, when she had made the bed, she asked him to go to bed with her, but his reply was: "No thank you, I am not worthy to sleep with the daughter of the highest, and anyhow, I am more comfortable here." So they slept separate from each other the very first night, when it should have been interesting to explore each other's kingdom. It was a hard time for the princess. All night long she moaned and sobbed. She knew that her life was going to be miserable unless she could get a divorce.

Again in the morning, the dwarf refused to have breakfast with the princess, but remained lying by the fireside. She grew so angry that she threw a pot of boiling water into his face, which took the skin off him.

One moon passed and another one and the magic ring told him that there was going to be a horse-race, at which the champion of the whole country would be present. Again the ring told him that he was going to be the champion. He couldn't believe this, yet he knew that it must be so. The next day the princess begged him to go to the races with her, but he replied; "I am not used to attending such occasions, but by all means go by yourself and tell me the story of it when you come back." Again she was very angry, but there was nothing she could do. She drove away with sadness to the race-course. She parked her car in one corner and sat there with her head resting on her knees.

Meanwhile at home the dwarf took off his ragged clothes and threw them into a drawer. As usual he opened up another drawer where he kept his cowboy clothes. The cowboy clothes changed him completely. He was no longer a dwarf. He was one of the most handsome cowboys in the country. He found his horse waiting in the backyard, and within minutes he had reached the racecourse. He rode up to his wife's car and sat next to her. She did not recognize him and she admired him a lot. He offered her a cigarette and she accepted it with appreciation. Deep in her heart she wished that she could marry that man; and one could almost read her feelings on her face.

In a few minutes the race was going to start. The ring reminded him again that he was going to be the winner. So there was nothing to worry about, and he waited patiently. Then the whistle went and all the competitors were off and away. When the competitors had a five-minute start, he galloped after them like an arrow. Soon he overtook them all and was leading the race. Yes, sure enough, he won the race: he was the man himself.

Having collected his prize, he galloped away as fast as he could to prevent the princess from seeing him. At home he changed back into his usual filthy clothes and lay there by the fireside, waiting for her to return. He was no longer the cowboy whom the princess admired.

Then the princess arrived, driving furiously. With all the power of the engine she crashed into the side of the house. The wall fell to pieces. Without a further word she went straight into the kitchen to break all their eating utensils. All this showed that there was pain in her heart.

"Will you come to dinner, you . . . .?" she asked angrily. "Who are you talking to?" he asked. "You better eat all that lovely food by yourself and keep your shape and beauty." She was so angry that smoke almost burst out of her nose.

Another day came, when the king and queen wanted to give them their share of the kingdon. The dwarf was called, but he said: "I can hear every word you say nice and clear from the fireplace here. Just give your daughter her share of the kingdom and then go back home quietly." The royal family left in disgust. They would have arranged a divorce, but were embarrassed to break their promise.

Some time later they heard that another horse-race was going to be held. The night before the race the princess discovered the cowboy outfit in the drawer. She knew now that her husband had been playing some nasty tricks on her. She packed the shirt back in the drawer and said nothing to him.

She woke up early the next day and asked to go to the races. He refused to accompany her. She drove off by herself, but hid her car behind some bushes and returned to spy on the dwarf. Hiding behind the flower beds she saw him change into his cowboy suit. As soon as he had galloped out of sight, she snatched his ragged dwarf's clothes and burnt them. When she was satisfied she drove to the racecourse.

She drove up to where he was waiting and sat next to him. She thought that he was not an ordinary man. Now that she had burnt his dwarf's skin, he was going to be her true lover.

The race started, and as the magic ring had predicted, he won it again. He collected his prize and galloped home, but when he arrived his beloved skin was gone. She felt happy when she found him, unchanged, sitting on the veranda. She embraced him with tears of love for the first time since their marriage. She kissed him all over: from top to toes to the pubic area and up to his forehead. Yes, this was the man she wanted a lot, and at last he was hers. She picked him up and carried him everywhere; around the house, along the pathway, into the bushes and anywhere else you can imagine.

They lived happily ever after. One day the good news reached the royal family, and they came to give away the share of wealth. The queen announced: "You will prosper and be productive as your older brothers and sisters of all colours are. I knew you had been stubborn, Mr Dwarf, but now it is my pleasure to see that you have changed a lot — I know that this is the result of my daughter's hard work. Your future, as I see, is brightening. I wish you all the best of luck."

"Thanks a lot," shouted the husband and wife together. "We hope that we will prosper like our brothers and sisters. Our first stubborn marriage represents the time when we accepted the old English pounds, shillings, and pence — that was when the Australian government acted as the daughter country of England. The new marriage represents the acceptance of kina and toea and independence from the Australian government — after years and years of saying that we could not govern ourselves!"

Kama Kerpi

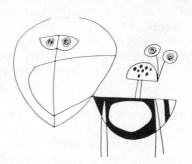

CARGO

"Cargo . . . cargo is what our people want. It has thrown everyone into madness," said Abram. "We must act now or never," he added as an afterthought, taking off the bandage around Cain's arm.

"It was as if a man who was eating a meal prepared by his wife suddenly jumped up with anger on hearing from his friend that at midday his wife was caught opening her legs to her secret lover. But I cannot understand why the white men are so greedy as to keep the secret to themselves," responded Cain, closing his eyes as Abram pressed his fingers around the boil on his right arm. "We are the proper owners and demand that secret to be torn open. All those endless debates at the men's house has brought us nowhere."

"It must be like this boil," said Abram, pressing Cain's boil a little harder. "I mean, the secret of our dead people's cargo."

"Someone has got to tear it open." He felt the pain shoot through his arm spasmodically, and he winced, feeling the blood pulsing around the boil. The pain was terrible, and he closed his eyes several times. The desire and frustration to obtain dead people's cargo must be like this boil that was bulging with pus. Maybe to certain people the secret was like a pain in their hearts, growing as their anxieties increased. As these thoughts entered his mind, Cain felt like driving a sharp nail into the centre of the boil to force out all the pus and let in air.

Reprinted from *Kovave* 5, no. 1 (June 1975): 30-36.

"Last week Bola's brother, returning from a coastal town, claimed that he brought with him the secret of obtaining cargo from our dead people. If what he says is true then it's the holy water and the Bible that is keeping us blind. And to think that the Church has prevented us from acquiring our property. It's a little hard to believe."

"Bullshit with the Church," said Cain as he ran his eyes up and down where new boils were developing on his arm. Maybe all the churches were like those contagious boils, he told himself. "They preach 'thou shall not steal', and yet they steal under our nose," he added.

Cain had never before spoken against the churches. Now that he was beginning to, the ugliness the boil created on his arm must have had some effect. Since the boil had been giving him a lot of physical pain he had begun to be more aware of another type of pain that occurs in the soul — a spiritual pain. But then all pains can be cured, and this suggested that there must be some hope in store.

"They preach the Ten Commandments, yet they soil their hands in things that are not theirs," said Abram. "We have become slaves to their teachings. Our people say when an enemy smiles at you his heart curses you and wishes you ill fate."

Abram, having finished bandaging Cain's arm, averted his eyes to the far ridges where his people lived and farmed. You are all blind, ignorant fools, he told himself. It's a pity they do not realize that it's the Church that's robbing them. The pity he had for them turned around to face him. This created a sense of mission that crept into his heart, and he began to wrestle with it silently. Sure enough, pity had created hope and hope in turn increased his anxieties.

"Abram . . . what can we do?" said Cain.

"Just you answer me one question," said Abram so quickly it was as if an idea that had crept into his mind was beginning to leave him. "If a man came at you with a spear intending to kill you, what would you do?" Abram moved closer to Cain's ear and almost whispered, "You would not stand and watch . . . at least I wouldn't."

"I wouldn't either . . . I would fight."

"Cain, you have got the point . . . you have got it. You defeat him by simply taking the spear from him. And that's what I have been thinking about. If the Church is using the holy water and the Bible to blind us, we make use of them to defeat it." Abram looked into Cain's face and blinked several times in the noon sun. He looked uneasy; he was planning something, and whatever it was it had to be checked twice if not three times.

"Bola's brother was simply saying that you defeat the Church by its own weapons. Bola must know more, at least the first steps of obtaining cargo."

"Yes, he must. You know his sister died last week. He is playing marbles over there. Go and bring him over. He might need some marbles."

Cain went over and brought back Bola.

"Do you need some marbles?" said Abram, rattling the marbles in his pockets. "You can have twenty. But before you have them, tell me about this secret your brother brought with him."

The question had taken Bola by surprise. A look of hate appeared on his face, and deep inside he sneered and wished that they would take a bee-line to hell. Bola's sister had died not long ago and he was planning to catch the Reverend Father stealing the cargo. And what his sister gave belonged to his family. He had just lost a game of marbles and the twenty marbles in Abram's pocket would help him to get his own back. From his confused mind a saying began to take shape and then hammer at him. His father had always said that when a man dances at the first rains of the wet season he is foolish, because the storms that will be coming will kill him.

"It's a mission. Our people need help in the dark; we must lead the way. We must be the beacon in the night," said Cain with emphasis, when he realized that Bola was not going to answer their question.

"And we can only do it by finding the secret of obtaining it . . . I mean the cargo," added Abram. He realized that he had to convince Bola, otherwise he had to make guesswork and start from there.

"You know ten pigs await anyone who discovers the secret," said Cain. "That's a lifetime wealth."

"Really? But I do not need pigs. My father has got a lot of them." Bola's tribe and Cain's and Abram's tribe had always been enemies. And Bola had not forgotten that their young men had killed a close relative of his father. He gave them a sullen look and went away.

"Greedy bastard. Son of a pig," muttered Abram.

"Just think, ten pigs. I will ask my grandfather, who died last year, to help me. He used to like me above my other brothers and sisters. Last week my father slaughtered a pig near the old man's grave. My father requested him to watch over my steps."

"That is probably the reason why you scored good marks in your schoolwork. I used to be better than you before." Abram then looked around to ensure that no one was about and continued, almost whispering: "A few days ago my father killed a pig in my grandmother's name, requesting that she should let my mother bear one last child in her old age; at least a boy to follow my footsteps in learning white man's knowledge. Our people have a saying that if you have a brother then in any fight your back is always protected — of course, you can apply it to anything."

Cain watched a small boy walk towards the bell. The boy lifted up a big object and hit the bell. It was time for class; if they were late a big cane awaited them. Taking a deep breath he said, "I have got a plan we might work at. We will talk about it after class. It may take a long time before the secret is in our hands."

"I think my plans are similar to yours. We can defeat them by their own weapons. When we discover the secret we will hand it over to the elders and at the same time claim our ten pigs."

"Yeah, we will do that."

The two boys walked towards the classroom, privately making great plans to find the secret of obtaining cargo. At times they were carried off into fantasy.

The half moon crept languidly from behind some low hills and poured its silver lights over the mission station. It was as if milk was poured on a table. The moonbeams danced on the leaves and the blades of grass like angels celebrating the homecoming of a prodigal son. The corrugated roof of the church reflected a greyish white colour, and in the silent atmosphere it resembled a mammoth statue. The stars twinkled in magnitude like countless Easter candles, while the trees stood in mute silence casting vivid shadows on the lawn.

Two dark figures darted across the playground in mortal hurry as if they were the last species making for Noah's Ark. They made for the church and were immediately swallowed up in the dark. Far up at the altar was a glow of light that burnt day and night. It was symbolic of God's presence. They felt secure.

"Hold the cross and the Bible. I will go and get some holy water. It's at the back of the altar. I won't be long." Abram's voice trailed off into silence. Giving the cross and the Bible to Cain, he vanished into the darkness.

Cain waited with the cross in his left hand and the Bible in his right. A good five minutes must have elapsed. His legs were beginning to pain a little, and the frigid air of the night began to send waves of shiver up and down his body. "What is taking him so long?" he asked himself. He made a firm decision that he would have to go for Abram if he didn't come in the next few minutes. But he warned himself that their job must be fruitful. The darkness seemed to be alive with moving figures. They were beginning to test his courage. "The mission must come to success," he shouted silently to himself, closing his eyes. "It's imperative that the elders have the secret of obtaining our dead people's cargo. We must not fail. Our people have been fooled by the white man. It must come to success," he whispered, impulsively folding his fist.

"Cain . . . where are you?" It was Abram's voice. For a moment Cain was taken aback.

"I am here. Did you get the holy water?"

"Sure I did!" exclaimed Abram, walking towards Cain's voice. "Cain."

"What?"

"I also got some wine!"

"But why wine? You will spoil our plans with . . ."

"Hold your tongue. Did they not say blood and water ran down his body while hanging on the cross? I have perfected the plan by bringing in wine."

"Yes . . . yes, you are right. I am beginning to have illusions of our kin dancing to the beat of the *kundus*!"

"Well stop it then. Let's get to work and have your daydreams come true," said Abram.

Far into the night their ears tuned to a monotonous cry of a night bird.

"That's the right moment. The dead people are stirring alive in their graves. We must track Reverend Father; otherwise he will elude our trap." Abram's voice became inaudible as he fiddled in his hip pocket for a match. He struck one and immediately it burnt, a yellow flame with a ring of blue at the burning end. Cain tore a page from the Bible and set it on fire. Immediately the light cast horror figures on the cement wall of the church. Then they set the Bible down, the cross immediately on top of it.

"Let's begin the ceremony," whispered Cain, holding up the light.

Abram poured a few drops of holy water into the cup of his hand and dripped it around the cross and the Bible. The church had not been swept, and, as the drops fell, round balls formed a ring around the objects. Then Abram drank half the wine, making the sign of the cross very slowly. He passed the bottle to Cain, who had not recovered from mumbling some prayers. Cain then began imitating Abram, and when he emptied the last drop of the contents he placed the bottle in front of him and, closing his eyes, awaited Abram to proceed with the prayers.

"The lord is my shepherd," began Abram, "of whom should I be afraid? If an enemy — ah — ah . . ."

"Encamps against," prompted Cain.

". . . Encamps against me, let him tremble and fall. If a friend is deceitful, let him grow hairs in his eyes. O Lord, we hear; Cain, son of Koirap, and me, Abram, son of Sua, request you, in the presence of the darkness and the silence of the valley, the moon above, and the dark ridges awaiting dawn, to help us track down Reverend Father. Open our eyes, we pray, and let the riches pass on to the rightful owners. We seek the guidance of Mary and all the saints and angels in heaven. In the name of the Father, Son and the Holy Ghost."

"Amen," they chorused. A smile of satisfaction hovered on their lips.

"You hold the cross, and if any devils attack us put the cross in front of you and walk towards them and say, 'Begone, devil.' I will hold the Bible." As Cain's voice trailed off into silence, they got up and walked to the back of the church.

Immediately behind the church were the graveyards of both missionaries and devout Catholics who demanded before their deaths that they should be buried near the house of the Lord. It was affirmed that their spirits would make an agonizing journey to the house of the Lord if they were buried in the tribal graveyards scattered on the hills and the ridges. The graveyard at the back of the church was well kept, with low flowers bubbling in profusion, like dripping on a hot frying pan. A few pine trees grew, with rich green natural needles. In the moonlight, they stood almost terrified, as if awaiting a death sentence. The Reverend Father's house stood parallel to the church with a neat lawn in between. His toilet was in line with his house, and because it was a few yards from the graves they had been suspicious about it. It was thought to be the passageway to the dead people's cargo beneath the graves. Previously, Cain and Abram had inspected the toilet and were convinced that the wooden hole was a passageway to the underworld, and if they followed Reverend Father they were bound to catch him tricking their grandfathers. Then they would explain where the cargo really went.

"We will wait under that coffee tree. It's near the toilet. Now, remember to recite the Hail Mary when your ears track the slightest movement!" They hurried across the lawn, kicking a few dried leaves. Sitting under the coffee tree, they waited tensely as if ready to pounce at their prey. The broad green leaves stole most of the moonlight but provided the best hiding place. And there they waited. The seconds crept into minutes and the minutes into hours. The half moon crept away from behind the *nop* trees. An instinctive fear of failing crept into them, threatening to smash their optimism to shatters.

Suddenly their vagrant thoughts were distracted by a door opening and closing. It came from the direction of Reverend Father's house. The beam of a flashlight danced wildly on the lawn and then took its place in front of a figure. For Cain and Abram excitement shot through them, setting their hearts in vibrant tattoo. The fluid language of Reverend Father's movements suggested that he was hurrying on an errand. A smile of satisfaction appeared on their lips. He was hurrying to receive the goods, they told themselves.

Cain and Abram immediately held the cross and the Bible in front of them and whispered as many Hail Marys as they could before he got any nearer.

"Do not lose sight of him," whispered Cain when he paused after the fifth quick Hail Mary.

"Em," grunted Abram with a tinkle of anger for having been interrupted in his prayer. The Reverend Father stood for a brief moment outside the toilet and, after looking around, gave the door a push and walked in. The door let out a groaning sound. The flashlight threw its light, splinters of which escaped through the cracks and cast long golden figures on the lawn.

"What do we do? Should we give him a few minutes more? Or go in after him?"

"We will give him a few more minutes. Say about two minutes. When we think he is down the toilet we will follow him. We will then tell our kin why their cargo does not reach our hands."

"You are right. We will tell them that it's the white man's Bible and holy water that has kept us blind."

"What's that over there?" asked Abram in a startled manner, his hands impulsively pointing at two dark figures crawling on their bellies towards the back of the toilet.

"Hell, who could they be?" said Cain. His voice was barely audible, as if questioning himself.

"Look! They are peeping in through the cracks!" The last word had not left Abram's mouth when the door was literally thrown open. The two figures sprinted away as if they had witnessed their dead grandfathers coming back to life. Meanwhile the Reverend Father flashed the light and surveyed the vicinity. For a brief moment the light fell on the coffee tree where Cain and Abram were hiding, and seemed to stop. Cain sweated profusely, while Abram threw open his lap-lap and urinated from fear. Fear of being caught crept over their desire to see the mission come to success. Both grieved but sighed when the Referend Father hurried away, buttoning his long trousers, looking over his shoulder as if to check if anyone was following him.

"It's their fault. They spoiled our plans. Did you see fear on the Reverend Father's face against the moonlight?" said Cain.

"He hurried away as if he was discovered," replied Abram. "Let us go and find out who spoiled our plans."

Cain and Abram dashed to the back of the church. There they encountered Bola and his friend Mickle. They were sitting trying to get back their breath after the fast run. Cain came forward and stood over Bola with a menacing look on his face.

"Why did you spoil our trap . . . you toothless ones?" he rattled as anger and bitterness flooded through him.

Bola was surprised to see Cain and Abram. They must have been after my sister's cargo, he told himself. If they wanted a fight he would give them one, but for the moment he would control his anger.

"We were after my sister's cargo." He spoke calmly, fighting to control his anger.

"But you spoiled our trap . . . stupid," came back Cain's reply.

"You were out to steal my sister's cargo . . . you fat thief."

"You cow. Did not my father push you to the ridges during the dark days of tribal warfare? Your father is a weak bull."

A new madness took hold of Bola. An angry look appeared on his face. He stood up. His eyelids narrowed his molars came together, his fingers folded and the muscles around his arms tightened. He shook a little. Bola could not recall anyone calling his father a weak man. And no one dared to. How could anyone dare call his father a weak man? He was the father of the seven clans living on the ridge. He was well spoken of, and when he was at war with another tribe his name would blow with the wind. How could anyone dare speak false about his father?

"Your father impregnated a pig . . . you are their product," shouted Bola.

This sparked a fight. At first they stood their ground and exchanged a few punches, then they grabbed each other, and as they rolled over and over on the grass they exchanged abuse. Both called upon the art of throwing each other that they had learned from older men. And at times wild fists were thrown only to scare the other.

Abram watched Cain. At first he seemed to do well, avoiding Bola's wild blows. But with boils all over his arms he would not last long.

"Let's stop them," said Abram when he realized that Bola was gaining the upper hand. It was some time before they pulled the two apart, and it was some time before the fighters calmed down from making attempts at getting each other.

"Listen, we are all after the secret of obtaining our dead people's cargo. Our people say that when a man gets up before the sun to work in the gardens he will get a lot of work done. Of course, he should shake off sleep, otherwise he would be a foolish man. I think we have been foolish. We must have some teamwork." Turning to Bola he said, "How about some teamwork?"

"We will think about it first," replied Bola grudgingly.

They were all embittered by repeated failures. But another adventure awaited them. They must track the Reverend Father stealing their cargo. And all the wealth flowing into the hands of the white Reverend Father would arrest their interest. Maybe tomorrow night they would work as a team.

The glamour of the moonlight on the quiet mission station was enchanting and allayed their failure, moving a faint excitement in them. They would not abandon themselves to despair, because tomorrow was a new day, and there another adventure awaited them. The moon was high above, smiling. Nothing changed.

John Kasaipwalova

BOMANA KALABUS O SORI O!

My name is Johnny Woka and right now the grassknife is eating up my hands and Bomana hot sun is hitting my back like one angry mother with the broomsticks. Last week the chief put me and my friends on "big line" to cut grass, to cut grass and to cut grass until our palms become very sore and very brown like the dead grass themselves. In Bomana prison (we call it *kalabus*) there is a war going on every day. *Maski* rain, sun, or sick, we still have to fight. We prisoners are the fighting soldiers for the warders and the judges in Port Moresby who have declared war on grass. So the big line is our front line every day to carry this fight against the green grass on the roads, off the roads, on the hills, down the hills and even inside and outside of the *pekpek* houses.

Anyway our big line punishment started one morning last week when the chief called us out after everybody has roll call and fall line.

"Johnny Woka!"

"Yes sir!", and I run out very smartly with everybody's eyes following me.

"John Bacardi!"

"Yes sir!", and my friend runs out with warders swearings following him.

This fragment of a novel ("Bomana Prison, Oh Sorry!") was written while John Kasaipwalova was in gaol (see Notes on Contributors at back of book). It is based on the adventures of a fellow prisoner.

"John Whisky!"

"Yes sir!", and my other friend runs out, making all prisoners laugh.

One thing that makes all the warders very angry every time is to hear us prisoners laughing when they are wearing uniforms, so when they heard the laughings they all roared out like mad bulls swearing *pekpek* and *pasim maus.* When everyone shut their mouths the chief continued.

"John Kalabus!"

"Yes sir!", and my third *wantok* runs out to join us.

"John Sweet Sherry!"

"Yes sir!", and my last friend came out to join us, making all prisoners laugh and warders swear again at us.

When everybody stopped swearing and making fun at us, the chief gave down his decision and our punishment. We didn't say anything because our ACO has already finished reporting and making court with the chief, and now we are just going to get our punishment. ACOs always right. Prisoners always wrong.

"OK olgeta, harim gut! Yu wokim rong ausait na lo i putim yu long kalabus. Yu man nogut. Yu man bikhet. Yu 'kriminol'. Yu brukim lo na yu kalabus samting nogut."[1]

The chief pauses a little to allow his ACOs to swear at us first before staring out and yelling coldly again.

"Harim gut! Yu mekim trabel ausait na yu kam long kalabus. Mi gat bikpela wok. Mi mas stretim yu. Em taim bilong wok, em taim bilong wok tasol!"[2]

He stops a little to let the words go inside our heads.

"Mi no laik lukim sampela kalabus i go i go na giaman nabaut nabaut nating! Lo i tok yu mas wok, yu mas wok tasol. Na lukim dispéla fopela kalabus. Asde i giaman long wok na i go haitim bihain kona na katim mambu nabaut. Taim bilong wok em i no taim long katim mambu! Nogat!"[3]

Then he turned sharply to give us his fierce eyes.

---

1. "Listen well, all of you. You did wrong outside, and now the law has sent you to prison. You are bad men. You are stubborn people. You are 'criminals'. You broke the law, now you are in gaol; that's no good."

2. "Listen well! You gave trouble outside, now you have come to gaol. I have a big job to straighten you out. This is a time for work. A time for nothing but work."

3. "I don't like to see some of you prisoners. mucking around. The law says you must work; only work. Now look at these four prisoners. Yesterday they pretended to go to work, but they were hiding in a corner, buggering around. Time for work is no time for buggery. Not at all.!"

"Go long bik lain nau. Yu pekpek man. Yu bladi 'kriminol'!"[4]
Well, that really shut us up very quickly, and we had to just go quietly to our punishment without complaining to the chief that he was all wrong and that we were being punished for nothing. It is very sad because in Bomana prison, if any of us prisoners talk back or argue with the warders, they always charge us and then screw our time. That means two or three months more on top of our jail sentences imposed by the judges. Me and my friends had to shut up, that's all. Inside we were boiling and feeling very ashamed because the chief had accused and punished us at the same time for *katim mambu*. We know we didn't *katim mambu*, but all the other prisoners had already believed the bad story from the chief's mouth.

Katim mambu is a phrase coined by the chief to describe the homosexual activities that are taught in Bomana prison. It is like "cutting bamboo" because when you cut a bamboo it gives a grating and jarring noise from lack of lubricating fluids. Nearly every week fights break out among some prisoners because of jealousies caused by their partners changing to someone else for *katim mambu*. Some officers do it to their ACOs and the ACOs sometimes do it to the prisoners. But the funny laws about *katim mambu* in Bomana prison is that if the warders do it to the prisoners that is OK because that is part of their duty to teach us to be good citizens when we come out of jail. Yet if they catch the prisoners *katim mambu* among themselves, there is no limit to the warders' jealousies. Sometimes they screw our time and nearly always find some other punishments as well, like solitary confinement or breaking rocks and big line.

Anyway, our real trouble was not *katim mambu*. It started last Tuesday. I and my friends were working in the Piggery Section and we were mixing cement for the new pens going up. Our ACO sent us with a wheelbarrow to the Industrial Section to bring some more cement. So the five of us drove our wheelbarrow taxi and came happily to the Industrial Section to get cement. But when we arrived there, something really terrible happened. It was like seeing the ghost of my great-great-grandfather come out of his grave. I could not believe it; right in front of my eyes were the ten bags of cement and on each one of them was my handwriting still very clear and still ver large: JOHNNY WOKA in large red letters and underneath that the words MADE IN JAPAN printed neatly and black by the manufacturers.

My heart jumped to block my throat as I trembled in fear. Maybe this was another one of God's punishments for my sins. It was too much for me. I tried but didn't succeed as my ears rushed out like a flooded river to knock me down crying to the ground. John Bacardi,

4. "Now go to the 'big line', you shit men, you bloody 'criminals'."

John Kalabus, John Whisky, and John Sweet Sherry all stood there very drunk with their own surprises too. At first they couldn't believe what their eyes were seeing, but after a while they tried to lift me from the ground to stop me from crying. If they couldn't, we were going to be in big trouble.

I tried again this time very hard, but still I could not stop crying, so they loaded up five cement bags and I wheeled our taxi with my head down to hide my cryings while my friends walked like a fence around me to stop the warders from seeing my tears. When we got through the gate of the Industrial Section, I became even more sadder and wanted to cry even more louder. By now my friends had become very worried, so when we came near a mango tree beside our road, they took me to its cool shade to finish my crying before we went back to our work.

So as I cried and cried very sadly, my friends started asking me how my name came to be printed on those ten bags of cement. My throat was stuck with a very big lump, but still my mind opened very clearly just like yesterday as I remembered . . . .

O sori O! Bomana kalabus samting nogut tru hia![5] My sorryness began four years ago when I was still singing and free in the hills of beautiful Melpa. The day was a very important one. Everyone from my Jiga clan had gathered with very many colourful feathers with many hundreds of pigs all tied up and lined with an army of dead rats. The beautiful blue sunshine filled the skies with excitements as my Jiga clan laid out their boastful gifts for the *moka* exchange with the Yamuga clan. All the families of both clans showed off their own importances for all the people to see. All except myself. No matter the excitements and the foods they still could not make my heart happy, because our councillors and other big men had decided two nights ago to take away something very important to me.

For nearly two months I had been in love with this girl, and every day I was really trying all my strengths to win her for myself. She is a Jiga like me, but from a different and distant family. In my eyes she looked very pretty, like a Honda motor bike. I tried everything, but I don't know whether she ever realized the pains she caused me many times, especially when I saw her smiling to some other young men. However, those pains were nothing compared to the death pains of our councillors' and big men's decision. They had decided to create a new sport altogether to mark the Independence Day celebrations going on in Port Moresby. They had passed the word to all the married and unmarried men of Yamuga clan that at the end of the

5. Bomana prison is something really bad.

moka exchange, the Jiga clan was going to offer a very special prize for all the Yamuga men to try their lucks. The beautiful girl that I loved was going to stand about four miles away and when the Jiga clan gave the right signal, all the Yamuga men could race for her. Whoever would get there first could have her as his wife. So as the sun started climbing down from its midday place, my heart also began to climb down until the *moka* exchange was completed. Then in the midst of excitement from the men and general jealousies from their wives, the new independence sport was announced proudly by our councillors and big men. Some eight hundred Yamuga men lined up in their colourful *bilas* and skin *diwai* with hunger for sex in their eyes. Two small hills separated the eight hundred men from the girl I loved. She was waiting half frightened in case some really ugly man was to prove the fastest runner of the Yamuga clan.

They stood with one leg forward and all of them worried as our leaders checked to make sure nobody was cheating. When the piercing yell was given the straight line broke up immediately and all the men started running forwards like some mad ants scattering everywhere. A long line of dusty cloud followed them as they raced towards my girl.

By this time I was already praying that God should somehow strike all of them very dead so that I could save the girl I loved. However, not even God nor anyone else was interested in my prayers. Instead, they were all laughing and greatly enjoying my sad spectacle. Everywhere the *tanget* (arse grass) of the running men jumped up and down like the trail ends of some crazy emus being chased. On their fronts their hanging *baal* swayed rhythmically from side to side to give everybody a good view of their penises waving up and down as they ran, while the *kak para* (skin *diwai*) rubbed painfully against their skins so loudly that the sound of all the eight hundred of them was like a sawmill cutting logs. The *puru puru* of the women didn't hide much between their legs as they jumped up and down to see who was winning the race. The younger men soon speeded ahead leaving the older ones panting very loudly for air and holding their stomachs as if some angry snakes were biting their sides. It was very funny for everybody except my sad me. After twenty minutes all the racing Yamuga men returned singing loudly and shouting the success of the new exciting sport.

The fucking bastard who won the race arrived back smiling proudly to everyone while his new prize followed shyly. His name was Maiyau Taxi, and he was only wearing a pair of blue shorts instead of the traditional *bilas* which weighted down the speed of all the other men. The bastard had tricked us all. He was a policeman on leave from his duties in Port Moresby. When my eyes found the girl, my sadness was immediately overcome by my sexy desires to touch all her young flesh and lay my body into her. Man, man, *em swit moa yet!*[6] *O sori O!* My young boy stood up straight like all the other men. She was very very sexy and prepared. All our eyes were fixed on her middle between the legs. She didn't hide much and was wearing only a *dagla seven* (seven strings) in front to make her body even more desirable. Unfortunately my strong sexy desires very quickly turned into unhappiness when I saw Maiyau Taxi smiling to the girl ready to take her away. I promised myself that he would always be my enemy.

Two weeks later I heard that Maiyau Taxi had finished his leave and had taken the girl I loved back to Port Moresby with him. All my hopes were completely destroyed. Everyone in our village started noticing my sadness, and from there on all sorts of gossips and stories began to jump from lip to lip to explain my unhappy behaviour. With each passing day the stories made me feel more and more ashamed until they were unbearable for me. I decided on a plan. I must run away from Melpa and go to Port Moresby too. Maybe after I became rich and important there I would come back to Melpa and find a wife to love me. So without saying goodbyes, I walked secretly to Hagen, bought one Air Niugini ticket, and flew to Port Moresby to look for some of my *wantoks*.

I found them and we joined up. They were living in a *boi* house behind a *masta's* residence on the hill overlooking the House of Assembly. They quickly told me all about Moresby and how to behave. Because many of our *wantoks* were often getting into trouble with the police, they told me that one of the first things I must do was to change my name so that if I get into trouble my family and clan at home will not be shamed for nothing. So my *wantoks* gave me my new name after their favourite drink — Johnny Woka. I felt very proud and happy that maybe with the changing of my name I would also change my luck to becoming rich and important enough to go back and win one wife or even marry one *meri* Papua. *O sori O!*

Well, my luck was really going up, so I got one good job as a cook at Papua Hotel. I started learning all kinds of cooking, and every day me and my *wantoks* had plenty to eat. The work was not easy because we would start in the mornings and work and work until

6. It is very sweet!

near midnight. But I was determined to work hard and save my pay until I had plenty of money. As I worked harder my sad heart started to disappear. I found out a new enjoyment in my job, especially at night. Every day there were always sexy women coming to dinner and dance at Papua Hotel with rich businessmen and important politicians from the House of Assembly. I got very excited watching them dance so very very closely until their private parts were touching one another. I knew that afterwards the rich businessmen and the politicians would take the sexy women away and sleep with them. This made me more determined to work harder so I could become like that one day. Gradually I forgot completely about my girl whom Maiyau Taxi had stolen from me and began to concentrate on making my new style more happier.

One Wednesday morning on my day off I met some of my other *wantoks* in town. After watching all the sexy girls walking busily in the streets we decided to go and have some SP and San Mig at the Papua Hotel public bar. Our watching and thinking how they would look like if we took their dresses off had made us very hungry, so we ordered some fish and chips with some brownies first. There were five of us, and the fish and chips tasted like heaven when we downed them with the beers. When our hungry meal was completed we were ready for drinking. We drank and we talked, and after talking we drank some more. We didn't care about our money, and I felt very proud to buy more drinks to show my friends that I had plenty because of my good job as cook. They saw the money, ten kina notes, inside my wallet, and soon our drinking party grew to ten as more *wantoks* joined us.

The afternoon passed very quickly, and soon four o'clock brought more people into the bar until it was full with men, beers, smoke, and happiness. My head was already starting to turn and turn, but I didn't care as much as I was feeling very happy and wanted to sing. The waiters by now had become like Uni Transport trucks speeding everywhere to take away our empty bottles and bring new ones to our table. They liked our group very much because each time they came we gave them each one bottle also, but because their boss might angry them for nothing, they would bend their bodies to the floor pretending to pick up rubbish and while our legs hid them from sight they quickly emptied the beers into their open throats. By five o'clock our waiter friends couldn't walk straight, and their smart speeding started to appear like they were dancing to our singing.

That was when their boss saw them. He gave a very loud yell and followed with bloody swearings. But our waiter friends didn't take any notice. Our beer presents had already full up their heads and our happy singings had grabbed their hearts. Instead of answering their boss, they put the serving trays on top of their heads and started to dance to our singing in front of everyone. All the other men saw what was going on and they formed a ring around our waiters to clap and help them to dance some more. Man, man, *em gutpela pasin moa ya! Maski boss!*[7] Everybody was having a good time, and the only thing that spoiled the happiness was that there was not the woman in the bar to make it more happier. The singing, the drinking, the dancing and the smoking grew louder and louder until the windows started shaking. Papua New Guinea style! *O sori O!*

Just then it happened very suddenly. The bar manager had come from nowhere and grabbed the necks of our two waiter friends. He was pushing them and yelling them to go back to their work. When I saw them treated like that I lost my temper straight away. I jumped up like a snake and started biting their manager on his neck. He let go of the waiters and quickly began shaking me off as if somebody had poured hot water on his back. I fell to the floor and struck my head very hard against the timber. That was the signal. All my *wantoks* quickly jumped to their feet for my revenge. Bottles, chairs, tables, and everything started flying or running about the bar like mad. Everybody was fighting everybody in no time.

When I opened my eyes again I saw my enemy Maiyau Taxi standing behind the bars at Boroko cells and smiling his revenge on me again. My shirt was very torn, and blood and smell of beers and whisky covered me all over.

All Wednesday my head was like Boroko sports ground where my drunken hangover played rugby league against the throbbing pains of black bruises made by police batons on my poor skull. My left eye was swollen upwards and my right one swelled downwards and both of them were pulling very hard to tear my nose apart. My handsome face was no more to be seen that day. I stayed all day and all night Thursday in the police lock-up getting very angry and very afraid because they didn't tell me what law I had broken. Just before four o'clock, however, one of the guards called my name and told me to be ready for Boroko District Court next morning. I still wanted to know what charges they were going to hit me with, so I called to the police with the keys.

"Ei wasman! Mi laik save long wanem trabel wokim mi ya. No inap yu sasim mi nating nating na paulim mi nabaut!"[8]

7. "Man, you are doing fine! Don't mind the boss!"
8. "Hey, guard, I want to know what kind of trouble you are making for me here. You can't just abuse me for nothing and foul me up."

The guard redded his eyes towards me as if I had just committed another crime by even daring to ask him such a question. He gave a long surprised whistle and opened his teeths to me.

"Yu husat? Yu bladi 'kriminol'! Yu ting yu masta o olosem wanpela pablik solisoto eh? Yu bladi pipia man long Hagen! Pasim maus na go bek long sel. Yu no inap askim mi! Yu bikhet, em wan we tasol! Bomana kalabus, harim aah?"[9]

It was no use asking further, because I could see that he was already preparing to open the door to come and hit me one if I asked any more. So I shut up my anger to myself.

Next day, Friday, they took us to Boroko District Court. The magistrate had also red eyes and very very sadly angered face. He appeared as if he had been drinking all night and his wife had refused to sleep with him. I could see that he was already deciding to end the case before we even started so he could get away.

"Johnny Woka, you are hereby charged before this court with the following counts: one, that on Wednesday seventh May you did unlawfully strike Inspector Maiyau Taxi, a member of the Papua New Guinea police, at Papua Hotel, and two, that you did use obscene language in a public place, namely by calling Inspector Maiyau Taxi a 'fucking bastard' on the same date at the same place. How do you plead? Guilty or not guilty?"

My head was still paining and I couldn't remember what happened after I hit the floor two days ago. This was the first time I heard that I had hit my enemy Maiyau Taxi.

"Your honour, I cannot remember what happened!" I said very humbly.

The magistrate became impatient straight away. Maiyau Taxi gave his evidence, and then another two police gave their stories. I didn't know what to say as I watched the police exchanging papers with the magistrate. They asked if I had any witnesses and I said no, so they instructed me to sit down for a while. After reading the papers the police gave to him, the magistrate commanded me to stand up to hear his decision.

"Johnny Woka, I hereby find you guilty on both counts and sentence you to four months imprisonment at Bomana gaol with hard labour."

My heart fell down dead. Fear and anger shook my whole body

---

9. "Who do you think you are? You bloody 'criminal'! Do you think you are a white man or perhaps a public solicitor? You rubbish man from Hagen! Shut up and go back to your cell. You can't question me. You stubborn fellow, there's only one way here; this is Bomana prison."

until sweat started falling down from my forehead like rain. It was all too much for me. I looked up again and saw the magistrate leaving his chair. Maiyau Taxi was smiling and shaking hands with the other policemen. Fucking bastards. I said to myself as my new anger started coming up. What for nothing now I must go to Bomana *kalabus.* What about my good job? What about my good name? I knew for sure that my old enemy had found out about my being in Moresby and maybe he was becoming jealous. So, that was why he wanted me in *kalabus! O sori O! Em no inap! Mi wanpis stret!*[10] The plan jumped to my head immediately. I think God must have sent his Saint Peter to put it there, so I quickly thanked him and tightened my muscles.

I didn't stop to see the shockness on the faces of Maiyau Taxi and his other police friends. I jumped over the rails of the witness box and shot out of Boroko District Court like a cowboy. I was ready to give one kung fu to anyone who might stop me, but fortunately nobody tried as I ran towards the Boroko Motors car display building. A lot of people were pushing to get into the buses for town and didn't take notice of my running. But then I heard the police siren screaming and coming into Hubert Murray Highway. So I cut the corner, jumped over the fence and ran behind the Boroko Motors building. I could hear now that four police Toyotas were crying their sirens very loudly. One was speeding towards Jackson's airport, another one was speeding towards Waigani, one was heading towards town, and I'm sure the one with Maiyau Taxi was busily running around Boroko looking for me. Because of the many people, the police didn't know where I had disappeared to.

In quick time I was back again to the Boroko District Court, but this time I was crawling along the backside of the building. My heart was beating very fast and having a race with my heavy breathing. The police siren continued to scream louder and louder as they went round and round the block hunting for me. If I remain on the ground I will not see what's going on and soon they will have no trouble catching me, I thought. So I climbed up the drainpipe and leapt onto the roof. Like a tiger I jumped from one roof to another until I came close to the Boroko Fire Station building. *Maski* the hot sun on the corrugated iron roofs, I didn't care. My life was more important. From there I lay down flat on my stomach to catch my wind a little bit. I could see what was going on along the three corners of the block as the roof was quite high above the ground. I turned carefully to see where my enemies were.

10. That's no good. I am really lonely.

When I saw Maiyau Taxi talking to some of the people at the bus stop, I realized they were pointing to where I had cut the corner near the Boroko Motors building. My heart jumped again, so I jumped again too. From the roof to the ground is not easy, but I cleared the wire fence and landed like a coconut inside the backyard of Boroko Hotel. Too many empty beer cartons and trees were blocking my sight, and that was really dangerous for me if I couldn't see where my enemies were. So I climbed quickly up the wall of the hotel and jumped smartly onto the roof. Then I ran from one roof to another until I came to a good spot where I could see what the police were doing. My throat was already very thirsty. I thought about all the beers sleeping away in the dark room below my feet, but that was impossible now as fear, sweat, and dust covered me all over. Too late to give up now and only one way for me to win. I must escape from these bastards. Their sirens were already catching me even though they couldn't see me yet. I looked back and saw the police already everywhere searching the grounds and the roofs of the Boroko District Court building.

I saw somebody pointing to the roofs of the Boroko Hotel where I had climbed. Well, that was the end of my short rest. I jumped from the roof to the narrow footpath below. I nearly broke my arms and legs, but there was no time to waste on small pains, so I shook the dust from my nose and face and ran quickly towards the Elcom building across the street. Elcom building is one of the biggest buildings in Boroko and has two floors. I pushed the glass doors and rushed inside hoping to find a good corner to hide from the police, but the office was already busy with the people working there. They didn't stop my rushing until one *meri* Papua came out suddenly and blocked my way. She had beautiful legs, beautiful hips and beautiful breasts, but her face was ugly with anger for my running into their office like that.

"Hey you! *Dakaka oi ura?*"[11] She fired the question to me in quick voice.

Get out of the way, you beautiful bitch, I thought to myself. There's no time to waste talking to you. Can't you see my enemies chasing after me. But I didn't want her to alert all her friends and I had to find something to say to her.

"*Lasi! Lasi! Mi laik wok tasoe!*"[12] I replied very quickly.

My voice was shaking very badly and I didn't keep my head straight to give her the anser because my eyes were shooting every-

---

11. "What do you want?"
12. "No! No! "I'm just looking for a job!"

where to find one good corner for hiding. But it was no use as there were too many people already on the ground floor. I could hear the police sirens already coming around near the Fire Station, so I ran along the corridor and started climbing the stairs for the second floor. I was breathing very very fast and bubbles were dancing on my wet lips. The coldness of the air-conditioning hit me very bad. Even though my inside was boilding, my outside skin started shivering with cold.

However, that didn't stop me. I knew that big bosses always have their offices on top floors. Maybe there I would find one of my *wantoks* to hide me until the police went away. I had heard a lot about the government localizing many of the top positions, so maybe one of the bosses would be Papua New Guinean who would easily understand me and give me help. When I reached the second floor I waited a few minutes to see where I should go and also to catch my wind. One of the doors was marked "Assistant Director — Installation Division", and it looked very important, so I decided to try that one first. I straightened my trousers and bravely opened the door suddenly.

Both of them gave a small cry of surprise but didn't hide what they were doing. His secretary's short skirt was pulled up above her waist and her purple panties were open for my eyes. She was sitting on his lap with one of his hands feeling her between the legs. They were kissing and touching each other like that when I opened the door. I was very surprised. The assistant director was from Manus and his secretary was quite a beautiful Australian woman. All three of us couldn't find words to break our surprises. Anyway my face smiled automatically and saliva started running out of my teeth as my mind started to think of something else already. *O sori O!* Shit me blue, I thought to myself and shook my head again and again. I wanted to continue looking at the sexy panties and the nice buttocks and thighs, but I knew danger was following me very closely. So I ran quickly to the glass window to survey the police down below.

I saw Maiyau Taxi and his friends get out of the police van and start for the door where I had come in. No more time to waste now, and my fears even grew bigger. I quickly left the assistant director to continue localizing with his white secretary and ran out again towards one of the far windows. I opened it, and with only a quick glance to see that everything is clear below, I jumped down from the second floor to the hard bitumen below. God must be really helping, I thought, because I still didn't break any bones, only my feet were bleeding. I swore many times to regain my strengths, and then I picked up my bleeding feet and ran them towards the buildings of New Guinea Motors.

I cleared the fence with no trouble and landed among the trucks and utilities that were waiting for display. I had to crouch down to avoid being seen and to regain my breath at the same time. Then I heard both the van that had gone to Jacksons and the one to Waigani had started coming back towards me. The Boroko one was already coming round the corner near Green Jade Restaurant. I knew immediately that if I tried to run far they would have no trouble catching me. Just then I saw a short piece of rubber hose lying beside me and a dirty drain bordering the New Guinea Motors yard a short distance in front of me.

It had been raining last night and there was still a lot of dirty water in the drain. To my good luck there was a fairly large pool where another side drain emptied its water into the main drain and it had dug a deep trough for me. I didn't wait. I grabbed the piece of rubber hose and jumped into the water. After a quick look to see that no one had seen me I sank to the bottom of the pool with the hose stuck in my mouth. I made sure that its top end was above the water and well hidden between some grasses along the bank. At first I gave up a lot of bubbles but fortunately the side drain was still pouring its dirty water onto the main drain so no one could see what was at the bottom of the pool or even notice the difference to my bubbles coming up. I lay flat on my stomach with my sore eyes closed so the dirty water could not fill them up too. With one hand I grabbed hard to the rock bottom to stop myself floating upwards and with my other hand I held the rubber hose to stop it from moving around. Each time I took one breath, dirty water found its way into my mouth, but it was better that way than being caught again by the police.

When the four police cars arrived near the New Guinea Motors area, they searched for me everywhere inside the cars and outside the buildings. They spent about one hour in the area trying their very best to catch me, but too bad for them. They had to scratch their heads finally and drive off somewhere to look for me. I didn't want to take any chance in case they left one of them to stay guard at the New Guinea Motors yard. So I stayed under water from three o'clock in the afternoon until six o'clock in the evening waiting for darkness to come.

It was already very dark in the drain when I pushed my head above the water for the first time. Street lights were already on and the taxis and PMVs were taking their last loads. I was very cold from the dirty water, and my teeth were bumping one another very loudly like a truck changing gear in half clutch. It was not only the cold making my teeth like that but also a new fear starting up again. I squeezed the water from my clothes and walked suspiciously towards Ikwanemu shop where one Pagini taxi was waiting. I opened the door and jumped into the back seat. The driver was half drunk and was trying to fill his watery stomach with fish and chips.

"Trowem mi long Murray Barracks, please driver!" I said confidently and holding up one ten kina note for him to see I had real money.

He reversed quickly and we started for my *wantok's* house. Only when we drove past Boroko did I let go of the door handle, because I was readying myself to jump out if he decided to suddenly drive me to Boroko Police Station.

I paid the taxi and ran quickly to my *wantok's* house. He was in the army, and many times we used to spark together at the Boroko dark room. He and his wife were very surprised to see me and knew immediately that I was in some trouble. I showered quickly to get rid of all the mud in my hairs and mouth. He told me to leave my clothes behind to be washed while I changed into his old army uniform. My blood was then beginning to cool down, but my fear was still very very strong. I had not eaten since this morning's one hard biscuit at the police lock-up cells. My stomach really cried for food, but when his wife put the foods in front of me, my throat couldn't open their doors easily. My mind was too busy with thinking about tomorrow and the next tomorrow. What would I do? I knew the police would continue hunting me until their dogs caught me.

At nine o'clock I thought it was safe for me to try for my house in town. So I caught one Buang PMV and rode to the bus stop in town just opposite the Papua Hotel. Some people were in the small bar getting their refreshments from the half time of the pictures at the Papuan Theatre. I felt safe and walked along the shadows towards them. Then I quietly walked up the hill towards the new Travelodge. I didn't want to climb along the main street towards the House of Assembly because there could be some police patrols along there. My eyes were everywhere looking for police and planning sudden escape as I made my way towards my house.

Bad news was waiting for me when I arrived at our house. My friends told me that a lot of policemen had been coming to our house to ask about me. Of course the news only made me sweat more on top of the hotness of climbing up the hill. I ate some more food and drank some green men to make me feel strong again. Then I quickly told my friends what had happened. They swore at the police and promised that one day they would pay back for me. This made me feel safe for the time being, but the beers suddenly made me feel so tired that I wanted to sleep maybe for one whole week. Yet I knew that the police would try to catch me that night while I was fast asleep inside. Another plan came to my head. I packed my pillow and blankets and climbed onto the roof of the boi house to sleep. The roof was not on a big angle and it sloped closely into the hill to make an emergency escape easy. Well, the sleep killed my eyes immediately, but one ear was open all the time for any strange noises as I rested on the roof.

My ears woke me up at about one o'clock in the morning. At first I thought I was only having a bad dream, but no, the bastards had really come again. I heard the crunch of their boots on the loose gravel, and the street lights showed that there were four of them and had two police dogs with them. From the roof I could see that they were trying to snake up the hill quietly, but too bad for them because I had already seen them. I didn't wait. I threw away my sleep with my blankets and jumped away in the opposite direction. I knew one secret track that ran between the houses until it came down to Papua Yacht Club near the water. I didn't think where I should go, only that I must get away from the dogs and the police bastards. Ten minutes later I heard the dogs barking at my friends where I had left them.

I held onto my sides as I waited for my wind to come back. My heart was nearly breaking with anger, fear, and sadness all at the same time. All the small boats were floating sleepily at anchor, and the coloured lights from the residences on the hills and the big ships at the wharf made a very beautiful picture on the calm waters of Moresby Harbour. Everything seemed to be sleeping peacefully except me. I left the shadows of Papua Yacht Club and crawled to the water edge where the dinghies were parked so that from the jutting cement landing I could get a good view of the corner towards town. I listened carefully and heard the dogs had stopped barking. I knew what that meant immediately, and I swore to Maiyau Taxi very loudly. Then I saw their bright headlights speeding down the hill towards Papua Yacht Club.

I jumped from the cement landing into the harbour and started drowning immediately. The salt water burned the cuts and bruises I had collected during the day and all my muscles were aching with tiredness. But somehow when I hit the ocean bottom my anger shot me upwards again to look for air. When I broke the surface I was in such a desperate hurry to breathe again that the air I swallowed was greatly mixed with gallons of salt water. I decided to swim for my life, at the same time to get away from the police as far as possible. There were hundreds of yachts and speedboats anchored around, so I swam from one to another and looking back all the time to see where my enemies had gone to. Then I saw them shining a bright flash light around the anchored boats. Fucking bastards, I swore to myself again as I realized that they must have seen me jump into the water. So as they flashed their bright torch around I decided to swim towards the large yacht that was anchored furtherest into the harbour. I swam and I swam until I reached the large yacht.

There was a small cabin light on, and the couple were completely naked with their love-making and enjoyment of themselves. The man was a German and the woman was a *meri* Kerema. Both of them were so busy digging *kaukau* that they didn't hear me climbing on board. I was completely exhausted. I lay panting on deck to get my strength back from the excited swimming and the good sight before my eyes. After about five minutes they decided to come out to check, and that's when they saw me half dead. The man was angered at seeing me lying there on his boat, and he quickly wanted to know my business.

"Was willst du? You bloody monkey!", as he mixed some German and English for me.

Fortunately the beautiful *meri Kerema* had pity for me and realized that I was in some big trouble the way I kept turning my head towards the shore. Even though she didn't have much clothing on her, she had plenty of brains and knew how to quieten down the angry German.

"Darling please, don't be hard on the poor creature." She rubbed her voice against him.

Shit me blue! The way you talk! It was too good that I even felt like jumping overboard again and drowning myself. The German melted straight away and I told them my sad story. As I finished the story we saw one speedboat starting up and I knew that my enemies were now going to come after me. The couple didn't want the police to spoil their fun so they gave me a pair of rubber flippers and told me to swim for my life. There was only one place to swim to without going back to the police trap. Macdhui was lying about one mile away from where the yacht was anchored.

Russell Soaba

FROM "WANPIS"

I found him talking with the elderly gentleman in front of the chemistry lab. Upon seeing me Just Call Me Joe beckoned. "Here he is," I heard him say to the gentleman as I approached them. "Brother," said J.C.M. Joe with a bow, then turned and bowed again to the gentleman, "this is Mr Goldsworth; Mr Goldsworth, our ex-deputy head prefect of All Saints'."

"Yes of course, of course," said Mr Goldsworth, extending his hand. "I'm more than gratified, my lad..." I felt the firm, humanitarian squeeze. "I have been looking forward to meeting you, my boy. And I must say..."

I let my mouth gape wide, thinking of suitable words to say and at the same time drowning the gentleman's words with my sudden shock of bafflement. But no words came out of me. Why, this *is* Archibald Goldsworth in person, whose name appears prominently in the history books of our old school; for whom we prayed every year on All Saints' Day and sometimes saluted or bowed before his portrait; and without whom most of us would never have had the chance to acquire the education we now have. And there he was, right in front of me, smiling and letting those blue eyes survey my profile with friendliness and paternity. I just did not know what to say.

An excerpt from the novel *Wanpis*, published by the Institute of Papua New Guinea Studies, Port Moresby 1978.

"Mr Goldsworth," I managed to say at length, "I—I'm — I'm proud to be an old boy of All Saints'." Somehow, deep inside my heart I felt that what I had just said was true. For the first time, it seemed, I felt the paradox of my whole life: of always wanting to go on walking in one direction, only to turn back remembering that there are also people like me; of always arguing, raising contradictory views, with an imaginary Father Jefferson in my dreams, then walking out on him, slamming the door hard in his face and running wild into the webs of the wide free world, escaping one net of confusion just to be caught in another, just to return to him a few years later in complete distorted state of mind and say, "Yes, Father, you were saying . . . ."

"I'm glad to hear you say that, my boy," Mr Goldsworth said. He paused, looked at each one of us closely, then fixed his stare on something somewhere behind us. His face showed an expression worn by dedicated men of the world in deep contemplation. "Yes, my lads," he then continued in a faraway voice, "yes; yes, yes, yes . . ." Mr Goldsworth turned his face away from me and Just Call Me Joe. He began now pacing the pavement with heavy steps, his hands behind his back with the fingers meeting and caressing each other into tight locks. We followed him: with J.C.M. Joe wondering what was in my mind and I listening attentively for the next words.

"I have received a number of letters from the principal of All Saints'," he said, still walking ahead of us and never looking back, "and each letter is an expression of deepest concern — not only from Father Jefferson but also from friends of the school here, in Australia, in England and in America too — for the vitality of education in this country. So much need there is for education for those who come after you, so much work there is to be done and so much money to be raised for the erection of the school's permanent buildings."

We followed the gentleman weekly, listending attentively.

"I am sure what I am saying is nothing new to you, my lads," the old man's voice came again, "since you two have been to All Saints' — and I am sure you do recognize the needs of the school."

"Yes . . . yes, Mr Goldsworth," J.C.M. Joe agreed.

"A man, my lads," Mr Goldsworth continued, "a man cannot go about slicing a piece of cake on his own. There must be other men, dedicated men of the same interests, men with enthusiasm and responsibility, men who are homogeneous in their common conscience, causes and so forth, to help make up the yoke the lone man has and help slice the cake for the benefit and betterment of all."

Nostalgia gripped my insides and in the distant parts of my mind I could hear a familiar voice calling "Cui bono?" and I responding at the top of my voice "Ego!"

"To put it another way," the old man continued walking towards the library, "there must be co-operation between those in positions of authority and those below; to have them work together in achieving this country's nationhood and unity — and this can only be done through education, my lads, education."

"Educate them all," J.C.M. Joe said suddenly and unexpectedly.The elderly gentleman stopped when we had reached the steps that fell to the student forum arena where the student politicians aired their views. He still had his back to us. Ahead of us emerged a few students who busily moved from door to door, going to and coming from lectures and tutorials.

"A popular example of what I am trying to stress now," said the old man, turning right and away from the steps to the forum, "and it's quite often used at All Saints', is: a twig alone can be easily broken; but where there are more than twenty twigs gathered and bundled together it is hard to break them. Consider then, my lads, that each twig is a person working for a particular purpose. Now then, and this is very tricky, would one twig last?" He paused, to allow us time to grasp the meaning of the parable. "That, my lads, that is what I want you to think about; for through this ideology, simple though it may seem, a society or a country stands fast on its own. And remember, lads, remember that without this form of co-operation, a country, however big or small, will eventually bring itself to chaos, and there may not be any room for those who will want to cry over its spilt milk."

The statement of the century, I thought sadly. Mr Goldsworth turned to confront us.

"I am growing old, my lads," he announced in a crisp voice; "yes, I am growing old. And some day, one day, I shall cease to be." He paused again, to let the sentiment sink into our hearts. "Yes, yes; rather an uncomfortable experience that all humanity must go through. And at times, therefore, I am inclined to think that within a man there is a certain duty, a certain promise, that must be fulfilled for a certain purpose before the ultimate end."

"Yes, Mr Goldsworth, we realize that," said J.C.M. Joe.

"I have seen much in my time," the old man said, turning away again and jutting his snowy head heavenwards; "and this, to an extent, enables me to assert that I know how things are, will be, must be. My experiences in the last war, for instance, made me aware of the wonders a man can see in this world, and of certain sacrifices he must make for a particular cause or causes."

Just Call Me Joe nudged me to show me a broad grin between his dimpled cheeks. I followed closely the footsteps of Mr Goldsworth to the library, as he spoke with authority and care.

"Twenty-five years ago I would have died," he said; "yes, my lads, I would have died if only God had not put me in the hands of those villagers without whose help I would have ended up ignorant of the meaning of my life. It was then that I saw things, and thought of doing something to help the poor villagers."

And I thought back, turning the pages of the old school's history and through Mr Goldsworth's speech I could see the villagers bearing a fatally wounded warrior on a stretcher to safety, humming "Onward Christian Soldiers".

"There was something they needed but knew nothing about," Mr Goldsworth went on; "They had to see the light while they had the chance. And somehow I felt it was my duty to see to it that they possessed this light as rightly and as much as any other human being upon this earth."

"Of course, of course," put in J.C.M. Joe, as if talking to the students ahead of us. Whether Mr Goldsworth heard him, I could not tell, for he kept walking towards the library.

"When I started talking about starting a school it was a one-man job at first, due of course to financial shortages and lack of interest from the people who should recognize what I had recognized. Then I had offers, mainly from churches in Australia, England, and America, which sent teachers, men and women, dedicated men and women, who were prepared to carry out my principles and, if possible, put them to fruitful practice. But alas, alas, some of these men and women died as martyrs and saints while trying to bring the light to the villagers, some of whom might have participated twenty-five years ago in saving me. Yet, these men and women who died had to die; they had to die, my lads, in order to have the villagers themselves open their eyes to see the light."

For no reason at all I suddenly caught myself thinking of Jimi Damebo. A random memory, random memory; I immediately dismissed the thought.

"And every time I think of the school itself," went on Mr Goldsworth, "there is something to add to it, my lads, something more . . . . So you see, All Saints' is, in many ways, part of me, part of a man's life, one might say; it isn't a gesture of mere gratitude to what the villagers had done for me during the last war. No. All Saints' is, in so many ways, my child."

By this time we had reached the door of the library. A group of students walked past us: some held up clenched fists in the air and called out "Black Power!" to Just Call Me Joe, who grinned; others just giggled and hurried on after making the comment "Ei taim bipo! i pinis, lapun!"[1] to Mr Goldsworth, who showed no response; and still others exchanged conspicuous secret glances and remarked, "Ai luk, dat's da kid u was tokin tu 'imself! Yeah, dat's im ourait! A saiko kais!" Mr Goldsworth turned slowly, still deep in thought as if he didn't hear the comments, to face us both. He rubbed his bushy white eyebrows free of perspiration and blinked two or three times as if he had at last discovered what was written in our hearts. J.C.M. waved to some students. I looked up at the old man.

"But I must say I was more than glad to hear you say you are proud of the school, my lad." He directed the words more to me than to J.C.M. Joe. "Bear in mind, young sir," he added, "that in a country that needs development and prosperity it is young people like you who must be its leaders, who must be its means of attaining economic, social, political, and perhaps cultural and religious integrity. It is through you that it will become a nation, a strong, united nation."

I listened in silence, thankful to learn that I would be one of the leaders of the country. Suddenly the old man shook his head vigorously, as if awakening from reverie.

"Well, I have talked too much," he said, and playfully threw a powerful fist which tickled my belly. "We'll have to talk about the school some other time, my friends." He smiled down at me. "How nice to see you! I must say, you are a cunning little chap, because every time I come here you don't seem to be around. I have been hunting for you all through last week, asking Joseph where you were, and all he could say was, "Oh well, he's around, but you only find him asleep in his bed late at night." He turned to J.C.M. Joe, laughing. "And how's our Black Power man? Always addressing himself as 'Just Call Me Joe'. Yes, good old happy days! Reminds me of my own academic years when the students at the university I went to could divide themselves to different groups of Rightism, Leftism, this and that, aha! ha! ha! Yes, yes, there never were times much happier than one's academic years."

Mr Goldsworth danced as he spoke, like a boxer in a ring, throwing his playful punches at me and then at J.C.M. Joe.

"Well, if you two don't have anything to do tonight," — he danced to me then to J.C.M. Joe — "would you care to come to dinner at my place?"

1. "Your time is finished, old man."

"Be delighted, Mr Goldsworth." I dodged his playful punches and looked up to J.C.M. Joe, who nodded and put on his usual grin again. "Oh, that's right! Today's Friday! Yes, we'd like to come, but please don't feel obliged to take us in, Mr Goldsworth."

"There is absolutely nothing to it, my lads. Nothing at all."

"Any beer?" asked Just Call Me Joe, who was too slow to dodge the old man's heavy arm which landed paternally on his shoulders.

"Oho, Joseph! Always talking about beer! I can imagine seeing you in a few years time, young man. An influential politician and a giant of a man all because of beer."

The dinner was profoundly delicious. Classy would perhaps be the right word. There were paw-paw drinks, fruit salad, sugared banana and custard, some taro and *kaukau* and a variety of imported vegetables enriched with coconut oil, sauces, and gravy of both Oriental and Western tastes. Meat was in abundance, and there was enough grog to last anyone with any amount of drinking apetite the whole night. It was more a party than dinner, as most dinners are to some influential people in Moresby.

A lot of people came to the Goldsworth dinner that night. There were university students and members of the academic and administrative staff: members of the House, ordinary people; senior public servants, junior clerks; guests of distinction, and *ol lusman bilong rot*.[2] They swarmed in merrily in Afro-Asian shirts, baggy long pantaloons, round-necked T-shirts and white spotless shirts, cheap looking thongs and high-heeled shoes, dusty or torn Hush Puppies and black shiny boots. It was a night for all to socialize: some people talked of the past with regret, others talked of the bright future; some talked politics, others talked culture; some cried for some unknown reasons after a few bottles of beer, others just laughed with everybody else; a few danced casually, or did the tapioca dance as the Trobrianders call it, to the rhythm of the music that came out from one of the rooms; and yet others just got drunk to kill sensitivity.

Mr Goldsworth was the happiest man that night. A satisfied man, with the usual bright and young personality, moving lightly from guest to guest like a butterfly, cracking a joke here, participating in a vital political discussion there; offering a beer here, amicably slapping a *boi* there. A senior public service acquaintance of his had once described him as "a worthy man, a great man of our country" — the compliment we remembered so well from the mouth of our history master at All Saints'. And no guest left the gathering without a word or two with the old man. After watching Mr Goldsworth for

2. "all the drifters."

some time, I could not resist wishing I were as content as he, in a way I had been wishing all my life, never stopping once to admit that my life was so full of silent dreams of a world only I could feel, think about, and live in. This particular world was so alien, so incurable if it were a disease, that my hopes for the future had turned out to be those of fear, uncertainty, confusion, and self-destruction. And the terror or it all was my own refusal to find ways of surpassing such a curse. It became part of me, my habit, my badge of honour, but a concept for which no other strong enough belief could help erase my internal stubbornness. I still was the *lusman* at heart.

Mrs Goldsworth was equally the happiest woman that night, entertaining the guests with the same amount of enthusiasm as the old man. She offered drinks to guests of all sorts, escorted some, the late comers, to the dining room to devour the unending supply of food, as well as shared and cracked jokes, conversed and cackled with them. Every now and then she would answer her old friends' questions on how young Jack Goldsworth was doing at the ANU, informing them that he was expected "home" next Christmas after completing his masters, or outline to the interested newcomers, like J.C.M. Joe and myself, her husband's history from the days of his youth to the night in Port Moresby.

I discovered, after moving among the crowd, that I had un-consciously consumed four bottles of beer. Fears of complete in-security and self-betrayal began to stalk my conscience. I knew that a rather rapid consumption of beer for a starter like me wasn't at all rewarding. Yet I felt at the same time that I needed some kind of release, an inner release. I moved amid the din of the gathering with some difficulty at first but tactically afterwards, no longer afraid of the dangers of self-exposure, thinking I had no choice but to pretend to live with the crowd: by the time I was tipsy I felt secure.

Just Call Me Joe, to my surprise, had come out of the Goldsworth castle talking louder than usual. Surprisingly still, he came out holding hands with a *dimdim* who was wearing a pair of liquor-crimson eyes that flickered freely at any mobile male in the gathering as if some magic had gotten into the dear daughter of the soil. At last, at last, we have a *lusmeri* in our midst, I thought drunkenly.

"You are not enjoying yourself," I heard some one say behind me. I looked around to find the old man towering over me. I understood then that he was superior.

"Oh yes I am, Mr Goldsworth," I returned. "But please don't bother about me."

"And oh, don't take too much of that brown and green stuff," the old man joked in an imitated Aussie accent, then strolled off. I admired him: Man is a social animal?

A typist I had seen in front of the library walked up to me and we talked. After some time she recommended that I should read Colin Johnson's *Wild Cat Falling.*

"Why?" I asked. "Because it was written by a half-caste?"

She left.

Then Just Call Me Joe walked over to me with his friend.

'Her name is La!' he shouted and slapped me hard on the back. I felt my back hurt from the *pum* of his palm.

"Who's La?" asked the *dimdim.*

"La?" inquired Just Call Me Joe, which proved that he too was drunk.

"Who is La?" the Australian asked again, slowly, as if a flood of jealousy was surging through her blood.

"Oh La!" shouted J.C.M. Joe in sudden realization. "Of course, of course — er, La is his fiancee —"

"Bullshit!" I said.

"Oh by the way," said J.C.M. Joe; "brother, this is Sophie."

Then he gave the *dimdim* my Christian name, after which she said, "Oh that's you, ah brother? Ah, my *wantok,* yu yet — yu winim olgeta."[3]

We shook hands. I felt I liked Sophie.

"Who was this La that you were talking about?" she asked a while later.

"Oh, it's the name of a girl at uni, Sophie," explained J.C.M. Joe. "Also prelim, like me and him here."

"I see. What about her?"

"She's interested in this *doga.*"

"Well, wish you tons of luck, comrade," said Sophie and tapped me on the shoulder.

"I wish I could thank you for that, my *wantok,* but J.C.M. Joe is a cold-blooded liar!"

"Aio Goudi!" laughed J.C.M. Joe mockingly. He then said, "Hey, Sophie, I'm going to piss."

"Okay, but don't fall asleep in the john."

"In the what?" asked J.C.M. Joe.

"In the john."

"What the hell's that?"

"That's someone's *tok ples* for the dung pot."

"Oh!" said J.C.M. Joe and let out an uproarious laugh that drew attention from the other guests. I was afraid I would be sober again.

3. "Ah, my friend, you surpass all."

"Go on," said Sophie, ignoring the stares around us. "Go on, before you wet your pants, Just Call Me Joe." He staggered into the enclosures of the Goldsworth haven to release the poison he had just consumed.

Sophie turned and stared at me, her pupils enlarged, revealing the slight crimson that glittered under the soft neon lights. That happens, I thought sadly; at beer parties. She leaned forward to let her cigarette fumes cloud my line of vision.

"Just Call Me Joe tells me you write some of his stuff for his forums," she said.

"Well, some of the ideas are mine, but a lot of them are J.C.M. Joe's own thinking. I don't contribute much, really." I stopped, to have a silent opinion on her but dismissed the thought. "They are a village idiot's confused, studentship convivialities, really," I then said.

"Oh, but some of the things J.C.M. Joe says are real — I mean, they project the facts of the whites — well, take his forum yesterday, for instance; what was it called again?"

"Looking Into Ourselves."

"Ah, that's it," said Sophie. She offered me a cigarette. I told her I wasn't a smoker yet. "I really enjoyed listening to it," she continued. "Somehow I felt that speech was far removed from the Movement's other speeches in that it created that sense of depth and clear understanding of what it means to be black, a subservient of some huge churning machine that sort of hypnotizes you, or something. It was a *creative* speech, anyway." Pause. No sign of Just Call Me Joe. What's Sophie explaining? "Tell me, do you really believe in Black Power?"

"What do you want me to say to that, Sophie?"

"Well, it's a straightforward question, isn't it?"

"I know." I felt my head spin.

"I mean, do you really think, judging from yesterday's forum, that the black Niuginian is undergoing torments that are very much different from those the African and American Negro goes through?"

"Different? I reckon all blacks are black — they can even be white and vice versa — but the torments, which must be spiritual if not psychological, are always there, within anyone, as a basis of all human suffering; very near to sadism, but not —definitely not — within sadism, since this is a developing country — this is Papua New Guinea — much as what J.C.M. Joe spoke of yesterday —"

"Yes — but don't you think that is sadism still, no matter how much you might strive to avoid, let's say, sexual and other perverse obsessions that should still reflect sadism, or are forms of sadism, anyway. I mean, let's face it: I can just take one look at you and know what's in that little head of yours. It *is* sadism!"

"But you must realize the importance of having to leave, in your definition, an individual Niuginian at the very doorstep of sadism."

"You underestimate your own people."

"There is none that convinces me I am no better," I said. And in sudden anger, I added, "You mustn't force them forward too quickly, *please!* Don't give them easy promotions!"

"Strewth!" said Sophie, throwing her head back and laughing. I looked all around me uneasily. "You are not being kind to your . . ." — she paused, surveyed by profile, then completed the phrase — "your people."

"You don't have to listen to me, Sophie," I said, thinking: I'm not educated enough; I'm still immature; I'm still Enita's useless, seventeen-year-old silence and perversity — O James, Jimi Damebo, where are you? I envy your intelligence, your serenity that knows no guilt. "But a restless Niuginian, now, isn't someone who indulges in the pleasures out of the pains from internal suffering. None would, anyway, let alone have him or her just *imitate* the beauty and satisfaction seen in the Christian tradition of martyrdom. Rather, even in his prime of — what? — having achieved or reached tertiary education and having acquired *raison d'etre* to glorify his personality, in reality, he still is that confused young Christian moralist!"

"An atheist and a Christian at once."

"Almost, Sophie: a profound Christian rejecting Christianity, rejecting himself. And a closer look at his self can easily reveal that he is a pretentious village nut! So in his self-rejection he is rejecting the self that is not his. And the result after the absence of this particular self, which is Christianity, is his original self which is void, but an emptiness that is filled by fruitless nostalgia for the traditional past. Sometimes, though, such an emptiness could enable him to start patching up his own being. Not many Papua New Guineans, not even your Just Call Me Joe, recognize that."

"Hell, you must be some kind of a philosopher or something," said Sophie.

I saw her eyes roll lazily, her head sway a little and her shoulders sag after a deep sigh.

"I can't think any more," she lied.

I liked Sophie.

The cold neon lights from the Goldsworth Garden of Eden began to spin before me. I lost concentration. Yet an instinct warned me to keep on going until I had not only reached but also crossed a thick dividing line between sanity and insanity. I knew I would still be alive then. And what would be there to confront me if I crossed the line even in my state of sub-conscious yet distinct, even faint, living mind? Peace? Tranquillity? Getting drunk was a stimulating exercise for the mind. I rose. I needed another beer.

"Sorry?" mumbled Sophie.

"I need another beer."

"Oh. Get two, please."

Just Call Me Joe met me on the way with three bottles. We sat down again just as the gathering was beginning to come to an end, owing to the din which was louder than was perhaps expected. People began leaving one by one and I realized it was time for us to go.

"Is Mr Goldsworth giving us a lift, J.C.M. Joe?" I asked, uncomfortably beginning to feel sober.

"Oh, I'll drive us," offered Sophie, and leaned over Just Call Me Joe to pick out a straw that was caught in his tightly-knotted hair. She missed the straw and found herself laughing against his tough body.

"Hey, come on, let's piss off!" said J.C.M. Joe, after watching the crowd for a while.

"Just Call Me Joe?"

"Yes, Sophie?"

"Our friend's pretty simple, isn't he? I mean, he doesn't find it hard to bring himself out to the open, or something. Hey, *wantok.*" Sophie then turned to me. "If I were in your clothes I'd feel like strolling down the streets with my fingers chokingly gripping my own neck! Release yourself, man; release yourself."

"Yeah," said J.C.M. Joe, almost defending me; "he's the only knowledgable idiot we have around here." But he was watching a Bougainvillian student who had somehow come to bad terms with a *dimdim.*

"Hey, watch where you are going, whitey!" shouted the Buka student while picking himself off the ground.

"Well, if you weren't too bloody drunk, you'd watch where you were going, mate!" retorted the Aussie.

"Don't speak to me like that, whitey!" shouted back the Buka student and reached for the other's collar; the Australian's spectacles fell to the fround during his unsuccessful attempt to jump clear. "Come on, someone — hold my beer while I teach this white bastard a lesson!" His friends joined him but were striving to pull him away.

"Come on, Camillo," they choroused. "Leave the guts-ache alone. He's too fat to fight for himself."

"Leave me be, idiots!" shouted Camillo. "I want to know why he called me black bastard before he tripped me. Oh yes, brothers, I want to know. I *need* to know! Come on, whitey — explain yourself, or I swear by my ancestors I'll spill your blood here and now!"

"Come on, Camillo," moaned his friends; "let's piss off!"

"What for?" cried J.C.M. Joe suddenly, startling Sophie and me. "Are you kids women to let the bastard get away with it? I heard him call Camillo *mungkas* bastard!"

"He what?" the Bougainvillians responded in startled anger, releasing Camillo.

"He called him *mungkas* bastard!" shouted J.C.M.Joe. He was grinning. "Now let me call all of you lot *mungkas* bastards and see if it doesn't hurt. Go on, *mungkas* bastards! Doesn't that hurt? Ei? Ei? Go on, *misinaris* — pissoofff!"

At this opportunity Camillo rushed his victim. "And you know what *mungkas* means?" he shouted into the throat of the Aussie gentleman. "Mungkas means black and black means power!" With the word *power* the student pushed the victim to the ground and was about to ride him when there was a commotion of hurrying figures, some of whom grabbed him in time. Someone had managed to turn the music full blast; with the music the blacks were off for their lives. They did not care who stood in their way: they wanted to spill blood: they wanted to kill: they wanted to survive, to live. Just Call Me Joe was within the black crowd. Soon the rest of the gathering swarmed to the trouble spot and Sophie and I found ourselves within the group, holding hands. Alone in the middle of the ring of the Mungkas the Aussie gentleman became his own misfortune, his own poor condition, his own sad destiny: he looked up to Sophie and me as if begging for mercy, as if wanting us to go in and rescue him from the blacks. Speechless, he stared at us expectantly. Calmy releasing my grip on Sophie, I turned my back on him.

"You are the one who rightly deserves the charge of White Fatherism," I heard Just Call Me Joe shout behind me. I turned, like a traitor, to observe from a safe distance. "Yeah, we always see you in the company of black people whom you are trying your hardest to turn into another group of whites. You know what's wrong with you? You are a white, soul-forgotten, common poofter who wants to be polite just so that blacks will think of you as a good man, a simple good man, or some shitted rubbish as that. You are a white bastard who has no soul, no beginnings, no nothing — you are empty inside, you hear! You are an exploiter, that's why you are too disagreeably fat! You are a moral teaching maniac, that's why you retreat every time a black man wants to approach you with something saner. The only blacks you want to be with are those that you think of as mere fools who must regard you as some Big Masta beyond their comprehension! Understand? Understand me, white bastard! Go on, *raus!* Get out of my sight before I kill you here now and give your flesh to the dogs in the streets to devour. Go on, away with you — you who turn my life into a dog-shitted venom!" And Just Call Me Joe's words echoed eerily down the brightly lit yet silent Goldsworth Garden of Eden.

The music died.

Yet J.C.M. Joe had managed to get the crowd under control. Sophie became hypnotized by Just Call Me Joe, whose drunken and angry form in the middle of the crowd resembled the axis of a vast, yet dead, ferris-wheel. In that instant I saw Mr Goldsworth extend two powerful arms far in front of him, his face twisted into contours of pain supported by a popping pair of blazing eyes, yet he remained where he was as if warned by some external command to keep still with the dead wheel. The crowd became a snap-shot, creating an atmosphere of alive, near-Rembrandtal abyss, although as soon as J.C.M. Joe resumed speaking, it slowly moved in lazy rhythm, all ears attentive.

"Away, away with you," continued J.C.M. Joe, lowering his voice to poetic tones. "For we know your kind, man. Come on, pick up your glasses and cause no more disgrace. You are simply a bastard. Ah!" J.C.M. Joe paused to spit, then raised his voice with a new kind of anger. "Ah! You don't even deserve a dog's name! Go on, piss off! Go into the darkest confinement of your room where you came from and masturbate there, in front of *Playboy* magazines. Or go on away from here and rape a random village idiot along the road and produce useless bastards and *ol lusman bilong rot!* That'll console you! That's all you deserve! And don't use our society as an excuse to hide from yours!" J.C.M. Joe laughed bitterly. "In fact, I've heard of people like you — I've been to one of them's flat at Paga Hill. Man! he was so pissed he's decided to masturbate in front of us-ehe yeah! And his only reason had been that not even a local money-minded bitch could love him! Because he was simply too fat, to froggy, too white like a dead fish bloating in Moresby's streets, devoid of flesh, devoid of beauty!"

Just Call Me Joe stopped to eye everyone at the gathering, including Mr and Mrs Goldsworth. The tone of his voice had again become calmer, more like a profound and concerned black poet.

"Now all of you, listen to me," he said with deliberate care. "You may think I'm mad. And yes, I can agree with you there — that what I say is all madness. But the fear in it all is that everyone of you might take my mania to be truth, the profound consequences of which will be that of salvation for a nation from the self-cheated noose of non-idealism, from the Australian government itself sending dogs like this fat slob here, from even our so-called politicians who commit themselves to this self-cheated noose of non-idealism out of false democracy that is completely white. And the black man? What of him? Answer me, somebody!"

He paused, his body quivering with the poetry of Negritude.

"Why, the black man that is of the soil is stripped, his youth far molested, cursed and gripped by a slow, smouldering spinning fire of colonial hell, turning him into a mere grain of a sad case composed entirely of his senses that are too numb to respond; and the music of that youth, that black youth, which is the soul of the forgotten village, is brought to a standstill! Why? Because of the perennial greed of the white man that helps to do nothing but chop him down like a tree, like that antique tree of time, like that —"

Sophie drove us to the campus.

John Kolia

A MEMO ON MISSIONARIES

One of the most interesting missionary stories occurs in Dostoevsky's *The Devils*. A poor Bible-seller has obscene material planted in her bag by some idle and vicious adolescents from the class of gentry; there is also a hidden political motive behind it. Later, the character of the innocent woman is cleared by the novel's most determined inquisitor. Many missionaries, however, suffer rather from an excessive whitewashing, but the point is clear: their motives are misinterpreted for either flattery of denigration. On radio programmes and in booklets intended for our primary schools quite misleading information is handed out. The London Missionary Society work — that is, by its South Sea Island Teachers and their Tongan pearl-fishing guide in the Western Province — is ignored. Vengeful Doctor Brown is venerated. But for that matter Queen Emma the awful is quaint and D'Albertis the disgusting is dapper. Only the armchair colonist, the Marquis de Ray, is not exonerated; and at least he had the decency not to intrude personally. Because intruding on an individual basis is the missionary method, but like Bulominski on horseback they do not really feel the roughness of the road on their soles. However much one can criticize our heroine, she cannot be accused of having remained aloof, and come to think of it, neither can Jesus or Mahomet or Paul or Master Kung. Newly recruited missionaries have for many years been arriving into

The epilogue from *My Reluctant Missionary*, a novel published by the Institute of P.N.G. Studies, Port Moresby, 1978.

organized Church systems which must slightly discourage the best of them. A very few have arrived as individuals relying on the support of faith, and one gathers from traders and administrators they have been a general nuisance to everyone. That's more like a missionary! That's more the brand for burning us with indignation! But I refuse to be humorous about it when any day now Satan will be let loose from his prison. Revelation is obscure on this point, but perhaps it means that it has already happened nine hundred and fifty years ago. I must ask my ex-mission lady. Because, of course, as the reader has already realized, I am interested in being converted by her also; perhaps if my tinea gets worse?

Perhaps she could also explain to me this mission poster; given out to encourage the faithful, apparently. It is the illustration to some text, not a biblical text but a message from or for the Billy Graham Evangelistic Association, 1000 Harmon Place, Minneapolis, Minnesota, editor (somewhat deliciously) Sherwood E. Wirt, but the text is by an Akbar Abdul-Haqq. Another article starts on the reverse of the illustration and is called "Don't Knock Christmas". But the illustration itself; well, there are camels to the left and a town to the right, so we're in the desert, and out of the wastes grows the most enormous tree, cedarish? From its top branches looms the ghost-like figure of a headless man with arms outstretched, olive skin, white semi-transparent garment. In place of a head is the banner DECISION. Well, 'tis too hard a knot for me t'untie. But it gives one an idea how ill-comprehended might be similar foreign posters to indigenous minds on first beholding them.

However, perhaps one should examine dogma rather than personalities or propaganda, though they are obviously interconnected. When dictator Moses came down with his alpine philosophy (and shortly afterwards massacred the rival party), he proclaimed certain rules which gained credence from their supposed supernatural authority. How relevant are these rules now proclaimed to Melanesia for Melanesians? Thou shalt have no other gods before me. Melanesians still pay respect to a number of supernatural beings, spirits, monsters, and others but perhaps all these are facets of what is meant by God. Even devout belief does not relieve them of their awe of these earlier gods, however; pastors do not ignore them, nor do they confine all of them to the person of the Devil. Perhaps monotheism is a convenience.

Thou shalt not make into thee any graven image . . . bow down thyself to them. Papua New Guineans have a rich art which involves the making of such images, and it is of great psychological support to their lives; its decay (but lately renewal) is part of their loss of stability. These images are perhaps no longer bowed down to, but older people suffer through lack of respect for their graven and respected images.

Thou shalt not take the name of the Lord thy God in vain; for the Lord will not hold him guiltless that taketh his name in vain. This has perhaps been taken too seriously by puritans. *Thank God* and similar ejaculations are the notice of God's existence taken by people not overtly devout. Melanesians repeat many of these sayings. An old commentary of last century pragmatically interprets the commandment to mean that one must not be a hypocrite in worshipping what one does not truly reverence, nor must one swear false oaths in God's name. The law then is a universal one and some villagers do go to church for social reasons and actually poke fun at the reverential parts of the proceedings.

Remember the sabbath day, to keep it holy. Villagers always did take days of rest, and the one in seven habit appears to be a healthy one. In villages, however, this is sometimes interpreted according to the letter rather than the spirit; for example, in some Central villages women will not hang out babies' nappies to dry on that day even though these are needed dry for the baby's welfare. A most mischievous laying of unnecessary burdens on men has been introduced by the Seventh Day Adventist mission in declaring Saturday the only sabbath day, whereas the Old Testament stresses the six days labour then rest, not the unreckonable day itself. The silly controversy has been taken up enthusiastically by Melanesians who find it easier than to think about the broader philosophical issues.

Thou shalt not kill. One must sometimes kill, in fact. There is no police control outside the towns and incomplete control in them. The line between self-defence and preventive attack is thin. In a bully's household it is no use the weaker physically waiting for him to come home drunk; much better to employ the sorcerer's weakening medicines beforehand — and these may prove fatal. It becomes necessary for an evil person to be eradicated for the good of the village community sometimes. Also, one can hardly fail to attack and perhaps kill, for example, the man who raped one's wife if the courts are super-lenient as they are, often letting the guilty off on a technicality, and if the result of not violently attacking one's wife's rapist is to have one's wife and children removed from one and awarded to the rapist by the sneering community.

Thou shalt not commit adultery. The whole *raison d'être* of village marriage is children. If one's wife does not get pregnant or if one is impotent then one doesn't want the world to know about it or oneself (that's adultery), but one is happy to have social children not necessarily one's genetic own. One must give children to an un-attached woman not one's wife to preserve her place in society and her sanity. Does that make her an adulteress? It often makes her a useful alternative wife.

Thou shalt not steal. When one is thirsty and near someone's coconut grove? It may be considered very bad behaviour, and there may be taboo signs on the trunks of the trees, but should one rather faint from thirst? Or of in Moresby starving, should one not steal a scone from a Chinese shop? One sometimes has to steal, if only in rich/poor towns to serve notice on the rich.

Thou shalt not bear false witness against thy neighbour. When *he* is bearing it against *thee* and the courts are blind? If one goes to gaol, one's wife and children (I am thinking of a particular case) will in a few weeks time be living in the house of another man, proud to have scored over one.

Thou shalt not covet thy neighbour's house, wife, servants, cattle, goods. Then the stimulus for improvement by self-reliance and hard work will be removed. In any case, one may have reciprocal shares in one's neighbour's goods.

It all, frankly, seems the product of the time, place, people, economic situation, social customs, and climate of a very different group of people.

But the most disastrous message of Victorian Christianity as introduced is the "gentle Jesus meek and mild" image. The very support of the women, the older, and the children depends on the unmeekness and the unmildness of the men. There is evidence from Mount Bosavi and elsewhere that men wanted their adolescent sons sodomized by tough men, so essential was it that every opportunity for gaining this aggressiveness be grasped. It was as if they were saying, "This is your role in life unless you are equally male." You don't have to like the method or the more, but try to picture gentle Jesus as an ideal of Melanesians in the three incidents that follow. They are from three different, unidentified Melanesian villages in highly Christianized areas, widely apart. I shall call the incidents the Poisoning, the Coward, and the Rivals.

At the first incident, The Poisoning, I was present. One evening in the village there was a great hullabaloo. "What's up?" I asked. Angry people were surrounding a young married man. It seems he was annoyed for some trivial reason: his wife was late back from the garden or his food was not ready — something slight of that nature. He deliberately filled a spoon with a noxious substance and poured it in the baby's mouth. The woman grabbed the child and ran to neighbours who washed the baby's mouth, made it vomit, and so on. The baby was saved, but the man had no reason to believe when he committed his crime that it would not kill the child. It was his child — no scandal attached there; the wife had not been unfaithful. A completely indefensible act. The man had no history of mental illness and is an upright citizen today. He regrets his act and loves his children. They are happy again. Apart from the cowardice of attacking a baby (he could have fought his wife and the people would just have laughed; but in the area the women fight back). Worse, the group was losing the population race and some of its land. They needed (and fiercely loved) their children. It would not assist them if the man went to gaol.

"Tomorrow", they decided and informed me, "we will hold a court at such-and-such a garden. You, being male, may come if you wish."

Naturally I did so wish, although I was unaware of what form the court would take. In the morning all the males except the smallest boys got in the canoe with the accused and paddled off. (Now, no guesswork, I respect their privacy. You are wrong, anyway, it's not there.) Up the river we went to Unaigardengabuna and disembarked. To my surprise the accused and one of the other young males stood while we seated ourselves in a circle.

"What's going to happen?"

"Shhh!"

An older man, I think the father or father-in-law of the accused, stood up. The youth next to me whispered in translation.

"This man had done a very bad thing," the senior man began. "We can either settle things in our traditional way or take him to the kiap. In that case he would go to gaol, and the very first night several men would be knocking at his wife's door." Everyone laughed and the accused grinned sheepishly.

"Therefore he has decided to settle things according to custom. They can fight till one is knock out or give up. If this bad man gives up and is coward this other boy takes his wife and child. We pick this boy because he is same size and age and can marry that woman too." (In fact, they meant he could take her as a second wife, but she would have accepted such a status in preference to a cowardly husband.)

"If this other boy is coward then he has big shame. When I say start you must start. Keep fighting till one is knock out. Any styles can be used."

God, I thought to myself, are they going to kill each other? But even the accused's brother seemed to be smiling. It was right and enjoyable, both, to them. And I winced as the battle began. Do you hate to read of this violent kind of thing? Then you are ignoring an important part of Melanesian life.

"Start!" shouted the old man after seating himself.

The two heroes — as they looked, in their ragged shorts and bulging muscles — leapt in to the attack. The defendant's and the prosecutor's fists connected more or less simultaneously, probably on each other's arms, but it was hard to see. They gave no quarter and did not step back and breathe like boxers do in rings. At first it was mainly fisticuffs, however, but that is something — slogging it out, I mean — that you can only keep up for limited periods. They were landing some heavy blows, under which I wondered they didn't reel back, but were fairly evenly matched. Soon they were grappling, however, and it was no longer a game. Their blood was up and their supporters were cheering them on, mostly cheering the prosecutor on, I noticed, even members of the defendant's family. Perhaps that was polite under the circumstances. Then it was a sort of jerky wrestling, with each one trying to trip the other with legs entwined — but, yes, they were actually trying to bite too and would have gouged no doubt if they did not have each other held firmly by the arms. Finally after what seemed round-lengths full of twisting and snarling and cheering ("Kill him! Kill him! Get him down!"), the defendant fell backwards with the prosecutor on top. I suppose the prosecutor's strength for the moment had prevailed — or was the defendant being tricky? But no, the defendant was firmly underneath as he bumped on the ground. He was stunned for a moment, I suppose, for he loosed hold of one arm on his opponent, who smashed him cruelly in the mouth. ("Kill him!") But only for a moment; then he was turning with his teeth in the prosecutor's neck, but the blood I saw was probably from his own cut mouth. At any rate the prosecutor jammed a thumb in his eye, and he let go and rolled away. The two jumped apart and kung-fued together. I think that is what it would be called. Anyway, the defendant's aim was luckier and he got in a strong kick to the prosecutor's belly, and as he crumpled up on the ground the defendant chopped him with flexed arm across the neck.

Surely he must be finished now, I thought. What happens now? Are they disappointed that the defendant is winning? Last century, would the defendant have now killed the prosecutor and proudly claimed that one's wife and any children? Certainly everyone including the referee was yelling, "Finish him! Finish him!" I realized that it didn't matter who won, as long as there was a decision. Queensberry Rules and points decisions were not for them. "Finish him!" The defendant, grinning with joy, I suppose, walked up to kick the prosecutor's head.

I'm going to see a murder, I thought. But that was his and my mistake. The prosecutor was barely supporting himself off the ground, but as the defendant got near him he suddenly catapulted forward and got the defendant's toes in his mouth, biting hard and twisting his neck. What a wrench he must have felt, but not as much as the defendant who came tumbling over and crashed face down onto the rough ground. The thrilled men and boys whooped for joy at the great attempt at comeback. Then the prosecutor was on top of the defendant and trying to cut off his wind with his flexed arm. The defendant was wriggling, trying to get him off.

"Give up!"

"No!" Cough, cough.

The crowd of males cheered his brave reply, because the bloke's eyes were sort of bulging.

"Give up!" Pant, pant.

"No!" Cough, cough.

Then I saw that what was meant by "any styles" was any tricks and treachery. The defendant grabbed a stone, and the crowd approved and cheered, but he couldn't quite reach the prosecutor for a damaging blow although they were rolling somewhat and at any moment he might get his chance and not waste it. But the prosecutor got one arm down and tore the defendant's shorts down. In a flash he was twisting the defendant's genitals. The latter screamed in agony.

"Give up!"

"No, ahhhhhgh!"

Remember, he was nearly choking also. Then the prosecutor gave him a terrific twist, he probably fainted for a moment, and the prosecutor leapt away then back and landed somewhat into his flank. The defendant was rolling in agony and let his rock go. The prosecutor snatched it up. "Kill him! Finish him! Any time!" *Bang!* to the side of the head. About to come crashing down again, but he is obviously knocked out. The prosecutor stands wary, to make sure. He glances at the referee, who says nonchalantly, "Finish him." The prosecutor delivers sentence with a mighty kick to the head.

"You win him," announces the referee, and they all run up to hug and embrace the winner.

It is obvious that in old times — or perhaps today if I, an outsider, had not been there — the defendant would have been killed. But there is no bitterness. They all, including the prosecutor, revive the defendant with water, and the prosecutor helps him up and they embrace, glad the village-disrupting incident is over. We all return singing and happy to the village. The defendant is smiling and the wife greets him, interested and pleased to see that he is still her husband. I do not think the defendant politely allowed himself to lose; they were too battle-angry for that. But no doubt if he had sneaked back to his father's house a coward who had "given in" in fear, the wife would have calmly picked up her baby and goods and walked smiling to the victor's house. They were dancing that night, and the boys said to the prosecutor, "You win him", and one of the smiling congratulators was the loser.

Well, that's the end of the first revolting incident. The second I did not witness, since it happened this century but before interference made it impossible. But still, who knows what happens in the privacy of the bush? The Coward, that's what I call it, and it's close to the very heart of Melanesian psychology and philosophy, perhaps. The informant was a witness as a young man. It was the custom to put the young men in the first line of battle. They either got killed or became men. So he was not only a witness, as we shall see. Again, his and their identity must be protected. They fought against the people not so far distant.

"After an exchange of ritual insults we ran forward, and boys of my own age, about fourteen at the most, I suppose, you know when you first get hair under the arms, faced me. I knew some of them. As we ran we threw spears, then fought with heavy strong sticks. A boy beside me fell down with a leg wound from a spear, but he died anyway because a boy from the other side crushed his skull in. That was allowed, as we say. Then we were smashing away with our heavy sticks, and I inflicted quite a few injuries; and like they say today in Moresby, I graduated, I felt. The men ran through us, and there were some terrible fights and injuries either side. I couldn't really say who won because the sun started to go down, so both sides retreated with their dead. But no doubt both sides claimed victory. I laugh with those old enemies today, because we are pleased with each other's brave performances, you see? But we had one terrible shame. The boy the other side of me — and I hadn't even noticed it myself — had run away. No one ran from the other side. We didn't even have a live captive to make the boy fight. They did that sometimes, and if the enemy won he was allowed to join our clan and live. But the elders had noticed, and when we got back boasting of our "victory" to the village, we saw this boy grabbed and brought before the elders, one of whom was his father or grandfather, I forget which, but his father was angry with the boy, not protective or making his excuses. He had already been through the preliminary initiation ceremonies.

"The grandfather, as if he had never seen him before, scolded the boy. As he said, our whole survival depended on nobody running away. It's not absolutely true, of course. If in a sneak attack the village is wiped out, the men who can run away do, and live as bachelors in the swamp trying to steal a woman when they can for their communal use. It used to happen." He meant nearly wiped out.

"Now you must fight another boy and he will kill you if he can. Then he said, 'Look at this good boy here. He killed many enemies today.' That was not really true, but I must have impressed them by my action. I think I had poked one boy's eye out, and they were pleased with me because when one of our men was fighting a big man I went up and hit his — what you call it — crutch with my stick. and our man then smashed his mouth with his weapon. So they were happy with me. 'This boy will fight you, and you must be brave and keep fighting till you kill him. Otherwise you are going to die today.' Well, I was very surprised. The boy was even slightly bigger than me. Taller, you know, but only a little bit. But he looked very frightened, and I felt hot with pride, I must admit. 'Right, get ready, only sticks.'

"In those days of course we just covered up our private parts a little bit, you know. In fact the cover was our initiation sign, and — ha ha — I can tell you it didn't hide much. Isn't it funny how customs change? Anyway, back to the fight. 'OK? You understand we want you to kill this boy.' they said. 'He is useless. Don't stop, just keep going.' And they placed us at a short distance apart with all the men and women and children watching, the women from verandas, but I bet his mother was hoping he would wake up and fight bravely, because she probably had experience of this sort of thing. It didn't happen very often; cowardice was a rarity with us, and she knew (but I didn't) that when we were nearly badly injuring each other the chief might say stop if the boy was brave, or he might get too excited and order me to kill him; so there was a chance for him, you see. 'Right, fight,' he ordered.

"Well, I certainly wasn't going to let him kill me, even though I used to play with him at the creek every day. In fact he was like my best friend, you know. But of course I had no thought of disobeying the chief. So I ran towards him, but he didn't. He was terrified, I know that now, poor bloke. Only boys, we were. Not ready for wives according to our custom. 'Kill him!' someone yelled. I knocked him hard with my stick on his arm, which of course he tried to fend me off with. He feebly tried to poke me away. Everyone was yelling. I can hear it now. But I should remind you how we enjoy to make another boy cry. I don't think men cry, but if we did we would enjoy that too. You know how those drunk men say I'm going to hit my wife and make her cry then sex her, you must have heard them. They do it, too. And you've seen how older boys enjoy to belt up younger boys; why, we tell them to do it and cheer them on, and if the other boy cries we tell the big boy to give him more. We get pleasure out of hitting a crier. You want me to tell the truth, don't you.

"Well, this bloke started crying, and so I got cruel with happiness. But anyway they were all egging me on. I even made them laugh by my sort of playing with him. When he covered up his face and weeping eyes and bleeding mouth and nose, I rammed the stick into his belly and did a little dance. 'Kill him!' the chief ordered, not amused. So I really crashed the stick onto his headside. 'No, no,' he begged. 'Well, fight me then.' And he did a bit, but I guess I already had him beaten. Oh, when I look back now I wished he had fought back. I would have enjoyed beating him even more. 'Kick him!' they yelled, because it looked as if he was going to stand there crying for ages, and my arm was getting tired. That's good idea, I thought. I kicked him and missed and nearly fell over. He should have lashed out at the moment and got me off balance. They would have liked him then. But I then had time to grab him with one hand as I steadied myself. I remember I got him with one arm around his waist, then I hooked one leg around behind his and tipped him down. 'Kill him, kill him!' they yelled. I kicked him and jumped on him, and he was screaming. I can't pretend I was not enjoying it. I felt hot with a great physical happiness.

"God, I punished that poor boy, kicking, jumping on top; he trying to roll out of the way with me catching up to him all the time, either with my feet or with my heavy stick. You know it's a special wood as hard as iron. Then he started to look sort of unconscious, and I glanced at the chief. 'Break his head and kill him,' he ordered. Everyone was happy, and the women too were calling out, 'Kill the bad boy, kill the coward.' They meant in our dialect kill the boy-thing with the fault in it. It's no good; throw it away. Like that. Well, that boy must have had a hard skull. I crashed down with the stick and the head bled but still looked the same shape, ha ha. Then I made my trick and they all thought I was wonderful, laughing loudly. I tell you, his father was so disgusted with him he was begging me to smash him. So what I did, I grabbed up a big stone and with two arms brought it crashing down on his forehead. He was lying on his back more or less, and stuff like brains or what came out. The men and boys ran up to hug me and like our custom is rub their chests up and down mine. 'You are a very good boy,' the chief said solemnly. The father of the boy came up and rubbed me and we rubbed our noses. 'Today you are my son-in-law,' he said proudly, but I didn't know what he meant. Then I saw him go up and kick his son's body and spit on it.

They carried me on their shoulders and we all had a big feast, mainly to celebrate our victory over the enemy, of course. Some dogs snigged at the boy's body until the chief told the boy's relatives to throw it away. It was not given our usual burial, but the idea was to throw it in the bush where the enemy might find it and it would cover our shame if they had seen him run away. In fact they had, and we didn't know it but in their celebration they had already made up a song about the cowardice of our boy, it was unusual. Had that boy still been alive we would have handed him over to them for their kids to practise on. And when I finally stopped dancing and went to my father's house, that boy's young sister, just a child she was, was already waiting on my mat. So I got married first before all the other boys and that girl was my first wife. She's dead now. But that first time I was so proud and rough with her when I spoil her first time I am at the same time boasting about killing her brother in her ear."

Well, that's the second obscene incident over, and I hope you did not enjoy it. There only remains the third incident, to which I was a witness, and I think I decided to call it The Rivals, didn't I?

In another area again, and I'll try to give no clues, there was the usual fights within the village, between the villages, and between groups of villages, the point being that rivals combine as soon as the group is attacked by an outsider group. I was sitting on a veranda one afternoon, a Saturday it was, and the sun was about to go down, when a truck roared in full of drunken town boys as they call them. I had been hearing something about some trouble. Well, there were all sorts of strands to it — a misused truck, a previous fight, a damaged house; who can trace the origin of such things? Anyway,

"We will kill those town boys when they come", that sort of thing was being said; and no doubt the town boys were saying, "We will kill all those village boys when we get there." The town boys, so we heard, had a great champion who had a reputation for successful fights with some boxing club. He was at the university too, part-time perhaps, I don't really know, but he didn't come home very often: but when he did, look out village boys. Of course the village boys pushed forward their own champion, one they imagined was the town boy's childhood rival, and it may have had some truth. They had egged him on so much he had insulted the girl who was to be the university student's village wife. You know they have two sometimes, one here and one there. He had grabbed the girl in a garden and made a very rough and shameful action of some sort; I didn't hear the details. But everybody was scandalized of course, and the man just jeered; and he was her brothers' leader after all, so they jeered too. He would deliberately hang round her when she went to visit her parents. Most of the time, of course, she was in her fiance's house, but this daredevil would infuriate them by going up close to the house and calling out sexy things to her as she blushed in shame inside. And here he was sitting on her parents' veranda when the alcoholic express roared into the station. Her brothers were probably urging her to marry their champion, but of course there had already been bride-wealth of some kind explained with the other boy's family, who referred to him as "that rough dirty boy".

Being a coward myself and only glad they hadn't found it out, I clutched my notebook and just hoped this wasn't going to be revelation night. The sun was blood red behind the truck, so the drunks looked like huge silhouettes coming towards our side of the village, straight towards the girl, her parents' veranda, and the rival champion. Just a thought: alcohol makes one reckless and dangerous but presumably interferes with balance and speed of reaction. I'm looking ahead, but just for then, well, you should imagine the scene: the town boys with bottles of beer and fairly good clothes and shoes, all their smart gear; the village youths in torn shorts or perhaps a pair of ragged jeans, the top button lost and the zip sagging; the village champion having leaped up and down the steps and standing there quite a man, muscles and all that, in fact rather light-skinned with freckles and gingery hair, quite an Esau, but no match for the hulking Martin Beni-type physique of his town rival. In fact all the town boys were heavier-looking; beer or better food or just better physiques, I didn't know. The village boys were without beer bottles or weapons, although one boy carelessly tore off a veranda railing as he passed some house and it leant handidly to him now just in case. The village boys were to the west of the veranda, the side I was on; the town boys somewhat to the east of the veranda but not far away. I suppose they had come to see the village champion belted up as if they had bought tickets when they'd borrowed the small truck. There was no exchange of insults; it was as if all had been said already. The town champion, huge shoulders hunched, tossed his empty bottle down and waded in, or at least towards. And I think the village champion did reel somewhat from the first blow which must have really stung his ear. Each side surged their champion on, of course.

Well, if I thought it was going to be over quickly I was mistaken, though the village champion looked frail and freckled beside the burly youth with the purple shirt. But he hopped about and got blows in here and there as he best could. Nobody interfered, although it would have needed only one movement from one side and they would all have been at it. The gingerish villager was set-faced and the town boy now looked furious, a killer for a night if ever I saw one. The villager would jump forward, punch, then jump back, and the town man would give a mighty punch which would have knocked him out had it hit his heart or chin but which usually smacked with audible force elsewhere. The rival age-group boys were yelling, of course, but the village otherwise was silent, and no doubt with reason. In a moment the town boys might suddenly start smashing up the village and hitting parents, wives, and sisters. Then freckles got in a forceful punch to the town man's belly, and the town champion got really mad and grabbed him. He was a bear of a man, and the villager looked crushable in his embrace, but he apparently brought his knee up smartly into the other's groin. Town bent forward slightly and Village got in a strong punch to the mouth and then a sort of kung fu to the legs which rocked Town. He jumped forward, however, and got his hands on Village's throat. That's it, I thought to myself, sorry for the village boys because I was rather in their favour. I didn't know the town boys, of course, but I have known one or two arrogant university students from the area.

But in some way the villager used whatever principle is involved in getting your enemy's weight and impetus to help you, and they crashed into the limestone floor of the village. The village boy had little chance of remaining upright himself and was somewhat underneath; perhaps they were on their flanks, for how else could he have in a moment got on top. Their legs and arms flailed and the town head got a bump on the limestone. Then in some way grabbing a leg and an arm, Village half-rose and with a mighty effort got Town on his face. *Bang*! He kicked the town boy's face down. And again. Town was not weakening and repeatedly tried to rise, but straight away Village would kick his head then jump on top. Finally he was lying on top of Town trying to pin him down, and you could see he hardly had the strength or weight to do it.

In a minute, I thought, the other town boys will be on him; they'll get him in a position with his arms behind his back, the town champion will have his pleasure of him, and the village boys, some of them thin an skeletal, will have to try and rescue him. But the maiden's two brothers came half-way down the steps menancingly and the town boys held off. I think they felt stunned with disbelief. Anyway, the village boy had the town boy by the hair and would bang his head down, smash his face down, his other hand punching and holding the heavy town man to prevent him getting sufficient leverage to rise. "Give up?" he asked him, and at length, to my relief anyway, the town boy must have said yes. The village boy leapt up and back, then jumped more or less onto the town boy's face as he rolled over. Wasn't his face a mess when you could see it? So much for the famous town champion. "Help me," he begged the town boys, and they warily did so.

"You win him," the village boys were saying as they walked towards the gasping village champion and rubbed his chest with their hands by way of congratulations. By this time the town boys had reached their truck; they weren't going to stay, apparently. As soon as the motor came to life, so did the village boys. They all ran after the truck, throwing some of the discarded bottles and stones. I think I heard the rear glass of the truck cabin shatter. The town boys tried to protect their faces with their hands. And so the interlopers were accompanied from the village. The village boys, those "rough dirty boys", came back with their grinning champion whooping what must be the modern equivalent of war-cries. The villagers were happy too, or politic. Some of them must have seen their sons and boyfriends chased away, and they mightn't have come back for months.

Then an interesting thing happened. I hadn't realized that the village girls thought the ginger one was ugly. Not only did he have an unfortunate pigmentation, in their opinion, but he had bad patches of sipoma, and no girls would agree to marry him. So perhaps he had frustration to spur him on too. Anyway, whether or not anything was said as he and the girl's two brothers were on their way back — I suspect it was; her older brother probably said, "Take my sister now", in admiration — the three of them strode up to the veranda and the freckled one pulled the girl up roughly by the hand. She screamed. He pulled her down the steps, the younger of the two brothers assisting her with his foot in the back. The mother rushed forward yelling, to pull her back, and the older of her two brothers landed the mother a smack across her face which ended her protest. But the girl didn't want to come to the ginger one's house, and she dropped to the ground on strike, as we might say. The woman sitting next to me said, "My brother is marrying her. His skin has very bad smell when it rains or when he sweats." I realized I was sitting on the veranda of the target house. Meanwhile the boy just roared with laughter, then belted the girl across the face and dragged her up to the house and up the steps with everyone except me grinning at her. I think the public exhibition was what upset her most. A pretty little girl, quite young; she had probably looked forward to having a modern house in Boroko with an electric stove.

He started bundling her inside and I had my first close look at him. I couldn't see that he was ugly. Fit and fine, rather, but certainly not smooth either. Freckly and hairier than most of them in that village, with very noticeable big patches of sipoma skin disease and, yes, a strong very sweaty smell. His shorts hung onto his hips by the grace of God, and very dirty from his garden or hunting they looked. He got her inside to a bedroom. Since she was still wailing, I suppose he must have started really hitting her, for I heard some — well, they sounded like strong backhanders. Not wishing to intrude (I might as well have been invisible), I made my way off. The marriage would very definitely be firmly if not roughly consummated by Sunday morning. A knot of excited villagers enjoyed the belting and laughed as they tried to picture the scene as they stood as close to the room as they dared. And I'm happy to say I never met up with the town boys again. They looked very tough to me.

That was unpleasant in the telling, too; but the happening cleared a lot of stale air away, I think.

No wonder the Old Testament is so attractive to our people. In Genesis they read of Adam's mistake in following a woman's advice; the violent revenge by God; the ideal man Cain's killing of weak Abel, who has no descendants, whereas Cain goes out victoriously, multiplies and flourishes; Noah's bloodless philosophy disproved by Nimrod's conquests; Canaan's laughter at his drunk father (as in villages) and his bold successes; Abraham's prostitution of his wife to defend the group; Abraham and Lot's hostility but combination in the face of outsiders, and particularly Abraham's slaughter of the enemy at the battle of Shaveh Valley; the punishment of the effeminate men of Sodom; Abraham's right to take other wives, the first being barren; Lot's impregnation of his daughters when like some village fugitives he has no other women; Sarah's genetic child accepted as Abraham's social child; Lamech's justification of his killing a man by Cain's example. There are many other examples. Virile Esau, first-born of twins, is tricked politically by cowardly Jacob but overcomes his enemies by aggression and makes Jacob submit to him in the end, even being offered women and children by Jacob. Jacob plans to let half escape if attacked by Esau (so some escape is permitted to preserve descent). This is inevitable conflict by Jacob's sons from different wives. Jacob, forced into a lengthy fight, learns to be strong too; but when Dinah's brothers punish the rapist, Jacob runs away. Jacob's son spoils one of Jacob's wives. Joseph's brothers make a mistake in not dealing with him more decisively. The bias in the Bible is disproved by facts — for example, Dinah's brothers save Jacob's group from destruction, but Jacob is made to say they will be punished by being scattered; in fact, in the eyes of men they are rewarded by aggressively spreading out and leaving many descendants. Jacob's philosophy therefore reads as introspective and unmanly. The same group (Levites) also saves Jacob's religious ideas later in time of Moses. Even Jacob admits Judah's fierceness will be important (Jesus descended therefrom). Benjamin's aggressive tribe will flourish (famous Biblical figures from this line).

In Exodus they can read how the soft Israelites living well in Egypt allowed themselves to be enslaved until the killer Moses organized them into rebellion, which is what the plagues probably mean, and the Egyptians let them go; how Miriam and the women-folk are thrilled with the Israelites; destruction of enemies, like village women; how Jethro advises Moses to control people by laws and organized religion; how the Mosaic regime is made valid by employing the Levites to slay the members of the other political party — but Aaron, being useful, is saved because he is a leader of the Levites, forming the Moses-Aaron coalition which successfully rules.

In Numbers they can read of the special honour given to the household troops, the Levites, that they might remain loyal; the legendary method of claiming that those destroyed by natural phenomena were in fact plotting against the establishment; the cowardly Israelites forced to wander in wilderness until they are courageous again when they overcome their enemies; their great cruelty in victory, but the saving of most women and children; Moses' rebuking of cowards; the payback murder approved; the marriage of daughters in accordance with the wishes of the menfolk. And in Genesis they can read of Tamar's right to be given to a younger brother each time her older husband dies. It's all so much in accordance with village custom. The so-called New Testament is not in accordance with custom. To quote just a few hymns: "Christian children all must be/ Mild, obedient, good as He"; "Jesus, meek and gentle"; "Jesus, meek and lowly"; not forgetting "Gentle Jesus, meek and mild, /Look upon a little child". In our towns it is against the law to carry an offensive weapon but almost suicidal to walk about at night without one. The village pattern is repeated in the towns. It's all right for the rich to be meek and mild, but to survive you have to be like the rascal gangs and try to stay alive.

Well, this hasn't really been a memorandum on missionaries, but I hope it has made a fitting conclusion to the novel. And if you are a missionary of the meek and mild persuasion, mightn't you devise a prayer for the rest of us? For without the aggressiveness and treachery and male chauvinism and cruelty and muscles and killer instinct of the fourteen sets of fathers and sons from Abraham to David, and of the fourteen from David to the carrying away to Babylon, and of the fourteen from them to Jesus' father Joseph, then there would have been no Jesus who was capable of losing his temper and belting up the temple businessmen.

Plays

Arthur Jawodimbari

THE SUN

CHARACTERS

BUNANI,	*a man from Towara village*
DOBANA,	*his wife*
OWADE,	*orator from Towara village*
TUNANA,	*Dobana's younger brother who has the magic of the sun*
KAMUSI	
PURERE	*young men of Towara village*
GETAPU	
MAITA	
GERETU,	*a dancer from Jinaga village*
BUNDEBA,	*villager from Towara*
SUNDARA,	*Bundeba's wife*
KUNJA,	*villager from Towara*
EMBOGO,	*Kunja's wife*

Children, Dancers, men and women of Towara and Jinaga

This play was produced at the first Papua New Guinea Arts Festival in 1971 and again at the Pacific Arts Festival in Suva in 1972. Reprinted from *Kovave* 2, no. 1 (November 1970): 46-57.

SCENE I

Outside BUNANI's *hut. Early morning. It is dark.*
Enter a group of children, singing:

CHILDREN:
> Sun, why do you hide so long?
> Sun shine, oh shine on us,
> come out of your lime pot.

> Sun, why do you hide so long?
> Come out, we have slept enough,
> come out of Tunana's lime pot.

> Sun, why do you hide so long
> in the darkness of your lime pot?
> Come out of your mother's womb.

> Sun shine. oh shine on us,
> sun look into our faces
> sun make us warm, make us laugh!

[*During the singing the light gradually fades in to bright daylight.*
BUNANI *is now seen in front of his hut, chewing betel-nut.* DOBANA
comes in, carrying a pot of food. BUNANI *looks up briefly, then goes*
on chewing. DOBANA *starts dishing up food.*]

BUNANI: Hurry up with that food! You are very slow. I am tired of
chewing betel-nut.

DOBANA: Chewing betel-nut? That's nothing new. Every night you
stay up, chewing, till you finish the whole bunch.

BUNANI: Stop that talk and pass me the food. My saliva is dry.
[DOBANA *hands him a dish.*]

DOBANA: There, eat it all. I am not hungry. These taros are tasteless. I
wish we had some fish.

BUNANI: Can you catch fish? Or aren't you a woman? Why grumble
about fish? Don't you see the waves are very rough these
days? I am hungry for food, not fish.
[BUNANI *starts eating his food.* DOBANA *too starts eating.*]

DOBANA: The wind blows all the time, but we don't have any rain.
Maybe the people of Beube are sailing to our place?

BUNANI: No, the people of Beube won't come till the moon falls behind the sea. But I think that the people of Busega are making the wind blow, so that we can't catch any fish for the feast.

DOBANA: Aeee . . . even if the wind didn't blow, you wouldn't go out fishing. You just talk about fishing, but you never touch the sea.

BUNANI [*angrily*]: Have you ever eaten a fish you caught yourself? You just shut up! And what about your brother? Ask him to catch some fish, instead of playing around the beach.

DOBANA: I see, you don't dare to face the sea yourself, but you want my brother to go out and catch fish.

BUNANI: He doesn't do any other work. So he might just as well catch some fish for you.

DOBANA: This is wife and husband talk. Don't bring in my brother. He is no longer a small boy, he is approaching manhood.

BUNANI: You are the one who started the talk. I don't like talking — but you force me to talk. You are a woman who says one thing one moment, another thing the next.

DOBANA: When is that feast going to be held? We have not brought our crops from the garden yet.

BUNANI: There is plenty of time. The feast will be held when the next moon comes out. There is no hurry. Many people have not brought their food crops yet. But tomorrow we will ask the young men and women to help us carry our food to the village. Our big men say that we must give more than what the Emoi clan gave us.

DOBANA: Yes, they talk a lot. They said they blinded us with their food crops. They said we can't give as much as they gave us. [DOBANA *takes another bowl full of food and places it in front of* BUNANI.]

BUNANI: What's all that in the big bowl?

DOBANA: That is Tunana's food. He is young, and always hungry. I know. Take it to him in the men's house.

BUNANI: How many stomachs has your brother got? This food is just too much. He did not follow us to the garden yesterday. Why give him so much? Have you left enough food for the children?

DOBANA: He is not a pig or dog to eat your leftovers. He does work in the garden, but yesterday he stayed home with the other young men. I put the children's food in the basket, before I dished up the food for us.

BUNANI: All right, let him sleep, play, and eat all the time. You can feed him like a piglet in a cage.

DOBANA: If I don't give him food, who else will? He has no relative to
go to: our parents are dead.

BUNANI: All right, give me the bowl of food and I'll take it to him.

[DOBANA *gives him the bowl.*]

DOBANA: Go well. I must see what the children are doing.

[*Exit* DOBANA.]

BUNANI: What has the fellow done to deserve this amount of food?
He has done nothing: except swimming in the sea and playing
on the beach.

[BUNANI *transfers the taro to another bowl which he hides. He
replaces the taros with stones and covers them up.* OWADE *comes in,
in time to see* BUNANI *disappear.*]

OWADE:

A man walks proudly in the sun
a man walks angrily in the warmth.
He takes his good fortune for granted.
He does not know what jealousy will do,
to him and to the rest of us.
A man walks proudly in the sun
he is going to offend an orphan—
he does not know that an orphan is guarded
by anxious parents from the land of the dead.
A man walks angrily to the orphan—
he does not know how closely he lives
to the spirits of the dead.
A man carries our fortunes in a bowl of stones.
May his foot stumble,
may his mind falter
and his heart lose courage . . .
Sleep soundly men and women of Towara
the time could be near
when you no longer want to sleep . . .

SCENE II

On the platform of the men's house. The young men are talking idly.

KAMUSI: Friends, my sister told me that the girls will be challenging
us in a moonlight dance tomorrow night. Girls from other
villages are coming.

TUNANA: Is it high tide or low these nights? Last time two girls nearly drowned me. Other girls poured sea water on me and my necklace was thrown into the sea.

PURERE: Had I been there, I would have forced one of them to drink sea water. At that time most of our boys were fishing on the reef. I went there after fishing, but no one was around.

[BUNANI *walks in smiling.*]

BUNANI: You all seem excited about tomorrow night's moonlight dance. Last time the girls said that they defeated the boys.

[*Hands the bowl to* TUNANA.]

Here is your food, brother-in-law. I must go to the garden now.

TUNANA: Thank you, my in-law.

[*Exit* BUNANI.]

GETAPU: Tunana, your brother-in-law must have been listening to our talk. I wonder how long he was listening . . .

MAITA: I hope he does not tell the girls, because we want to surprise them. Since they are inviting girls from other villages, we will invite boys from other villages too. We will let the small boys join in the dance; then we'll come later and surprise the girls.

TUNANA: This time I'll get revenge on these girls for what they did to me last time. But my friends, let us leave this talk. Come and eat with me. My sister has sent me a big bowl of food. I bet all of you are very hungry.

[*They sit around the dish and pick out a stone. Each boy tries to bite it.*]

KAMUSI: Aeee . . . this is stone! My teeth can't penetrate this solid stone. Where are the taros? My mother never gave me stone instead of taro when I was hungry.

PURERE: Who ever ate stone to fill his stomach before? Our friend of no shame asked us to share his unusual meal. After all this friendly conversation, he sets a bowl of stones before us!

TUNANA: My friends, I am sorry. I cannot understand how these stones got into the bowl. They can't be from my sister. They can't.

GETAPU: Aaah — shut up! You told us lies and I almost broke my teeth on this stone. You should eat some of your unusual meal yourself, before offering it to us.

MAITA: Our friend has planned to get rid of our teeth. Let us get out of here, before they bring us some more stones. I don't want to go home with my mouth bleeding.

TUNANA: My friends, I am shamed before you. I have no bad feelings

against you. I can't understand why my sister gave me stones
instead of food. I am sure it was not her. . . .

GETAPU: That is not true. You and your brother-in-law want to get rid
of our teeth.

TUNANA: Oh no. Believe me my friends, really, I don't know . . .

MAITA: Let's go. I suspect Bunani will be back with more stones . . .
[*They contemptuously throw down their stones in front of* TUNANA.
TUNANA *sits with his head bowed.*]

TUNANA:
Oh shame, shame!
How can I live with this?
No one will ever forget this day.
Whenever I show my face
people will say:
"This is Tunana, who fed his friends on stones."
I must leave this place
I will travel down the coast
till I come to the dark land of cannibals.
If they kill me — well, let them kill me
and eat me.
But if they spare me,
I will give them the warmth of the sun.
[TUNANA *packs his belongings. He gets his large lime pot and puts
his sun magic inside. As he does so the stage lights fade.*]
Father, see the shame of your son.
Help me to get my revenge.
Before you died,
you left all the magic to my sister,
but to me you left the magic of the sun.
Now let darkness fall on this village.
Let the cold enter their bones.
Let the taros dry up in the ground.
Let the children die with hunger.
Let pale creepers entangle their houses.
Let all joy and happiness leave this place.
I will take my canoe and paddle to the east.
Better to be at the mercy of cannibals than to endure this
shame.
[*There is darkness for a while and silence. Then from a distance
the children's song is heard.*]

CHILDREN:
Sun, why do you hide so long?

Sun shine, sun shine on us,
come out of your lime pot.

Sun, why do you hide so long?
Come out, we have slept enough,
come out of Tunana's lime pot.
Sun, why do you hide so long
in the darkness of your lime pot?
Come out of your mother's womb

Sun shine, sun shine on us,
sun look into our faces
sun make us warm, make us laugh!
[*After this song there is a very brief silence, then confused and
anxious voices all at once while people rush on the stage.*]
MEN AND WOMEN:
What happened? He is not coming!
No sun! No light!
Something is wrong!
Tunana! Tunana! Where is Tunana?
I am afraid! I am afraid!
What shall we do? What shall we do?
[*Admist the shouting and confusion a solo voice is starting the song
again, anxiously, nervously.*]
WOMAN:
Sun, why do you hide so long?
Sun shine, oh shine on us,
come out of your lime pot.
[*The crowd joins in. They sing wildly, desperately.*]
Sun, why do you hide so long?
Come out, we have slept enough,
sun make us warm, make us laugh!
[*The song breaks off suddenly on a kind of desperate shriek.*]
WOMAN: It's no use! It's no use!
MAN:
Behind the black palm tree
the sun is hiding.
There he sits,
by the old woman,
the witch who kills our children.
WOMAN:
Let us cut the black palm tree
till it comes crashing to the ground.

MAN:
>Let us kill the witch
>let us kill the old woman!

MEN AND WOMEN: Let us kill her, let us kill her!

OWADE: Stop!
>[*He speaks with both sadness and authority.*]
>Don't atone for a crime with another crime.
>The sun is gone from you for ever.
>Tunana is gone.
>Driven out of the village by shame.
>The orphan walked out of our village
>and the sun went with him.
>From now on
>the night will make its home
>with the people of Towara.
>The cold will follow us like our shadow.
>Retire to your houses
>and digest the last fat meal you have eaten.
>From now on
>lean days will commence in Towara!
>Retire to your houses
>to spend this long dreary night . . .
>[*Silently and slowly the people walk off the stage in different directions.*]

SCENE III

Enter TUNANA *in an almost dark stage. He puts down his string bag, and mumbles to himself. He seems frightened.*

TUNANA: I can go not further. In this lonely place, I'll make my home. The sun will shine on this land: but what will it see? Who lives here? Are there cannibals to kill me or sorcerers to bewitch me? But my eyes are heavy. I am too tired to build any shelter. Better not to make any noise, that might attract people. Father, protect me during my sleep. Whoever finds me here, let them accept me in their midst. . . .
>[TUNANA *falls asleep. Beating of drums is heard, first faintly, then louder. Warriors rush in with their spears. Some are beating*

Kundu drums. One of them sees TUNANA. *There is a shout and they dance a mock attack on him. But the women come in and beg the warriors to spare him.*]

WOMAN: Spare him! Look at the necklaces of pigs' tusks around his neck! He must be a man of great importance. Let the stranger live among us and be one of us.

GERETU: Ah, this is true. We must not kill a man who sleeps peacefully on our dancing ground.

[*The warriors retreat with a sigh, lowering their spears. The women sing and dance around* TUNANA. *He stirs. He wakes up confused.*]

TUNANA: Am I dreaming? I fell asleep in a lonely place. Where did all these people come from?

[*The women stop dancing and retreat to stand with the men. There is a moment of anxious expectation on both sides.* TUNANA *reaches for his bag to get the lime pot. Instinctively* GERETU *raises his spear, but one of the women stays his arm.* TUNANA *takes the sun magic out of the lime pot. The light fades in rather quickly. There are cries of admiration, fear, and delight. Some of the women cover up their eyes. They begin to feel the warmth and give sounds of well-being and comfort. They throw off the bark capes in which they are wrapped. Suddenly they remember* TUNANA. *They all kneel down facing him and they shout.*]

MEN AND WOMEN: Oro, oro, oro, kaiva! Oro kaiva!
Oro, oro, oro kaiva! Ora kaiva!

GERETU [*steps out and gives* TUNANA *a string bag*]: Arise, our chief! Who you are, we do not know, nor where you come from. But the wonder that you have brought to our land is greater and more beautiful than anything we have ever seen. Stay with us, be our chief! Chew our betel-nut and marry our women. Stay with us, and keep your light with us, to warm our blood.

[*The drums start beating again, and the women dance before* TUNANA. *Somewhat overwhelmed, he stretches out a hand, hesitantly, towards three of them in succession. Immediately he does so, the women sit down by his side. The dance stops.*]

GERETU: Let these be your first three wives. Chief from the unknown land, bringer of light and warmth, rule over us. We all shall obey your command.

[*The drums start beating wildly again and everybody joins in a dance to pay homage to* TUNANA, *who sits centre stage, with his three wives.*]

MEN AND WOMEN: Oro, oro, oro, kaiva! Oro kaiva!

SCENE IV

The sad note of a flute. Back in Towara village the people sit in groups in the dim light and deplore their fate.

BUNANI: Woman, aren't you tired of sleeping? Wake up and make fire. Our children are dying. They lie around like lifeless logs. They have had little food since darkness fell on our land.

DOBANA: Where will I get the firewood to make fire? Go out and bring dry leaves of coconut trees. We have used up nearly all the rafters of the house. Before long the roof will collapse on us.

BUNANI: It is becoming more and more difficult to move around the village: these deadly colourless creepers seem to strangle every plant and every tree.
[*A wailing sound is heard from afar.*]
Can you hear that? It sounds like Kunja and his wife are crying. Maybe one of their children has died.

DOBANA: My eyes are still unused to this darkness. Whenever I open them, this thick wall of darkness closes in on them. I wish I knew where Tunana went. He left at night — so the land breeze must have guided him to the land of cannibals. Has he taken the sun to shine on them? Will they have spared his life? Or will they have killed him and destroyed the sun for ever?
[*Enter* OWADE.]

OWADE:
Men and women, sleeping, sleeping, sleeping.
Boys and girls, sleeping, sleeping, sleeping.
Wake up, wake up, you have slept too long.
Wake up, your children are dying of hunger and cold.
Crawl on your hands and feet,
collect firewood and dry coconuts.

BUNDEBA: Where is the light of the sun? Shut your mouth, orator, and go away. What will your words bring us? I have lost three of my children. Now my eldest son is dying. Will your words bring them back to life?

SUNDARA: Let not the sun show his face. He will bring me great sorrow. Let him hide in his house till I die. All my lovely flowers are plucked and I am left with the thorns. Let me not live to enjoy the warmth of the sun, when my children can no longer see his beautiful rays.

KUNJA: We are too weak to paddle up the coast or down the coast. My stomach is as clean as the inside of a bamboo. Let the stalk fall on the ground where the flowers withered.

OWADE:
Sleeping, sleeping, sleeping.
Men and women, boys and girls, sleeping.
Wake up! Wake up and rub your eyes.
It is not yet too late.
Pursue the sun! Search up and down the coast
and find out its new abode.
Find Tunana and ask his forgiveness.

EMGOGO: If you can see in the dark, pursue the sun and bring it back to us. We are perishing. Why do you cry like an owl in the gloomy night? Help us, we are very weak and sick.

BUNANI: And even if you find him, do you think Tunana will forgive? He has always been mean and useless and he will prefer to let us die..

OWADE: Be quiet, Bunani. Have you a mouth to talk, after you brought this calamity upon us? Were you not the one who offended the orphan, who drove him out with a bowl of stones?

[*Grumbling voices all round:* Bunani be quiet. It's all your falt, *etc.*]

DOBANA: If you men are too weak or too cowardly, then I will go myself. I will find Tunana.

BUNANI: You can't. You are too weak. And what about your children? . . .

KUNJA: You will lose your way. . . .

SUNDARA: You will die in the dark. . . .

EMBOGO: He will not speak to you. . . .

OWADE: Let her go. Her father's spirit will guide her to see her brother.

DOBANA: I'll go. My father gave me all his magic, except the sun. Had I been a boy, he would have given it to me. But he had to give it to Tunana, who has always kept it near him. When he sees me, Tunana cannot refuse me. He will come down the coast with me and bring the sun back to us.

BUNANI: My wife, stay back and let me go instead. You cannot go to the land of the cannibals, and there is little strength left in you.

DOBANA: No, my husband. It was your unkindness that drove Tunana out. So let me go and atone for you. Let me go and ask for restoration of the light. Stay well, my husband. Stay well, people of Towara.

MEN AND WOMEN: Go well, Dobana.
OWADE:
> Go well, Dobana, in search of the light.
> May your hand be firm on the paddle,
> may the land wind guide you along.
> May you soften your brother's heart
> for we have suffered enough.

SCENE V

A feast in Jinaga village. Very bright lights. TUNANA *is surrounded by beautiful women. Other women dance before him. People sit around in groups, eating.*
DOBANA *staggers in. She tries to make her way to* TUNANA, *but people push her back. There is a quarrel,* DOBANA *is pushed and falls to the ground. She shouts her brother's name desperately.*

DOBANA: Tunana!
TUNANA: Who is that?
> [*He jumps up, raising his hands. Music and dance stop abruptly. He walks over to* DOBANA.]
> Sister!
> [*Everybody steps back, as he lifts her up and leads her to where he is sitting with his wives.*]
> Dobana . . . you look sick. You are weak. . . . Rest and have some food.
> [*Several women rush forward with food dishes.*]
DOBANA:
> My brother, I will not eat.
> Let me talk first.
> How can I eat, when my people are starving?
> How can I warm myself in the sun, when my people
> in Towara are cold?
> Tunana, my children are dying.
> Since you have taken the sun from us our taros do not ripen, our coconuts have neither flesh nor milk. Our men are too weak to go and fish — many of our children are dead.
> My brother, come back to us. Restore the sun to our people.
TUNANA:
> That cannot be.

I was driven out in shame
from my own village.
What has befallen your village
did not happen through my fault.
These strangers have received me kindly.
They have spared my life,
they have made me their chief,
they have treated me better than my own kin.
I cannot return to Towara.
But you, my sister, stay with us.
Be happy here, find a new husband,
bear new children.
Come now — eat and strengthen yourself.

DOBANA:
No, my brother.
I cannot eat, while my children die.
Give us back the sun!
I implore you, by our dead father,
give us back the sun.

TUNANA [*visivly moved*]:
My sister, never will I forgive Bunani.
But for your sake, and your sake only
I will save Towara.
For your sake, I will return,
and once again, the sun shall shine on good and bad alike. For
your sake, the people of Towara shall live and Bunani too shall
be saved.
[*He turns to his people.*]
My people! We must leave at once.
Prepare the canoes. Load them with food to feed the people of
Towara. Let everyone get ready. Only the old, the lame and
the blind shall stay to look after the children.
[*Busy activity on stage as everyone is getting ready.*]

TUNANA: Arise, sister. Let us walk to the beach. The big canoes are
waiting. Let us set sail.

GERETU: Beat the drums, young men of Jinaga! Let the rhythm of the
drum calm the waves. Let it inspire us to sail fearlessly across
the sea.

SCENE VI

Back in Towara. Darkness. The people lie around weakly.

BUNANI: Two weeks have passed and Dobana has not returned. I should not have allowed her to go.

KUNJA: What will have happened to her?

EMBOGO: Poor Dobana. She has perished on the dark seas.

BUNDEBA: Bunani, you should have gone yourself. What if the cannibals killed her?

OWADE: You men of little faith. Nothing is lost. There is still hope. I can never believe that a great magician like Dobana's father will let his daughter die like that.

[*A conch shell is heard from afar.*]

BUNANI: Did you hear that?

KUNJA: What was that?

BUNDEBA: Someone is coming!

[*The conch shell is heard again, louder. The lights fade in gently. Excitement among the people. They scramble to their feet.*]

OWADE [*ecstatically*]: Stretch out your arms, people of Towara, the darkness is lifting from our land. Our sufferings are coming to an end.

[*The conch shell blows the third time, very loud.* TUNANA *and followers enter from centre back stage. A very bright light shines from behind* TUNANA *almost blinding the audience. The actors on the stage appear like silhouettes.* DOBANA *rushes to her husband.*]

BUNDEBA: The light of the sun hurts my eyes! Oh, I can feel the warmth flowing through my blood. But how dare I enjoy the light without my sons?

SUNDARA: Oh sun, if only you had come earlier, to rescue my child!

TUNANA [*turning back to his people*]: My people, go back and bring food, and feed these suffering people of Towara.

KUNJA: Look at the chief! Is it not Tunana, the playmate of my son, Kamusi?

BUNDEBA: How did he become so big? So important?

PURERE: Is this the same boy, whom the girls threw into the sea and made him drink salt water?

[TUNANA *'s followers return with the food, and they are beating the drums.*]

EMBOGO: Let us not talk about our sons. Or we shall bring great sorrows on ourselves. Let us listen what this big man has to say.

[TUNANA'*s followers give out the food.*]

GERETU: Beat the drums, young men of Jinaga. Let us entertain our friends of Towara. Dance till your feet are heavy. Dance till your legs are wet with sweat.

[*While the Towara people are eating, the Jinaga people dance. After a while* TUNANA *beats his lime pot with his lime stick. Everything stops. Everybody listens.*]

TUNANA:
My promise to my sister is fulfilled.
I brought you food. I brought you warmth.
But now I must return to my new home.
For never again shall Towara be my home.

BUNDEBA: Stay, big man, stay. Be our chief and live among us. Ask your people to bring their belongings and live among us.

TUNANA: We must return. My people are anxious, because we left our children, with only the old and the lame and the blind to guard them.

BUNANI: Stay, brother-in-law; stay, big man, stay. We'll work for you. We'll hunt and fish for you. We'll fight for you.

DOBANA: Don't leave us in darkness! Why can't you stay here? The bones of our parents lie in his land. You are going to a land that is new to our ancestors.

TUNANA: My sister, I have returned you to the land of your fathers. All your wishes I have fulfilled. All your wants I have provided. But let me go and find my own happiness in Jinaga. As for the bones of our parents, let them stay with you. Their spirits are with me, and they can follow me to any strange land.

DOBANA: My brother, if you leave us — what will happen to the sun? Will we be left once more in the cold?

TUNANA: I will leave you — but the sun shall shine on all. No man is big enough to keep the sun a prisoner. Today, I'll break my lime pot and set him free. Released from bondage the sun shall roam the sky, removed from human reach.
And he will wander, from place to place and shine on everyone in turn!

MEN AND WOMEN: *Oro, oro, oro, kaiva! Oro kaiva!*

OWADE: This chief is truly great! Only a great man can resign the power of his magic for the benefit of all!

MEN AND WOMEN: *Oro, oro, oro kaiva! Oro kaiva!*

[*The drums beat again and everyone is dancing. Everyone joins in a modified version of the sun song.*]

ALL:
Sun shine, sun shine on us,
come out, we have slept enough!
Sun make us warm, make us laugh!

Don't hide behind the black palm tree,
don't hide with the old woman,
sun, come out and shine on us!

Come out of the darkness of the womb,
come, break the lime pot and shine!
sun make us warm, make us laugh!

Sun, roam over the sky, be free
shine on the good and shine on the bad
warm their blood, make them laugh!

Kumalau Tawali

CHAUKA

CHARACTERS

POMOTOU,	*a village man*
NIALIN,	*his wife*
PAPI,	*cousin brother of Pomotou and Posangat*
CHAUKA,	*nephew of Pomotou and Posangat and adopted son of Posangat*
POSANGAT,	*younger brother of Pomotou*
PIWEN,	*wife of Posangat*
HIPAPI,	*sister of Pomotou and Posangat*
FIRST MAN	
SECOND MAN	
LITTLE BOY	
A VOICE	

SCENE I

It is evening. At POMOTOU's *household a little hurricane lamp gives light.*

POMOTOU: Nialin.
NIALIN: Yes.
POMOTOU: Bring me some betel-nuts. I have people coming to my house tonight.
NIALIN: There is no betel-nut.

POMOTOU: Bring them out.

NIALIN: I said there is no betel-nut!

POMOTOU: Woman! Once is enough. I don't want to hear that mouth of yours again.

NIALIN [*brings the betel-nuts and drops them beside* POMOTOU]: Here, the betel-nuts that you brought from the market.

POMOTOU: I said I don't want to hear that mouth of yours again. Now shut up! Did your mother teach you anything about man?

NIALIN: Day after day it's like this. When things come to this house, they just go out again like water. Does everyone in this village owe this house something?

POMOTOU: Listen to me, woman. Whether betel-nuts, sago, or fish come to this house by my own hands or not, once they are here, they are mine and they belong to people. Only the big man opens his door to all. If you close your door, others close their doors too. Listen carefully, if you have not heard it from your mother.

NIALIN: All is heard, great chief. Or trying to be like one.

POMOTOU: And why not? My fathers were great chiefs, and I have the right and authority in all the villages to look and live like one. Was the great, well-known chief Kumayon your grandfather? Ah? Tell me. [NIALIN *is quiet.*] Well? Why don't you return my words?

NIALIN: You win, great chief. [*Speaking away*] Those who know so much about our customs also know that they should not mention things about their mother-in-law.

POMOTOU: If you want to say something, say it loud and in front of me. I hate people who mutter away in a corner. But I heard what you said. I don't want to hear that sort of talk again. It stings.

[*There is a knock outside. Enter* PAPI, POMOTOU *'s cousin.*]

PAPI: Greetings my cousin. I have come.

POMOTOU: Oh! Your coming is welcomed. Be comfortable. Seat yourself. Betel-nut, my cousin. Let us chew. Then we can talk about this great thing that has brought you all the way here.

PAPI: *Uroh.* [*Looking at* NIALIN] *Uroh*, wife of great chief.

NIALIN: You and your cousin are great chiefs. We are just common women. How is everyone in your household?

PAPI [*pointing to* POMOTOU]: That's the great chief. Great chiefs make great feasts. [*They all laugh.*] Everyone is well in my household.

NIALIN: You excuse me. I'll let you two do your talking. I left the two women in the kitchen. I must go and talk with them now. [*She leaves.*]

POMOTOU: Yes, my cousin. Now you can say the thing that has made you come all the way from the east.

PAPI: Oh, my cousin, I find it hard to pour my thoughts to you. I have come with tears. The tears of your dead aunt.

POMOTOU: Yes my cousin, come out with your thought and let your sacred tears bless me and my children.

PAPI: My cousin, I have come to ask a son of yours to marry a daughter of ours. My cousin, this may sound strange to your ears, you who understand so much about our customs. But the previous arrangement made for her did not come through because they say I was not the one to have the girl married, and the words from the young man's side say she is not worthy of him. When I heard this, I felt as if an obsidian spear was thrown into my heart. My tears fell. So I said, let the eastern wind blow and carry me with my tears to the home of my uncles. My cousin, the blood of my dead mother will help me dry my tears.

PROMOTOU: My cousin, I have heard your cry. And I have seen your tears. Leave this to me. It is true that it is not right in our custom for the girl to go looking for the young man. But your case is special and different. And I know that this will receive the approval and blessing of our ancestors.

PAPI: My cousin, you are the only one in this land who can say that with authority. I believe you.

POMOTOU: By the way, who is the young woman?

PAPI: The daughter of my brother, Pomu who is gone.

POMOTOU: She is . . .?

PAPI: She is Molong.

POMOTOU: Molong? Oh yes. I remember her face now. She is a good girl. I have always wanted to see the sons of my household marry that kind of girl. Those with open hands and hearts for people. Their house will always be filled with people and laughter. Their house will never be empty of food.

PAPI: As you say. My cousin, I want you to know one thing.

POMOTOU: Yes?

PAPI: Remember, she is of my blood. She is your daughter too. You know what I mean?

POMOTOU: I see what you mean.

PAPI: When the ceremony of the bride-price comes, you, my cousin, will give and receive at the same time.

POMOTOU: My cousin, our talk has been good tonight. But it's not going to be easy, as I have no son of my own. Our only son, the son of your deceased cousin, is far away. As you know, he has been part of the household of my younger brother. And that is another storm to face. As you know, these days are bad days. They are not as the days of yesterday, when younger members of our family listened to the older ones and obeyed. O Papi, many new ideas have weakened our loyalty and honour to our families. Today when older people speak the younger people shut their ears or run away as if we were snakes. But, my cousin, leave the burdens of your heart with me, I assure you. Others may have their strength for this sort of thing. I have mine too. [*Pointing to his mouth.*] There is fire here.

PAPI: I knew you could do it. That is why I left my house and came all the way here. My strength, the strength of my mother be with you.

POMOTOU: Your coming was good. Goodbye.

PAPI: Goodbye.

POMOTOU: Let us work quietly.

[*NIALIN enters.*]

NIALIN: Goodbye.

PAPI: May you all rest well until I see you again. Pomotou asked me to stay for the night, but I said I must be back while the wind is still in good direction. Goodbye. [*He goes.*]

NIALIN [*after PAPI has gone*]: When the women were gone I was quiet in the kitchen and was able to hear part of your conversation.

POMOTOU: What do you think? Honestly, I want to know what you think.

NIALIN: I feel sorry for you.

POMOTOU: Why?

NIALIN: I don't want to appear to tell you what to do, but I think you are going to face a big fight. And I wish I were somewhere else when that takes place.

POMOTOU: That may happen, that may not happen.

NIALIN: It's not a matter of if it may. It is going to happen, I assure you.

POMOTOU: If that is so, then we shall see who wins in the end.

NIALIN: You have no hope.

POMOTOU: Who says. I am the oldest in this family, and what I say goes.

NIALIN: You are the eldest for nothing. You have not authority. Who is going to listen to you?

POMOTOU:Shut up, woman! Stop ridiculing me.

NIALIN: OK, I'll shut up. But I tell you, you are going to look like a real fool when that sister of yours whose tongue is sharp like the blade of morning grass starts opening her mouth.

POMOTOU: I am the oldest in this family. And all the children are my children. I have the final say in the marriage of each one of them. And if that sister of mine opens her mouth, it shall feel the sting of the back of my hands.

NIALIN: We shall see, as I have said; we shall see. But the final way must be backed up by something. Look at things realistically. What are you going to say when they ask: How many bowls of food of yours lie in the stomach of that boy Chauka? When he was running around naked how many pieces of cloth did you give him? What would you say to all these? Remember, the fruits of the future are sown by yesterday's sweat.

POMOTOU: Enough! It is already late, into the night. I don't want to wake people up.Are you afraid?

NIALIN: Who is afraid? Me or you? Who has been foolish? Me or you?

POMOTOU: Enough! I know I have no authority. I know I have done the wrong thing in the past, but I believe the ancestors are with me, because in me lies their authority. If I should call upon them, you know what would happen. Oh, yes. But my cousin has come to me with his tears, and as a man I must honour him, even if it means I stand alone.

SCENE II

At the home of POSANGAT. *It is evening. Several months after* PAPI *and* POMOTOU *'s meeting.* CHAUKA, *who has arrived that day, is reading a newspaper which he brought with him on the plane.*

CHAUKA [*shaking his head*]: You old people, what is going to happen to us? We are already going crazy in this country.

POSONGAT: What is it?

CHAUKA: What money should we use to pay for food and what money to pay for air-fares, rents, and electricity bills? And what money should we use to help pay for you old people's air ticket to come and see us your children?

POSONGAT: What are you saying?

CHAUKA: I am saying what this newspaper says. Everything is so foolishly expensive. Then there is that bride-price. These days if one family does not pay a bride-price which goes above the thousand kina mark, everyone starts gossiping and looks down on that family.

POSANGAT: I understand, son. But that responsibility is a family responsibility. You remember the son of Posanau? He paid five thousand for his bride-price. He did not pay all that by himself.

CHAUKA: What happened then?

POSANGAT: He is one with a warm heart and open hands. And for all those years that he was a single man his money and clothes and other things went far and wide to all his relatives. That was his security. That was his strength. So when the time for his bride-price came, he faced the occasion with joy and confidence. He probably paid only three hundred kina. The rest was given by his family to show their appreciation for his past care and generosity towards them. But I understand your feelings. We older people are many and we have our different ways. Some of us come to see you our children just for the sake of making a good plane trip. And, I could say we particularly exploit you.

CHAUKA: Thanks, uncle for those words. I still have to learn a lot more.

[*Enter* PIWEN.]

PIWEN [*quietly to* POSANGAT]: Food is ready.

POSANGAT: Good. Bring it. The boy must be really hungry. He has had a long trip from the town all the way here.

[*Enter* HIPAPI.]

HIPAPI: Oh! Chauka, always eating, eating, as if you have someone in the kitchen to cook for you.

CHAUKA [*smiling*] Yes. I have three. Come in, auntie.

HIPAPI: Where? Let me see the mark.

CHAUKA [*pointing to his temple*] Here.

HIPAPI [*sitting down near* CHAUKA]: Hm! you smell as if some young woman has been sitting close to you. Young woman's perfume, I smell.

CHAUKA: That's right.

HIPAPI: Oh, yes. That one. The daughter of . . . I don't want to say it, otherwise the waves break.

[CHAUKA *laughs.*]

Ah? Did I tickle you? The laugh is the recognition of truth, so they say.

CHAUKA: Where is she? Bring her here.

[*They both burst into laughter.*]

PIWEN: Hipapi, your food.

HIPAPI: Yes. Let's taste the food of newly married people like Chauka.

[*They all laugh again. They eat quietly for a while.*]

POSANGAT [*to* HIPAPI]: Have you heard of it?

HIPAPI: Heard of what?

POSANGAT: Have you heard of your cousin Papi coming to Pomotou?

HIPAPI: I think I have heard of it. But I have not heard of the reason for his coming. I am sure it must be of a matter bearing some significance. For why should he sail such long distance to come here for nothing?

POSANGAT: You are right, my sister. He came with some serious, important matter.

HIPAPI: Oh? What was the great talk of the cousin about?

POSANGAT: Arranging marriage. A girl from their side.

HIPAPI: To marry whom?

POSANGAT: Who else could it be, but your son sitting here. [*Looks in* CHAUKA's *direction.*]

HIPAPI [*suddenly angry*]: Who said! I don't want to hear of that! [*Almost shouting*] It makes my ears sore to hear such things.

POSANGAT: Sh. Take it easy. People love carrying untrue words around in this village. It may be all just rumour. Piwen, you said you heard of it?

PIWEN: Yes, yesterday evening. I heard it from some women who were with Pomotou's wife, when Pomotou and Papi were talking about it.

HIPAPI: Do you hear that? Is there any sense in it? Him? Chauka, give me some cotton wool to block my ears with. Him? Just because he is the oldest in this family, he thinks he can do anything without telling us. Wait. [*She tries to rise to speak loudly but is restrained by* POSANGAT.]

POSANGAT: The day for that has not yet come. The boy is a man now, and he can make up his own mind about whom he wishes to marry. But I want to remind you, son, of the words of your father, words which came from his mouth just before he gave up his last bit of breath. "My son, my only son Chauka, is yours, Posangat. You were like my son. Your ears were always willing to hear me and your hands were always willing to do what I told you. I have nothing to give you, no canoe, no big house, no dogs' teeth. So take my little boy to be yours. Give him a wife when he becomes a man." Those. Those were the last words of your father.

HIPAPI: Chauka, have your ears received what your uncle said?

CHAUKA: Yes. Yes.

HIPAPI: What do you say to it?

CHAUKA: I want to do what my father wants. But — but — I — I feel uneasy. I feel this is going to set aflame a big fire in my own household. I — I —

HIPAPI: Son, listen. Listen to my words. The words of my lips. The words of power.

POSANGAT: You understand her?

CHAUKA: Yes. I understand her. Yet I feel that because of me a tide will flow through this household and take us all in different directions.

HIPAPI: No, it's not you. It's some of us. One of us who thinks he can use people to make a big name for himself. And by the spirit of my dead brother and father, I will see that it does not happen. [*She spits onto the floor to show her contempt.*] He says he is a big man. Where? I don't see any sign of it in his acts. The big man gives plenty and big things to people and the people give him greatness because of that. But him? I see nothing!

POSANGAT: I think we have said enough tonight. Words blow around like the winds of the north-west. And let us hope it does not grow into a big storm.

HIPAPI: I hope and believe not. But if there is trouble, the truth will win.

PIWEN: I fear for my son. I know he is not of my blood and flesh but I love him as if born of me. Please do not tear my son, the way you tear a *karuka*. Let your anger eat yourselves but not my son.

POSANGAT: Your words are good. But don't let your mouth utter any more concerning this affair. My father did not pay you a thousand dogs' teeth to come and make noise. You were chosen and paid to serve, so serve quietly this household.

PIWEN [*almost sobbing from sadness and fear*]: Yes. Yes. But please let your anger eat yourselves. Do not let the flesh and spirit of my son be burned up by the fire of your hatred.

POSANGAT [*shouting*]: Woman! I said no more words. Do not make me go beyond the bounds of my words. Or would you rather taste the sting of my hands instead of my mouth?

PIWEN: Yes. Yes. I understand. But, please, please. . . .

SCENE III

At the home of POSANGAT. *It is evening.* Enter POMOTOU *and* NIALIN.

POSANGAT [*standing up*]: Welcome, come in, my respected brother, you two.

[CHAUKA *gets up, finds a place on the floor, and settles down.*]

PIWEN [*placing some betel-nuts beside Nialin*]: Betel-nuts?

NIALIN: *Uroh!*

[*There is silence, silence of uneasiness.*]

PROMOTOU: Who is not yet here?

POSANGAT: Hipapi, I've sent her words.

HIPAPI [*from outside*]: I am coming. Why the hurry? Are we going to war? We have plenty of time. So let us sit down properly like the blood of one father and talk truth.

POSANGAT: That's enough. Come and sit down.

[*Enter* HIPAPI.]

HIPAPI: Where? [*She seats herself where* POSANGAT *indicates.*] What was all the rush for?

POSANGAT: That's enough! We are going to start talking.

POMOTOU: Well, first of all I want to say, it is good we are together here. But my inner self is not at ease here.

POSANGAT: Is there anything bad here?

POMOTOU: Well, just that my inner self is not at ease. [*Pause.*] I am saying we are in the wrong house. It is our custom to always have talks of such important in the house of the oldest member of the family. [*He gets up.*] But as it is, I am treated like a child.

HIPAPI: This is bad talking. If you wanted this to happen in your house, you should have called us there. We haven't told you we don't like your house.

[POMOTOU *looks at her with sudden flash of anger.*]

POSANGAT: Let your mouth be silent. We have come here to settle something, not to start a quarrel.

POMOTOU [*controlling himself*]: Some time ago, our cousin Papi came to me and with tears poured out to me the burden of his heart, which concerns our young men over there. [*There is an air of electric silence.*] He came to ask of Chauka to marry a young woman of his household.

HIPAPI: Who is this young woman? What is her name?

POMOTOU: That you shall know soon.

POSANGAT: It was good of him. I respect him for his approach. But what was your reply to him?

HIPAPI: Yes.

POMOTOU: I told him everything was good. There is no problem. I feel it is good to continue the tradition that our father started.

HIPAPI: But at least you should have heard us before accepting his request. Why didn't you? I want to know!

POMOTOU: Because I am the oldest in this family and I have the right and power conferred by our father to make such decisions without consulting you.

HIPAPI: Yes, but on what basis did you make your decision? Eh? Tell me. I tell you, not a single bowl of your food lies in the flesh of Chauka. No clothes, no money.

POMOTOU: That I am the oldest in this family and Chauka is my son. Isn't that a strong enough basis to say yes to the request of our aunt's son?

HIPAPI [*bitterly*]: Chauka? Your son? The blood of my dead brother is *your* son? Come here, the spirit of my brother, and shut the mouth of the liar.

POMOTOU: Shut your mouth! You are just a woman. Go to your husband's house. You have no more say in this family.

HIPAPI: eeh! Just now he says Chauka is his son. He is your son now because of his money. But who is this Chauka? Wasn't he the same little boy you used to whip so terribly like a dog?

POMOTOU: You, woman, your mouth is very sharp. You shut up or I'll make it blunt with the back of my hand.

POSANGAT: You are wrong. Liars justify their wrongs by violence. You are the oldest for nothing. Your thoughts are those of a child.

POMOTOU: My God, I can't stand that. [*He gets up and goes towards* POSANGAT.] I am not a child.

POSANTAT: Come on, I am ready for you.

[*They swing at each other.*]

[*Enter two men.*]

1ST MAN: Ooo! No fighting! No fighting!

2ND MAN [*holds* POSANGAT]: What madness is this! This is unusual for this household.

POSANGAT: I cannot tolerate liars. [*To* POMOTOU.] You are our oldest, but there is nothing in your head. When our brother died, his last words were that I bring up Chauka as my son. But I thought all along that he was *our* son. But you treated him as if he was not of your blood.

POMOTOU: You are just a boy, and you want to be the chief of this house. [*Angrily.*] Who told you? Ah? Who told you? Your people of this village? Have you ever heard of an elder being told by a little boy what to do?

HIPAPI: An ungiving man is an ungiving man. The fruits of this, the stars and moon look down upon sadly. And the seasons will tell. All you do is listen to your wife. Are you a man ? Why do you wipe your wife's excreta?

NIALIN: Eh! Eh! Eh! What have I done wrong? What wrong drags my name into your quarrel? Ah?

HIPAPI: Stop lying! You are the one cause of all this. You push Pomotou around like a ball. You control his money and would not allow him to give a single toea to his brother's children. You wanted everything for yourself and your family.

NIALIN: Eh? Lie! Lie! Lie!

POMOTOU: Shut up, Nialin, and go back to your house.

NIALIN: I will go, but I don't want to hear lies.

HIPAPI: If you tell lies, then you must hear the truth. You have been the poison in the blood of this family.

NIALIN [*as she goes out*]: Eeh! Hey! Hey! Hey!
[*Lights dim. There is silence.*]

CHAUKA: My father, restore the spirit of peace and dignity which you once brought to fruition in this household. Let the people of this land know that this is your household. Give me a portion to play in this restoration of sanity, father, even if it costs me so much.

SCENE IV

At the home of POSANGAT. *It is evening. The room is lit by a lantern.*

CHAUKA [*getting up*]: Uncle, it is our tradition for you to choose a wife for me. I accept that. I respect you, my uncle, but I hate lies and exploitation.

POSANGAT: Son, what you say is true. And you know which of us your uncles is doing the right thing. Ambition makes people hard and unfeeling. We hurt people without second thoughts. We want to succeed at all cost. [*Pause. A bird sings outside.*] But you have heard the last words of your father?

CHAUKA: I have heard them, and they have sunk to the depth of my spirit like a heavy anchor. And I know who has the right to have the privilege of giving me a wife. [*Pause.*] It is you,

Uncle Posangat. That is the truth I feel in my blood. Yet
Pomotou is the brother of my father, and you are his brother.
There I cannot find reconciliation within me. You know,
uncle, what happened last night really wounded me. It
wounded me so deeply. Even my soul, the very depth of my
being, was wounded.

POSANGAT: I want to see you happy. That is my highest wish, since
you are the only young man in our household. Yet. I don't
really feel to do what I want. Because I am only doing the wish
of my deceased brother, your father. If I don't do that, bad
things will bedevil my own children. And your aunt. I must
listen to her too. For her words are a powerful curse or blessing
once uttered.

CHAUKA: The wish of my father is clear. I am willing to fulfil that. But
it is the war between you and Uncle Pomotou that worries me.
I hope my father [*looking out*] is listening to me at this
moment. I know, uncle, that I am the one is causing this
division and sadness in my own family. And that is not giving
dignity to the name of my father.

POSANGAT: Chauka, the son of my dead brother, my son, you know
that man Pomotou. He has always been the one who brought
shame to the name of our family, even when your father was
still here with us. No. We will just have to wait until the people
of the hidden world who understand all truth make their just
act on the wrongdoer in our family.

CHAUKA: Let it be. Let the people of the unseen world act according
to the truth they know. Yet even as my father was a true man,
I must also be true in his steps.

POSANGAT: What is the meaning of these words that escape your lips?

CHAUKA: Let me disappear. Let my eyes be seen no more by your
eyes, for the sake of unity in our family.

POSANGAT: What is going to happen, son?

CHAUKA: I must leave, so that neither you nor Uncle Pomotou is the
victor of this present war but both brothers together in a
household. Let the girls you and uncle Pomotou have chosen
for me be free. Let their fathers consider them for young men
of other households, where there is dignity and peace.

POSANGAT: My son, do not speak like that. If you leave us, I will die.
Your father's spirit will set fire to this house. And his wrath
shall be upon me and my children. I shall not be counted as a
true man in front of our people.

CHAUKA: My uncle, my father was always for truth to be alive. He held the belief that forgiveness was the highest act of justice in the land, that reconciliation demanded more courage than revenge. It takes a greater man to heal wounds of the past. And since we have no great man in this household, it gives me much shame. Therefore I must leave.

POSANGAT: Yes, son, I understand your yearning. But I cannot let you do that. It would bring the greatest of shame to our family. When people know that the only son of this household left because we the elders worshipped our prestige, our status, our ambition and our hunger for big name more than the happiness of our own son, it would bring untold shame and ruin. No, son. If you do that, you might as well get this axe and kill me and bury me before you disappear for ever.

CHAUKA: My uncle, understand me. When I am older I shall be the head of this family. But now I must go away to complete my obligation. Your years of sweat, tears, sorrow, and struggle must be honoured.

POSANGAT: No! Your words are part truth. They do not reveal to me all the secrets of your heart. I fear something.

CHAUKA: I must go. It is best that I do so.

SCENE V

In the house of POSANGAT *some months later.*

POSANGAT: Did the boy say anything to you before he left?

HIPAPI: Not very much. But he said a kind of goodbye which means more than just a goodbye. I feel he is deeply hurt about our quarrel with Pomotou.

POSANGAT: Yes. He is hurt. And he said something which I have kept secret in my heart all these last months.

HIPAPI [*eager to know*]: What did he say?

POSANGET: He said he was deeply ashamed of the division in our family. But then he also holds the burden in his heart that he is the cause of the turmoil that we have. Therefore he had to go away. He is a strange young man. He is very much like his father. He feels and thinks like his father even at his young age. You see, the thing that hurt him most was that he felt we were bringing disgrace to the name of his father.

HIPAPI: A coconut is always a coconut. True. And what about his marriage? Did he say anything?

POSANGAT: He said I am the one with the rights to his marriage. Yet. Yet . . . .

HIPAPI: What is it? What happened?

POSANGAT: Yet he said he does not want to marry any of the girls I and Pomotou have chosen for him. He said he wants to sacrifice his marriage for the sake of peace in our family.

HIPAPI: Oh! Oh! My father! My dead brother. This young man. I thought he was so normal, so gentle. Yet I feel now, I have a feeling now, some kind of fire burns within him. But what have I done wrong, my father, my brother, that your son is behaving this way? Have I let some evil words slip out of my lips? Oh no! I don't understand all these.

POSANGAT: Yet he said his money and his possessions he'll share with us. But himself, he wants to hide from our ryes.

HIPAPI: What has gone wrong, my brother?

POSANGAT: I don't know. I am at a loss.

HIPAPI: Is it really that he is hurt by the conflict in our family? Or is he really hurt and saddened that he cannot share any of his new wealth with his father because he is dead?

POSANGAT: He never said anything about that. But I think there's something to that. Yes, that may be it.

HIPAPI [*to* PIWEN]: My dear sister-in-law. You have been silent all this morning. Is there something hidden in your silence? For this is your son. No one has done more for this boy than you. He is your son. Maybe you understand more about him than any of us.

PIWEN: Yes, even though he is not of my flesh, yet he is buried deeply in the affection of my heart. I am his mother. I do not want to see him hurt. The things that happen between you — you quarrel about his money and his possessions, but you seem to feel little for him: the flesh, his thoughts, his feelings, his inner needs.

HIPAPI: Piwen, you have expressed your thoughts and you have said them well. They bear truth.

POSANGAT: He is my son, too. [*Addressing his wife*] But if everyone in this family were like you and me, this son of ours would not be woulded like this. But those people! [*Looks outside.*]

PIWEN: I had a dream about him the other night.

HIPAPI: Was it a good one?

PIWEN: No. I am afraid it was a bad one.

HIPAPI: Please tell me. What was it about?

PIWEN: It was so frightening, I cannot tell you what I saw in it.

Dreams sometimes don't come true. So I will wait for its
meaning to be revealed.

HIPAPI: You make the air stand on my skin, my sister-in-law. Please
tell me, I can't wait.

PIWEN: No, no. I'll keep it in my heart, as I have said, Hipapi. I want
to share the pains of the wounds that my son bears. And if it
seems he might never come again, I'll take this pain with me
to the grave.

POSANGAT: I don't like this kind of talk. I am as obliged to him as you
are or even more. Because he is the blood and flesh of my
brother. It is my obligation to see that he marries, no one
else's. Now tell us.

PIWEN: No. I'll keep my mouth shut, as that is my duty in this
household. I will serve and wait. I will wait for the people of
the spirit world to do their performance.

POSANGAT: Let them act. Let them perform. Let their judgement
come to pass. I am not afraid. I want them to strike and strike
hard, so we can see with whom the truth lies. But I tell you, if
the breath of the unseen people touches any of my children, I
will not hesitate to use my axe on those who have caused their
wrath to come to my house.

PIWEN: You and your brother have chased that boy away.

POSANGAT: Shut up! I am angry enough already. I have the right to
choose a wife for Chauka, and I will stick to that, come wind
come rain.

PIWEN: Well, there may be rain falling down from our eyes, if you
and your brother don't change.

SCENE VI

At the home of POMOTOU. *It is nearing dawn.* NIALIN *has a dream and
cries out in her sleep.*

POMOTOU: Nialin. Nialin.

NIALIN: Um?

POMOTOU: What was it?

NIALIN [*sleepily*]: I saw someone standing there at the door.

POMOTOU: Who was it? What did he look like?

NIALIN: It was. . . . . It was. . . .

POMOTOU: Come on. Who was it?

NIALIN: I am afraid it was your brother. Yes, he looked exactly like your dead brother, and he was saying something. I could not hear what he was saying. Yet somehow I seem to understand what he meant.

POMOTOU [*in an urgent tone of fear*]: What did he say? Tell me.

NIALIN: He was saying, I am taking him away. I am taking him away.

POMOTOU: Taking who away?

NIALIN: Can't you see? Can't you see the meaning of all this?

POMOTOU [*getting up*]: I am taking him away. I am taking him away. Can that be really true? You are taking him away? O my son, my flesh, the flesh of my brother. O my respected brother, why are you taking him away? Is it true? Really true? No! No! It cannot be. It is nothing but a woman's dream. A woman's nightmare. No, it is not true. It cannot be. It cannot be. [*Silence.*] Yet, dreams sometimes come true. If it is so, in this dream of my life, this family shall be no more. There will be no fruit, no seed to give flowers to this house. This house is going to vanish forever. [*Addressing his wife*] Nialin, it is almost dawn. Please run swiftly to the house of my brother Posangat and ask him and his wife to come here urgently. [*A rooster crows in the background.*] Then go to the house of my sister Hipapi and ask her to come here too.

[NIALIN *exits.* POMOTOU *sits there in silence. Then there is a whistle outside. He gets up.*]

Is that you Papu? Is your coming good or bad? Oh, my brother! My brother! I understand your visit, I understand . . . .

[POSANGAT *and* PIWEN *enter.*]

Come in, my dear brother. Come in, Piwen. Please sit yourselves. Whistles of the spirit people and dreams about them have come to my house. And this is bad, bad indeed. My brother —

POSANGAT: O Pomotou, I cannot make my lips work. I — my wife too had a dream a few days ago, but refused to tell me. Now, I know it is of the same nature as that of your wife.

PIWEN: True. True.

[*There is a knock and a little boy enters with a letter in his hand.*]

LITTLE BOY: A letter for you. [*Gives it to* POMOTOU.]

POMOTOU: For me?

LITTLE BOY: Yes, for you and him together. My father's canoe arrived late last night.

POMOTOU: Thanks.

[*The little boy exits.* POMOTOU *reads the letter.*]

Dear Pomotou na Posangat,

        Pikinini bilong yutupela, Chauka em i dai long Tunde i go pinis. Taim em i bin go long haus sik, ol dokta i no bin painim wanpela sik long bodi bilong en. Tasol em i stap i no long taim, na em i dai[1] .... [*He puts his arms around* POSANGAT *and cries.*] My beloved brother, it is my — my evil intentions that have taken him away. My wrong, my brother, no one else's, no one, not even you. I am the one and only cause of the death of our son. My brother, I am sorry, so utterly sorry. My hidden pride and desire for prestige, seen only by the unseen world, have born their terrible fruit. My brother, my brother .... [*He cries again.*]

POSANGAT: My brother, my beloved brother. I too am the cause of his death, O Chauka!

    [HIPAPI *and* NIALIN *enter.*]

HIPAPI: Is it true? The son has gone to join his father?

    [*She breaks down and weeps. They all cry for a while.*]

POMOTOU: Will it be enough for a while? Hipapi? Piwen? Nialin? We fought and caused the death of our only son. But his going away has brought us together again. O how cruel is my heart. O how hard is my heart. So hard, it has torn to shreds the flesh of my flesh.

    [*While all sob quietly,* HIPAPI *chants a mourning tune, a Western Manus tune.*]

VOICE [*over the tune sung by* HIPAPI]:

I am the tide
Who washes and purifies your shores.
I am the current who brings life
In the depth of your seas.
Let me sweep through again.

I am the pulsating *garamuts*
I am the vibrating *kundus.*
I am the river of festivity.
Let me give you feelings
Let me give you sensitivity.

---

1. Trans.: Dear Pomotou and Posangat, Your child Chauka died last Tuesday. When he went to the hospital, the doctors could not find anything wrong with him. However, he did not stay long and he died.

Let me offer of myself to you.
That you may be moulded and restored:-
    to yourself
    to the past
    to the present
    to the future.

I am the *chauka,*
I sing the song of a new day.

The singing of a bird, the chauka, is heard. As this slowly fades, there are the sounds of Manus drumming and people shouting and dancing.

END

Nora-Vagi Brash

WHICH WAY, BIG MAN?

Adapted for radio by Peter Trist

CHARACTERS AND CAST OF ORIGINAL RADIO PRODUCTION

GOU HAIA, *a public servant*	Anton Kaut
SINOB HAIA, *his wife*	Cecilie Noga
PETA, *domestic servant*	Gundu Raka-Kagl*
HEGAME, *Gou's cousin*	Rob Awai*
PRIVATE SECRETARY	Roslyn Bobom*
PAPA, *Gou's father*	Johnbili Tokome
MARIAN, *a clerk/typist*	Nell Pajen*
JAMES, *a clerk*	Benjamin Mumong*
CHUCK BRAGGIN-CROWE, *a businessman*	Ian Boden
Vi BRAGGIN-CROWE, *his wife*	Martha Corbett
SAGA, *a university student*	Pengau Nengo*
PROFESSOR NOUAL, *a linguist*	William Takaku*
MRS URA KAVA, *a reporter*	Roslyn Bobom*
DR ILAI KAMAP, *an academic*	Ian Boden

* Members of The National Theatre Company also in the original stage production.

First broadcast by the National Broadcasting Commission in April 1977. Produced by Peter Trist with original theme music composed by William Takaku.

SCENE I

SINOB [*calling*]: Gou, darling? Do you prefer the plain or the stuffed Spanish olives? I'm just making up the shopping list.

GOU [*calling*]: Oh, I don't mind, Sinob. Listen, come in here to the lounge and have a drink. Vodka and tomato or something different?

SINOB [*sighs*]: I'll have some Martini vermouth.
[*Sound of pouring into glass.*]

GOU: There you are dear. [*Pause.*] Ice? [*Sound of clinking glasses.*] Cheers! [*Pause.*] Ah, that's better. [*Sigh.*] Well, what did you do today?

SINOB: Have you forgotten already? I've been at the New Amengo Embassy, organizing that cocktail party. We're to raise funds for the Drop-out Rascals. I'm on the committee, you know.

GOU: Oh, yes, that's right.

SINOB: It was just heavenly. Carpets wall to wall, air-conditioning — *and* a gorgeous indoor swimming pool. Oh, that reminds me. I had a letter today from Gloria. They've moved into our new PNG Embassy residence over there. And *they* have an indoor swimming pool too. [*Sigh.*] O Gou, perhaps one day we'll be in a position to get one. [*Pause.*] If ever you get that *promotion!*

GOU: Perhaps . . . one day. [*Pause.*] Any new faces there — apart from the usual crowd?

SINOB: Not really. Just the usual. Mostly *nice* people, though. Oh yes, there *was* someone new. The wife of the managing director of Nirez. You know, the new perfume company set up by National Promotion. It will be just like the French perfume.

GOU: I suppose the fashion-conscious ladies of the city will be pleased.

SINOB: There were also some village women there. You know, mothers of the Drop-outs, and so on. Goodness knows why they asked *them* to come. They just sat by themselves in a corner and didn't say a word. Don't know how to behave at such functions.

GOU: But we must educate our village people. It's our duty to help the less fortunate.

SINOB: Quite frankly, I don't approve of it. Oh, by the way, I heard at the meeting that the PM is to form a new ministry. Is that true?

GOU [*whispers*]: It's not official — so don't say anything yet.

[*Pause.*] What's the time now?

SINOB: Nearly six o'clock. If that digital electric clock is correct.

GOU: I'd like to hear the news, if you don't mind.

SINOB: Oh, you don't want to hear that gibberish in Pidgin and Motu. Why not wait till the main news at seven o'clock in English? [*Sighs.*] Gosh, I'm feeling peckish — haven't had a thing since afternoon tea. [*Calling off*] Peta! What's for dinner? Come in here.

PETA [*moving on*]: Yesa misis! Nau mi wokim rais, na kaukau, na pis na kokonas.[1]

SINOB: Yuck! *You* eat that! Make us a salad and grill the T-bone steaks. There's plenty of lettuce and tomatoes in the fridge. Hurry up now!

PETA: Yesa misis. Mi go nau.

SINOB: Wait a minute. I haven't finished yet. Now Peta, next time you ask first *what* I want for dinner, *before* you cook native food. I can't stomach it. Now, take these glasses. We'll go out on the patio. [*Moving off*] Come on Gou, darling, let's sit on the new white iron chairs. [*Fade.*] They're so goregeous. Bring us new drinks outside, Peta.

[*Sound of door opening and closing.*]

PETA [*softly*]: Yes misis! Yes misis! [*Sign.*]Bladi shit! Dispela em wanem kain meri? Em sindaun na singaut — "Peta! Peta!" Ahh! Dispela kanaka meri kamap wanpela waitpela misis stret![2]

[*Short bridge music.*]

SCENE II

GOU [*fade up*]: Oh, I had a very busy day, I'm afraid. Had a meeting with the Admin. staff at ten. Then coffee. Then the director called me in for a chat and coffee, then we went to a long lunch with the minister at the Lakatoi Hotel. We had smorgasbord. Nice turkey and ham.

SINOB: So we've both had a busy day. [*Calling*] Peta! Peta! How are the steaks? Don't burn them. I want mine medium rare. [PETA *enters.*] Oh *there* you are. Well?

---

1. "Yes, missus. I made rice, sweet potato, fish, and coconut."
2. "What kind of a woman is this? She is sitting down and shouts, 'Peter, Peter!' Ah, this bush woman is exactly like a white woman!"

PETA [*moving on*]: Kaikai i redi nau. Mi putim long tebol. Nogut bai i kol.[3]

SINOB: Bring the portable table out here on the patio. We'll eat here in the cool. Hurry up now, Peta. I don't want that steak to be spoilt.

GOU: I'll go and help him.

SINOB: No. He's the servant. What do we pay him for? He's got little enough work to do. Sit down, dear. [*Pause.*] Oh, I do like that rose-bush we got from the University garden lady. It's going to look lovely when it grows along the railing. Just like the one at Professor Noual's place. Oh, here's the food now, at last.

[*Sound of utensils: plates forks, etc.*]

SINOB: Put them straight, Peta. And don't forget the napkins and the finger bowls.

PETA: Yes, misis!

GOU: The streak looks good. Like some salad on your plate, dear? Thank you, Peta, you can go now.

[*Sound of knocking on door.*]

GOU: Oh, I'd better see who that is.

SINOB: No. You go, Peta.

PETA: Yes misis!

SINOB: They can wait. It's very bad manners for visitors to come at mealtimes. [*Pause.*] Hmmm. This steak is lovely and tender, but I don't think I'd better eat it all. I've had too much. I'm not *really* that hungry, after all.

[PETA *comes back.*]

GOU: Yes, Peta? Who is it at the door?

PETA: Em brata bilong yu. Hegame. Em i stap ausait.[4]

GOU: Tell him I'm having my dinner. Tell him I'll be with him when I finish.

PETA: Yes masta.

SINOB: Oh, these people! I suppose he's come for money. Man! You can't educate these people. You keep telling them we pay rent, electricity, food, servants. And they still come here begging. Tell him to go away, Peta.

GOU: *Maski* Peta! I'll go and see him. Besides, it's nearly time for the news. [*Fade.*] Excuse me, dear.

SINOB: But you haven't finished yet. [*Calling off*] Money doesn't grow on trees. We just paid four hundred kina for school fees,

---

3. "The food is ready now. I've put it on the table. Don't let it get cold."
4. It's your relative, Hegame. He's outside.

and besides, I don't know where I've put my purse.
[*Pause.*]

SCENE III

GOU: [*Moving on*]: Oh, hello, cousin Hegame. It's been a long time
since you have visited me.

HEGAME: Sorry Gou, for this unusual visit. I know you are a very
busy man, but I had to come to you because there's no one
else to go to. My wife's given birth and I need to borrow ten
kina, please. I'll be able to pay you back next fortnight when I
get overtime pay.

GOU: Oh, cousin, I can only let you have two kina. This month I've
got a lot of expenses. You know, bills. It's not easy living in
the city. You village people are lucky because you have your
own gardens to get food from. Here in town we have to buy
food. Why don't you stay and have some food with us? Here's
the two kina before I forget, and I —

SINOB: [*calling loudly*]: Peta! Clear the table. Give the rest to the dogs.

HEGAME [*embarrassed*]: I — I — er — thank you, cousin, for offering
food. But I — er — I ate before I came. I must go now. [*Fade.*]
Thank you, cousin. [*Fade.*] Thank you, cousin.

GOU: Oh, I'm sorry, Hegame. I — er —
[*Door closes.*]

SINOB: [*moving on*]: Well, where is he? [*Pause.*] Oh, he's gone. I
couldn't help hearing what he asked for. I *knew* he'd come for
money! How much did you give him?

GOU: Only two kina. Poor man. Remember he *is* my cousin.

SINOB: Oh, this *wantok* business! Look,, we can't afford to flash our
money around — not even fifty toea. You know how
expensive things are. Don't be so soft, Gou.

GOU: Look, it only came out of my cigarette budget. I've never felt so
embarrassed in my life. Telling Peta to clear the table and give
the rest of the food to the dogs. I'd asked him to eat with us.
And he hadn't gone out of hearing when you started accusing
me of giving out too much money.

SINOB: I'm sick and tired of people coming here for money. This is
not a Development Bank loan office. The whole reason we
have this decent house is because of me. Do you understand?
I made it possible for us.

GOU: That's enough, Sinob. One more word about it and I'll be out

that door to the pub for some peace. Hey, it's time for the news! Switch on the radio, please.
[*Sound of radio switch.*]
NEWS ANNOUNCER [*fade up*]: And here are the headlines: A new government department has been formed and the appointment of its first director has been announced. An increase in the number of crimes in the city has been attributed to unemployed school-leavers. Now the news in detail. The prime minister has announced the formation of a new department to be known as the Department of National Identity. The new minister will be Mr Selap Rilai Ansi. The new director will be Mr Gou Haia. The spokesman added that this department will promote the image of the Melanesian way of life both here and overseas. The statistition announced today that figures for crime rates in —
[*Radio switched off suddenly.*]
SINOB: Oh, congratulations, darling! This is terrific news. Just what we've been waiting for.
GOU: Well, there you are. That's why I was waiting to hear the news. Director of the Department of National Identity. How do you like the sound of that?
SINOB: Let's have some champagne. And we *must* have a party to really celebrate. I can't wait to tell everyone the news. Listen, Gou, can you get your secretary to come here first thing in the morning, to help me with preparations?
GOU: Sure. She won't mind.
SINOB: It's her job to assist in every way. Oh, there's so much to do. I'm so excited I can hardly think. I hope my new dress will be finished from the dressmakers. [*Fade.*] I'll probably need new shoes, and of course will have to get my wig set, and then there's the food and . . . .
[*Music bridge to end scene.*]

SCENE IV

PETA: Misis, wanpela kuskus meri i kam na wetim yu insait.[5]
SINOB: Tell her to come in here, Peta. I've been expecting her.
[*Calling*] In this way, if you don't mind. [*Pause.*] Sit down.
SECRETARY: Thank you, Mrs Haia. I hope I'm not late. It's just ten o'clock now.

5. "A secretary girl has come and she is waiting for you inside."

SINOB: Oh, I've only just got out of bed, Now, get your pad and pencil. I want you to take this list down for your boss's celebration party. For his promotion, you know.

SECRETARY: Yes, Mrs Haia. We are all very proud of his success. He's worked hard to get it.

SINOB: Oh yes. But you know the old saying: Behind every successful man there's a woman. Anyway, down to business.

SECRETARY: I can take shorthand. You just dictate to me, Mrs Haia.

SINOB: First, of course, the minister for national identity — Mr and Mrs Selap Rilai Ansi. I don't really like his wife — she's hardly more than a village woman — but still we must invite them both — it's only proper. Oh, don't write all that down.

SECRETARY: No, Mrs Haia. I understand.

SINOB: The managing director of Nirez, the perfume company, and his wife — Mr and Mrs Braggin-Crowe. They are *terribly* nice people. Do you know them?

SECRETARY: No, Mrs Haia.

SINOB: Oh well. Now, Mr and Mrs Maus Wara — he's in Information, just back from New York.
Dr and Mrs Ilai Ikamap — the medical people. And, let me see, we should ask some *nice* academic from the university. Some of those Africans are smart. Oh yes, Professor and Mrs Noual of the university. And that Mr Saga — the young man who has been getting all that publicity. He's a bit radical, but everyone's talking about him.

SECRETARY: What about people from your husband's staff?

SINOB: Oh yes. I *suppose* they will have to come . . . How many so far?

SECRETARY: That will be about thirty, including the office staff. Now, this party is to be on this Saturday night. Is that right?

SINOB: Yes. Get in touch with the catering people. I want the best of everything. Just like the Embassy parties. Hot and cold savories, wines, beer, everything. Order good glasses for the important people and plastic cups for the office staff.

SECRETARY: Betel-nuts, Mrs Haia?

SINOB: Of course not! There are never any at the Embassy parties. Make all those invitations out to be sent today. And show me the catering list this afternoon. Now, I'll have to ask you to go. I have an appointment at the hairdresser's.

SECRETARY: Yes, Mrs Haia. Good morning.

[*Music bridge.*]

SCENE V

GOU [*calling*]: Hurry up in the bathroom, dear, it's almost seven
o'clock. The first guests will be arriving about eight.

SINOB [*calling off*]: I'm just fixing my make-up. Don't rush me, Gou.
These false eyelashes are hard to set.
[*Doorbell rings.*]

GOU: Oh gosh, there's someone already! I haven't even got my shirt
on! [*Calling*] Peta! Leave what you're doing in the kitchen and
answer the door. I'm going to the bedroom.

PETA: OK. Mi lukim husat i stap.
[*Pause. Sound of door opening.*]

PETA: Ahh! Papa! Yu kam insait. Kam insait. [*Calling.*] Masta! Misis!
Papa i kam.

SINOB [*whispers*]: Gou, it's your father! Why has *he* turned up *now*?
Just as we're flat-out getting ready for the party. What a time
to come! Make it clear that we're having important people
tonight.

GOU: Shh! Sinob, he'll hear you. [*Calling*] OK, Papa. Come inside.
I'll be out in a minute.

PAPA: Eh! Peta! Pren bilong mi. Man! Mi kam longwe, na mi les
liklik.[6]

PETA: Eh! Papa. Na yu sindaun long dispela sia. Pikinini bilong yu i
kam nau.[7]

PAPA: Man! Mi no sindaun long sia, mia sindaun long graun tasol.
[*Pause.*] [*Sighs*] Ahh! Em nau![8]

GOU [*moving on*]: Father! How are you?
We — er — weren't expecting you.

PAPA: Eh! Pikinini bilong mi! Yu tok Inglis. Na mi traim tok olosem.[9]
Your house here, is too far up hill and road. My bones tired
from walk. Now I find you is good.

GOU: Father, I have been promoted. I'm to be the director of the
Department of National Identity. Do you understand?

PAPA: Pikinini, yu tok wanem long dispela? Mi no save. Yu tok
Inglis, na mi no kisim as long tok bilong yu.[10]

GOU: It means I'm to be the boss of a big office. The number one
boss.

PAPA: Number one, eh?

6. Peter, my friend! Man, I've come a long way, and I'm a little tired.
7. Papa, sit down on this chair. Your son is coming.
8. Man, I'm not sitting on a chair. I only sit on the ground. Ah, there we are!
9. Ah, my son, you speak English. I'll try too.
10. Son, what are you talking about? I don't understand. When you speak English I
can't get to the bottom of what you say.

GOU: Yes. Tonight, Sinob and I are having a party to celebrate. [*Calling*] Peta, bring some food for Papa, please.

PETA [*off*]: Yassur!

PAPA: Ahh! Mi amamas tru long dispela tok. Na yu baim pik bilong wokim dispela singsing?[11]

GOU: No, Papa. It's not a singsing. Its — well — a *party,* where people come to drink, eat biscuits, olives, peanuts, and talk. Then maybe dance a little bit. In town this is called a cocktail party.

PAPA: Ah, kockitel pati. Olgeta taim mi save harim dispela kockitel pati. Mi tingim em pulim tel bilong kakaruk! Tasol em i wan kain singsing, ah! [*Pause.*] Na, dispela opis bilong yu — ol i kolim Nasem Andenti — em wanem samting?[12]

GOU: You mean National Identity? Yes . . . . Well, it means — er — something like knowing ourselves — what we really are. Samting bilong yumi yet.

PAPA: Na bilong wanem yu no salim pas i kam long ples? Na mama na lain bilong yu kisim planti kaikai. Mi kilim planti pik na kisim buai. Mi amamas tru long mekim bikpela pati bilong yu![13]

GOU: Tenkyu try Papa! But — I — I must now do things in the way of the town. This is the way things are done here. It would not be right if we had a feast here in town.

PAPA: Ah! Pikinini bilong mi! Ol man bilong ples bai lap long yu, sapos u no wokim singsing. Ol i bai tingim yumi rabis man.[14]

GOU: This party is the town's way. My friends come from Australia, England, and America, and we must do things to please them.

PAPA: Maski pikinini! Em i tingting bilong mi tasol! Yu wokim long lain bilong yu, na wantaim pren bilong you.[15]

GOU: Papa. You go with Peta to the bathroom and wash. Peta will give you some clean clothes of mine. Then you come and see the party. But Papa, my wife doesn't want us to chew *buai* here. But there's plenty of beer and cigars. Peta will look after you.

11. I'm very happy about what you say. Will you buy a pig for the singsing?

12. "I always hear about this "cocktail party". I wonder are they pulling the tail of a cock? But I think it's a kind of dance, isn't it? And this office of yours, *Nasem Andenti* — what is that?"

13. "Why didn't you send a letter to the village? Your mother and your relatives have lots of food. I would kill a lot of pigs and I have betel-nuts. I would be really happy to make a big party for you!"

14. "All the people in the village will laugh at you if you don't make a feast. They'll all think we two are rubbish men."

15. "Never mind, my child. That was only an idea of mine. You do things according to your own way and that of your friends."

PAPA [*off*]: Tenkyu. Tenkyu tru.
[*Door closes.*]
GOU [*calling*]: Sinob! Come out here, please.
SINOB [*off*]: Where is your father? Did you tell him?
GOU: He's gone with Peta to clean up and change clothes, then come to the party.
SINOB: To the party? The last thing I wanted was for your father to stay for the party? What will the people think? You better introduce him — and say he doesn't speak English. Tell him not to smile either. His teeth are as black as the bottom of a village cooking pot!
GOU: That's enough, Sinob! Tonight is supposed to be happy. And besides, I didn't ask the old man to come. Besides, you had better understand that we still have a bond between us and the village people. Despite the fact we rarely visit them. It's only the proper thing to do.
SINOB: All right. But I'll hold you responsible for any disasters that might happen tonight. Don't forget that.
GOU: What about Papa's things here on the table?
SINOB: Peta! Peta! Quick time! Gou, you go to the bedroom and finish getting dressed.
GOU [*moving off*]: All right, Sinob. But don't forget what I said.
[*Door slams.*]
PETA [*calling*]: Yes, misis.
SINOB: Take these things outside. Bring a can of air freshener and spray this room out. It smells like Koki market. Use *all* the spray if you have to. [*Fade.*] Just get rid of the smell — understand? Hurry up now . . .
[*Door slams.*]
PETA: Yes misis. [*Pause.*] [*To himself*] Ah! Man! Dispela meri olgeta taim tok klinim, klinim, wok, wok! Wanem kain hia? Mi les long dispela kanaka misis. Em winim misis kwin pinis![16]
[*Sound of spray can.*]
PETA: Ah! Papa yu kam? [*Laughing*] Ah! Man yu luk namba wan! Klinpela tru![17]
PAPA [*happy*]: Tenkyu, Peta! Ah! Yu wok long pikinini bilong mi, ah? Yu tink wanem? Em gutpela man, laka?[18]

---

16. "Yes, madam. Oh man! This woman always says: clean, clean! Work, work! What is all this? I am tired of this bush madam. She thinks she is bigger than the queen."
17. "Ah, Papa, are you coming? You look marvellous. Really neat!"
18. "You work for my son. What do you think of him? Is he a good man?"

PETA: Ah! Papa! Masta Gou — em gutpela man. Meri bilong en i no gut! Mi no laikim em. Olgeta taim i laik kros tasol![19]

PAPA: Mi no laikim en tu! Olgeta taim i save kros long pikinini bilong mi na i save toktok planti![20]

[*Distant sound of door closing.*]

PETA [*whisper*]: Eh, Papa. Maski! Tupela i kam nau. Nogut tambu bilong yu rausim mi. [*Fade.*] Mi go insait long haus kuk?[21]

GOU: How are you feeling now, Papa?

PAPA: Very good. Gutpela waswas. Mi amamas tru.[22]

SINOB [*calling*]: Gou. Come out here on the patio, please.

PAPA: Yu go lukim meri bilong yu.[23]

GOU: You sit down there, Papa, and rest for a while. [*Moving off*] Yes dear, I'm coming. [*Pause.*] Well, what is it now?

SINOB: Look, why did you give the old man one of your good white shirts? He'll only put betel stain on it. And why has he put those flowers in his hair? It's stupid.

GOU: Sh! He'll hear you. He looks all right. He's creating a party mood.

SINOB: He's creating a mood in me all right. Remember, it's you they'll laugh at, not me! [*Pause.*] [*Hard*] He's *your* father!

[*bridge music.*]

SCENE VI

SINOB: Gou! Quickly, someone's arrived! I can hear the doorbell. Does my hair look all right? Quickly. Come to the door.

GOU: All right. Take it easy. Relax.

[*Pause. Sound of door opening.*]

GOU [*off*]: Oh, welcome! Do come in. I'm Gou Haia. [*Moving on*] Do you both know my wife, Sinob?

VI: Of course. We're on committees together.

SINOB: Gou, this is Vi Braggin-Crowe — and her husband, Chuck. [*Whispers*] The manager of the Nirez perfume company.

BRAGGIN-CROWE: Great to see you. Hey! You folks have a really *nice*

---

19. "Master Gou is a good man, but his wife is no good. I don't like her. She is angry all the time."
20. "I don't like her either. She is always angry with my son and she talks too much."
21. "Never mind, Papa. They are coming now. I don't want your daughter-in-law to give me the sack. I'm going to the kitchen."
22. I've had a good wash. I am really happy now.
23. "Go and see what your wife wants."

house here. It's like the one we moved from at Boroko. We're on Touaguba Hill now, you know.

GOU: Now let's get you both some drinks. Come this way, please. [*Pause.*]

MRS BRAGGIN-CROWE [*off*]: Why, thanks a lot, Gou. It's real good to meet you.

GOU [*off*]: There's some more guests coming, Sinob.

MARIAN [*moving on*]: Oh hi, Sinob. How are you? Haven't seen you for ages. It seems years since we both worked in Admin. typing pool. Gosh, you look really beautiful tonight.

SINOB: Hello, Marian. I didn't know *you* were working in my husband's office. [*Pause.*] Listen, come over here, there's something I have to tell you, it's rather important.

MARIAN: Oh sure. By the way, these are my friends from the office — Tau and James.

JAMES: Hello, Mrs Haia. Good evening, Mr Haia.

SINOB: How do you do? You both go inside. I want to talk to Marian for a minute. [*Calling*] Oh, there's Professor and Mrs Noual. Good evening, Professor. Glad you could come.

PROFESSOR: Ah, my dear Sinob, I'm glad I could come.

SINOB: Go on inside. My husband will get you drinks.

MARIAN: Now, what is it, Sinob?

SINOB [*whispers*]: I'd like you to know that now I'm the wife of the director of National Identity — and with due respect to my husband, I'd appreciate your calling me *Mrs* Gou Haia. After all, you're only a typist.

MARIAN [*surprised*]: Well! [*Pause.*] I beg your pardon, *Mrs* Gou Haia. I'll go in to join my friends now — that is, if you don't mind?

[*Sound of party music, distant.*]

I hear the music's started! This promises to be a *very* interesting party. [*Fade.*] See you later then — *Mrs* Gou Haia.

SINOB [*mutters to herself:*] Oh! You'd better just watch your step, young lady. [*Pause.*] Oh, there you are, Vi. Hope Gou got you a drink.

VI: Thanks, honey. I've got a bourbon. Who was that girl you were talking to? She's a pretty little thing.

SINOB: She's a cheeky devil. Someone ought to teach her manners. Or I should have her fired. Calling me by my first name!

VI: Good for you. I don't even let my husband's secretary call me by *my* first name.

SINOB: You're so right, Vi. People have to realize where they belong.

Otherwise we'll have everyone crawling around for everything they can get out of us.

[*Music up slightly.*]

vi: I'd keep an eye on her if I were you. Just look at the way she's dancing with that boy. The hip movements! By the way, who's that young fellow in the Toana outfit?

SINOB: He's a Kiwi — you know, New Zealand? Incidentally my husband wants him to join the staff — as an adviser. He was in Welfare in Auckland. I don't think much of his wife —mousy little thing. Oh, have you met Mrs Ura Kava from the newspaper. This is Mrs Braggin-Crowe, Ura. You know, of Nirez Perfume.

[*Crowd chatter. Music stops. Crowd chatter up.*]

URA: Hello there! We must have a feature from you for our women's section. Hey, Sinob it looks a lovely party. All credits to you. Tell me, how does it feel to be a director's wife?

SINOB: Heavenly. I might even be able to go abroad on a trip with Gou.

vi: What about an overseas appointment?

SINOB: I'd love to go to Switzerland.

URA: I don't see much relevance between PNG and the Swiss. Why not Africa or another Third World country. At least we've a lot in common with them.

SINOB: We can learn a lot from the Swiss. Anyway, they're the bankers. You never know the future. Come on, girls — inside and join the fun. [*Fade.*] I'll just go and check on the hot savories.

[*Crowd chatter up, then under.*]

GOU: Oh, hello there, Marian. I saw you enjoying that dance with young Tau.

MARIAN: Yes, I'm enjoying the party. Now, you should let your hair down, as the Aussies say, and enjoy yourself too. It's your big celebration night.

[*Music over crowd: then under.*]

GOU: That sounds like an invitation. Come on, let's dance.

MARIAN: OK. [*Laughing*] Hey, you're not bad.I've never thought of you as a dancer.

GOU: Perhaps because I never had time. [*Laughter.*]

[*Music and crowd up, then under.*]

SINOB: Oh, there you are, Professor. Hope Gou got you a drink.

PROF. NOUAL: Thanks, yes. It's a good party. Your husband seems to be enjoying himself dancing with that pretty girl.

SINOB: It don't know why Gou is wasting time with her. She's just a typist.

PROF. NOUAL: Quite a bouncy little thing, isn't she?

SINOB: Bouncy, all right! She should go on a diet. She's that type, you know, Professor, without any *real* educational qualifications. Not university material.

PROF. NOUAL: She used to go around with one of the students. Saga — he's over there with Dr Ilai Kamap.

SINOB: Oh yes. I haven't really met him — but of course I've read about all his statements. Very radical, isn't he?

PROF. NOUAL: Well, that's a matter of opinion. Let me introduce you to him. [*Calling*] Saga! Over here a minute, will you? [*Pause.*] Saga, this is our charming hostess, Mrs Sinob Haia.

SINOB: How do you do. Hope you are being taken care of. You too, Dr Ilai Kamap.

SAGA: I'm looking after myself quite well. [*Fade.*] Think I'll have another drink.

SINOB: Oh, he's gone back to the bar. Oh. Er — have a savory Doctor? They're imported smoked salmon.

DR KAMAP: Thank you. Delicious. Did you notice a piece in the paper today about the national language question?

PROF. NOUAL: A bit presumptuous, don't you think?

SINOB: I don't think there should be any change in language. It's only the village people who speak Pidgin and Motu. All the school-children are taught English, and it would cost a lot more to re-write the texts. I mean, everyone should speak English. Er — will you excuse me for a moment?

DR KAMAP: Of course. [*Pause.*] My theory is that, because there are seven-hundred-plus languages here — I propose a new language which would include elements from each basic dialectal area. From this a new language would be created.

PROF. NOUAL: Pidgin is already a national language.

DR KAMAP: Anyway, there should be another committee set up to discuss the linguistic issues, the lexical and semantic dimensions most appropriate to the registers of discourse needed for particular occupations.

[*Party music up.*]

PROF. NOUAL: Well, yes . . . . I think you have a reasonably valid point, old chap. [*Fade.*] Now what I believe is necessary is that the whole language question should be in the control of experts and . . . .

[*Music up and under.*]

URA: That's a lovely dress, Sinob. It really suits you.

SINOB: I had it *specially* made, Ura. You know, that lovely shop in Lawes Road! It's based on traditional PNG patterns. My private dressmaker is so artistic.

URA: It's really attractive, Sinob. And the colours are so sophisticated. [*Fade.*] Those full sleeves are so flattering — I always like sleeves more than a dress without any arms and . . . .

[*Music up and under.*]

MARIAN: Hey, Saga, did you hear those two talking about dresses? I saw some dresses just the same as the one Sinob's wearing in a trade store yesterday. I thought she was too high class for the trade stores. [*Laughs.*]

SAGA: Well, what a load of *maus wara* they go on with! Hey, I wonder if they've got any *buai* at this party.

MARIAN: I doubt it, Saga. I'm sure Sinob wouldn't want to upset the whities with *buai*. But let's go over and ask Gou's father. He might have some.

SAGA: Yeah. He looks a good old guy. But out of place at this phony party.

[*Music out, crowd under.*]

MARIAN: He's lonely over there. It looks like he could do with some company. Hey, Saga, haven't you had enough to drink?

SAGA: No, I can take plenty more yet. [*Pause.*] It's ridiculous our people just aping the expatriates. Why not have our traditional sinsing? [*Fade.*] Isn't that good enough for them?

[*Crowd noise distant: hold under.*]

MARIAN [*fade up*]: Hello there, Papa! You all right, eh?

SAGA: Hey, Papa! You got *buai?*

PAPA: Yes. Mi gat. Tasol nogut ol i krosim mi.[24]

SAGA: No ken wari. Em ples bilong yumi tasol.[25] Man, this our country!

PAPA: Plis! No ken meknais! Tambu bilong mi kros tru.[26]

MARIAN: Ah, Papa! Em i orait. Mipela sindaun wantaim yu, na toktok.[27]

PAPA: Plis, no ken larim meri bilong pikinini bilong mi, i lukim! Mi no laik bai i krosim mi![28]

---

24. "I have some. But I don't want them all to be angry with me."
25. "Don't worry. This place belongs to us."
26. "Please! Don't make a noise. My daughter-in-law is very angry."
27. That's all right. I'll sit down with you and talk."
28. "Please don't let my son's wife see it! I don't want her to be angry with me."

SAGA: Ah, that's good *kambang!*

MARIAN: Sh! Saga! Here comes Sinob!

SINOB [*moving on*]: Look here! If you people want to chew that stuff — get outside. I don't want that in my house. Now go!

SAGA: You've gone really crazy. Look at you imitating these neo-colonials. This party — the atmosphere — everything. You're just bloody crawlers. The lot of you.

SINOB [*very angry*]: You're a fine one to talk about imitating the colonials. Just look at you — with the white man's beer in one hand and cigarettes in the other. You're drunk and disgusting! [*Calling*] Peta! Come and sweep up this mess!

PETA [*moving on*]: Yesa! Man! Dispela pati i givim planti wok long mi.

MARIAN: Saga, let's go — come on! You've had too much to drink. I'll drive you and —

SAGA [*interrupting*]: No! I'll say what I have to. [*Calling*] Listen, all you people! Come here and listen!

[*Crowd noise up and under.*]

SAGA: You lot are exploiting our taxpayers! Living high and draining public funds!

SINOB: Shut up! Get out before I call the police! Get out!

GOU: Sinob, please! Calm down! Everyone's watching. I'll get the driver to take them home.

SINOB [*half crying*]: I don't care! They can all go to hell! You take that *pamuk* typist away too.

MARIAN: Are you calling me a *pamuk?* How dare you speak like that to me!

SINOB [*screaming*]: I saw the way you were dancing with my husband! I've got eyes! [*Grunting*] There! [*Slap.*] That's for you!

MARIAN: Don't you hit me, Sinob! [*Grunt.*] I can fight too! [*Slap.*]

[*Crowd excited up.*]

GOU: Stop this at once, Sinob! You're drunk! I'm sorry, everyone, terribly sorry this has happened I really —

SINOB [*shouting*]: Shut up! You brought her here to humiliate me. I know now why you come home so late. Saying you've been working. You've been with *her!*

[*Excited crowd murmur up and under.*]

MARIAN: That's not true, Sinob.

GOU: Sinob! That's enough! Marian, you and Saga should leave now. Please . . . .

SINOB [*very slurred*]: It's not enough! Not enough! [*Crying*] Why can't you all get out! And get your father out too! [*Moves off, crying*] I — don't ever want to see them again.

[*Door slams.*]

PROF. NOUAL: Well, Gou. This was all most unfortunate. I'll say goodnight.

GOU: Thank you. Goodnight — er — everyone — I — I'm — I — VI [*sarcastic*]: Goodnight! And thanks . . . a lot!

[*Crowd. Voice:* Goodnight, Mr Haia. *Then fade. Doors slamming off.*]

PAPA: Pikinini, no ken wori long mi! Bai mi go na slip long haus bilong Hegame. Mi bringim planti trabel long yu, wantaim meri bilong yu. Eh! Planti trabel![29]

GOU: Nogat, Papa. Mi sori tru, yu bin lukim dispela samting i kamap. Em i no rong bilong yu! Em i pasin bilong taun. Dispela taun i bin bringim dispela long mipela.[30]

PAPA: Tru! Ol pasin bilong taun narapela kain. Tasol pikinini, mi papa bilong yu! Mi mas tokim yu wanpela samting. I luk olosem meri bilong yu i bosim yu. Yu no ken mekim olosem! Kam na lukim mi, na Mama bilong yu — long Krismas. Na bai mipela mekim bikpela kaikai long yu. Long pasin yet bilong ol tumbuna.[31]

GOU: Tasol bai yu westim planti moni tumas Papa! Yu no ken westim moni long mi.[32]

PAPA: Tasol yu pikinini bilong mipela! Ol pipel bilong ples bai lukluk long mipela. Mama na mi i sem, sapos yu no laikim kaikai bilong mipela. [*Pause.*] Nau bai mi slip.[33]

GOU: Papa . . . . Bet i stap long narapela rum. Bai yu slip gut insait.[34]

PAPA: Ah! Flo inap long mi! [*Sighs.*] Bet i malumalu tumas! [*Pause.*] Gut nait. Mi slip . . . nau . . .[35]

GOU [*softly*]: Gut nait, Papa bilong mi. Em ya. Putim dispela pilo aninit long het bilong yu, Papa.[36] [*Pause.*] There! [*Pause.*]

29. "Don't worry about me, my son. I'll go and sleep in Hegame's house. I cause lots of trouble for you with your wife. Lots of trouble."
30. "No, father. I am really sorry that you saw all this happen. It is not your fault. This is the town life. It is the town life that has done all this to me."
31. "It is true. Town life is different. But my child, I am your father. I must tell you something. You allow this wife of yours to bully you. You mustn't allow that. Come and see me and your mother at Christmas. Then we'll make a big feast for you, in the way of our tradition."
32. "But you are wasting too much money, father. You shouldn't waste money on me."
33. "But you are my child! And everybody at home is looking at us. Your mother and I feel ashamed, if they think that you don't like our food. Now I go to sleep."
34. "There's a bed in the other room. You will sleep well in there."
35. "The floor is good enough for me. The bed is too suffocating. Goodnight. I am going to sleep now."
36. "Goodnight, my father. There you are. Put this pillow under your head."

Ah-h-h, already you are asleep. [*Sighs.*]
And so . . . here I am, your son . . . the director of National
Identity.
[*Theme: "Which way, big man?" Fades up.*]

John Kolia

A PAIR OF LOCKS

Adapted for Radio by Peter Trist

1. THE LOCKED-UP LIBRARY

CHARACTERS AND ORIGINAL CAST

LIBRARIAN	Molly Nicholas
RESEARCHER	Tom Sinari
COFFEE-MAN	Kippaa Tebala
INTELLIGENCE AGENT	Ian Boden

LIBRARIAN: I'm sorry we're late in opening, sir. First I forgot the key and had to go back for it. Then we ran out of petrol on the way and had to borrow from some people we know who were passing by; and even when we were within several kilometres of work, we ran over a broken promise and got a puncture. So in the end I had to walk, and here I am with the key.

RESEARCHER: Oh, that was very self-reliant of you. Have you a section on —?

LIBRARIAN: The glory of this library is its memories of the past; and if you look in the catalogue you'll find your evidence fast. We've follies of the foreigners from old colonial days; we've lists of capes and rivulets, directories of bays. From *A* to *Z* you'll find we've filed statistics and opinions which make our shelves the envy of her majesty's dominions. So if you want to read the past in Motu or Tagalog, I'd recommend you read the cards residing in the catalogue.

These two plays were first presented by the National Broadcasting Commission on 3 July 1977, produced by Peter Trist.

RESEARCHER: Well, thank you very much; you're most kind; but I've already read your prepared brochure — when I first applied to be allowed in here nine months ago. What I really wanted to see was —

LIBRARIAN: In alphabetical order are administrative laws, subsection something, paragraph and any-numbered clause. Our mission books reveal the names of marriages, baptisms, and even those anathema and heresies and schisms. Reports we have from far and near and one remote outstation, which hasn't been located since we first became a nation. By filling in these orange forms our staff will most assist you; but if you had not entry gained, we hardly would have missed you.

RESEARCHER: Well, what I was actually after was — oh, she seems to have gone. Well, there is a set of green drawers here and some neat white index cards. Perhaps if I start from the beginning, I might find what I'm looking for. Here are all the *A*'s with everything from abrasive officials to azure skies — ah, here's an interesting one, *A* — Abau, where Spanish ships once called, but earlier still and later, the entrapped Austronesians got swallowed up by the non-Austronesian-bloc-Adventurers and active boats were frightened from its shores. An annual trading-voyage from the Trobriands brought stores, and articles and artefacts were passed on to the west. Well, it looks overcrowded, so I think I'll leave the rest.

COFFEE-MAN: Apim tupela lek bilong yu. Na mi laik brumim flo.[1]

RESEARCHER: Perhaps if I move on to this next drawer, I'll not be in your way and it will save you sweeping me up too.

COFFEE-MAN: Laik bilong yu.[2]

RESEARCHER: Ah, *B*, to or not to; Bamboo, Bena Bena, Bismarck, Boroko, Butibam . . . ah, here's an interesting one, Beche-de-mer. Take sea-slugs from the ocean-reef and boil them on the beach, then get the girls to dry them in the sun until they bleach, remembering to pay the workers half the cost of labour, for business rules last century required you trick your neighbour. Well, I don't like the sound of that. I never did fancy eating slugs somehow. I wonder what they've got under *C*? What a lot of cards they have. I didn't think any vernacular words started with *C*; must be some strange mission orthography. Let's see, *C* for —

---

1. "Lift up your feet. I want to sweep the floor."
2. "As you like."

COFFEE-MAN: Masta, yu laikim kopi. Faipela toea i kam. Wankain pe long olgeta strongpela na wara nating.[3]

RESEARCHER: Oh, that's very kind of you; yes, I'll take a cup. Have you any sugar?

COFFEE-MAN: Tasol, masta, "S" i stap long we tru long dispela "ABC".[4]

RESEARCHER: You're right. My word, the staff here are smart. I'd better hurry on to the *D*'s before dinner-time arrives.

COFFEE-MAN [*moving off*]: Mi nogat taim long kaikai long dispela ples. Taim mi pinisim wok long moning kopi — taim i kam kwik long wokim kopi long apinun. Na taim bilong pinisim wok i kam.[5]

RESEARCHER: Here we are; Dobu, Dutch New Guinea, Dimdim, Dani, Dagua, Development. That might be an interesting one. Development, subsection Rural, subsection Higher School Fees. Oh, what interesting ideas these developers have. Who else would think of helping the villagers by charging more for services?

INTELLIGENCE AGENT: I hard you had a great crowd here this morning.

LIBRARIAN: Yes, we do have one customer.

INTELLIGENCE AGENT: And who's this person?

LIBRARIAN: Oh, she's our regular eccentric. She's convinced that if she looks under alcoholism she'll find her late husband. He was a plantation manager, you know. Of course we never let her in.

INTELLIGENCE AGENT: You should. Expatriates like her late lamented have helped to make Papua what it is today.

LIBRARIAN: Whatever you say, sir.

INTELLIGENCE AGENT: But who's this other unaccustomed figure I see making free with your files.

LIBRARIAN: Oh, he's a genuine student.

INTELLIGENCE AGENT: Then he probably needs careful scrutiny. I'll go in and talk to him. Remember, miss, the perfect bliss of records in inaction, and therein lies for rebel eyes their possible attraction. Secure here fast the scandals past don't irritate your patron, whose yearly grant uplifts each plant, each citizen and matron. Of casting doubt on friends without,

---

3. "Master, you want some coffee? Give me five toea. It's the same price for a really strong one."
4. "But, master, *S* is a long way down this alphabet."
5. "I don't have time to eat here. I've hardly finished making morning coffee before it's time to make afternoon coffee. And then it's time to stop work."

librarian, beware, remembering your rendering of "Advance Australia Fair".

RESEARCHER: *E,* let's see, Eastern Highlands, East New Britain, Echidnas, Economic Planning, Economic Policy, Economy, Indigenous; why this economy thing is like a new religion. Education, Educational Evasions, Educational Retrogressions — oh, what a highly civilized place the world is! Educational Classes; how true! The present system is aimed at separating the elite from the egalitarians. Electric Power; I must remember to put a cross on my bill or they won't send back the receipt and the computer will try to overcharge me again. Enga, Environment, Eri, Ethical Attitudes, Ethnobotany, everything. Oh, what a wonderful thing a catalogue is, everybody can be filed away for eternity. It's endless, endless, there's a positive epidemic of explorations and external relations.

INTELLIGENCE AGENT: What is it you're looking for, sir?

RESEARCHER: I've already ordered coffee, thank you.

INTELLIGENCE AGENT: No, no. I'm loosely affiliated with the staff here. What is it you seek?

RESEARCHER: To tell you the trugh, I've forgotten. It's so long ago since I put in my application. But don't let that offend you. It isn't discouraging me at all. In fact, I've fallen in love with these wonderful cards you have here. Look at these numerous *F*s; Fish, sharks and shovel-nose rays, sawfish and herrings, barracudas and eels, catfish and garfish, fish that fly and skip, mackerel and barramundi, fish of all descriptions, oceanic and fluviatile; why, it's better than going out in an uncomfortable boat, and cannot become polluted by oil spills.

INTELLIGENCE AGENT: Perhaps I can help you, sir, to find whatever it is you are really searching for.

RESEARCHER: Oh, that's very kind of you. What do you suggest?

INTELLIGENCE AGENT: What about Government, sir? You aren't someone's official adviser, are you? Have you been in touch with a foreign government lately?

RESEARCHER: No, I don't think so.

INTELLIGENCE AGENT: Or Highlands Pressure Group? You aren't trying to find out anything that will embarrass anyone, are you? or Highland's Planters' Association? Or Highlands Zone Rugby League?

RESEARCHER: No, I wasn't trying to find out why imports score more goals than exports.

INTELLIGENCE AGENT: Well, I'm glad of that, sir, but I certainly hope you weren't trying to discover any new I —
RESEARCHER: Ideas. That's it; I was trying to discover some original ideas.
INTELLIGENCE AGENT: Very dangerous proceeding, sir, if I may say so. In any case, you won't find any here, sir. They're all safely locked away in the classified information section to which nobody is ever admitted — except members of the staff, blindfolded. In any case, the surgeon-general has warned that ideas can be injurious to your health.
RESEARCHER: Just a moment; don't jump to conclusions. I'm joking, of course. I'm jesting. Really, I'm interested in the . . . .
INTELLIGENCE AGENT: *K*s.
RESEARCHER: Kainantu, Kapa'uku, Keveri, and Kalam.
INTELLIGENCE AGENT: Kerema, Kingfishers, Kiwai, and Koita. You've got the idea now, sir.
RESEARCHER: Komba, Koriki, Kula, Kukukuku.
INTELLIGENCE AGENT: That's it, sir. Kuma, Kunimpaipa, Kuru, and Kutabu. Nothing controversial, sir.
RESEARCHER: Oh, you mean like Kaputin, Kiki, or Kasaipwalova?
INTELLIGENCE AGENT: There you go again, sir. Now you've spoilt it. We may have to withdraw your permit to come in here. A library's not necessarily a place for the dissemination of information, you know.
RESEARCHER: Well, perhaps I'd be safe if I move onto the *L*s.
INTELLIGENCE AGENT: Don't overwork yourself, sir.
RESEARCHER: Labour Law, Landforms; mmm, there's a big section after Land with blank cards; must be classified section, the cards even feel warm. Languages, what a muddled section; Lowland subfamily, Lemben, Lala, Lingua Franca: and then we go on to Legal System, Leeches, Legumes, Leprosy, Livestock, Lizards, Local Government; and leaving the *L*s there's a big section for —
COFFEE-MAN: Milik, husat laikim susu long kopi bilong en? Strongpela na wara nating. Blakpela na waitpela, tanim na seksek, olgeta faipela toea moa i kam.[6]
RESEARCHER: Really, this cup of coffee's such a long time coming. I'm beginning to think I'd rather have a cup of tea.
COFFEE-MAN: Nogat ti? Yu tink mi no les long mekim planti kap kopi long olgeta de? Kisim kap, kap, kap. Long dispela graun i gat

---

6. "Who wants milk in their coffee? Who wants it black? Black or white, stirred or shaken, costs five toea more."

planti doti kap bilong wasim. Yu tink olsem mipela i nogat skul, bilong wasim kap tasol? Sampela taim, mipela ol lain bilong wokim kap i ken kamap strong na brukim ol kap na kirap buringim dispela graun wantaim.[7]

RESEARCHER: Well, I'm sorry if I offended you in any way. I really didn't mean to. Have a cigarette.

INTELLIGENCE AGENT: No smoking in the library, please sir. A lot of the material is highly inflammable.

RESEARCHER: Oh, sorry.

INTELLIGENCE AGENT: Do you really mean to look through the whole catalogue, sir? Wouldn't you rather leave it for another year?

RESEARCHER: No, I would not. It's nice of you, but nothing will stop me until I find what it is I lost.

INTELLIGENCE AGENT: What have you lost, sir?

RESEARCHER: My memory, perhaps. I can't remember what it is I wanted to look up. Not Northern District or Orchids. Perhaps it was Papua.

INTELLIGENCE AGENT: Oh, that card was moved long ago, sir, you'll find it under *N*.

RESEARCHER: Let's see, was it Quaint, Quixotic, Querulous? No, that wasn't it.

INTELLIGENCE AGENT: Rabaul, Rai Coast, Religion and Magic, Rodents, Rubber. How about *S,* sir?

RESEARCHER: Sh! Don't say it aloud or the coffee-man will ask me how many lumps of sugar I want.

COFFE-MAN: Suga? Putim faipela toea antap! Masta, wan o tu spun?[8]

RESEARCHER: I don't want any coffee. I hate coffee.

COFFEE-MAN: Yu mas kisim kap. Olgeta kisim wan wan.[9]

INTELLIGENCE AGENT: What about Tea, Trade, Ticks, Tasman, Transport. Do you really mean to go right down to the end of the alphabet? Surely you'll be finding it difficult to think of topics to fit.

RESEARCHER: Oh, I don't know. Vanimo; Woitape; Exophthalmia; Yaws; Zamberigi.

INTELLIGENCE AGENT: Clever, aren't you, sir? I doubt if we can extend your permit. I might even have to send your file to the CIA.

RESEARCHER: Oh, are you a member?

7. "There's no tea. You think I don't get tired of making coffee all day long? 'Bring me a cup, bring me a cup!' There are too many dirty cups to wash. You think I'm an uneducated man only fit for washing cups? One day we tea boys will rebel and break all the cups and mix them with earth."
8. "Sugar? Five more toea. Master, one or two spoons?"
9. "You must drink one. Everybody else does."

INTELLIGENCE AGENT: Only an honourary member, sir. But haven't you left out the letter *U*?

RESEARCHER: That's it. Umbrella. I left my umbrella in here two years ago when I was allowed in one rainy afternoon.

LIBRARIAN: Here it is sir, under lost and found.

RESEARCHER: Thank you, thank you. Well, that's all, I think.

COFFEE-MAN: Masta, masta. Bilong wanem yu no kisim kopi bilong yu.[10]

RESEARCHER: Oh file it away, would you? I'll probably be back next year.

COFFEE-MAN: O yu trikman! Yu giaman dispela meri long wokim long ol buk.[11] Ah. [*Laughs.*]

INTELLIGENCE AGENT: Well, I might as well go to lunch too. It's nearly eleven o'clock. Goodbye.

LIBRARIAN: Goodbye, sir. Oh, he's coming back again. Yes, sir?

INTELLIGENCE AGENT: I left my tape-recorder behind. I want to play that researcher's conversation to the trade commissioner.

LIBRARIAN: I'm sorry sir, we've filed it away already under Spies.

INTELLIGENCE AGENT: Well, I'll have to come in and get it.

LIBRARIAN: I'm sorry sir, that isn't fair, and under regulations, the agents bold of masters old are foreign administration's!

INTELLIGENCE AGENT: I've created a robot.

LIBRARIAN: The stated rules are made for fools and state in language clear, you cannot cope so give up hope, all ye who exit here.

INTELLIGENCE AGENT: Why don't you build a capital that looks like Canberra?

LIBRARIAN: A bureaucrat knows this is that by looking in his manual. The public need is but a reed but we're a hardy annual.

INTELLIGENCE AGENT: You've become more colonial than the colonizers.

LIBRARIAN: Just fill in this yellow form, sir, and post it to the box number which has been left out of the new telephone directory. If you haven't had a reply in two years' time, make a complaint in triplicate.

INTELLIGENCE AGENT: I can't stand it. I'm going back to Queensland where it's more refreshingly backward.

COFFEE-MAN: Mi no ken wori tumas, masta. Yu laikim wanpela gutpela kap kopi? Susu? Suga? Em tenpela toea antap, tasol.[12]

10. Master, why don't you want to have your coffee?
11. "Oh, you trickster! You lied to the librarian."
12. "Don't worry, master. You'd like a nice cup of coffee? That's ten more toea."

INTELLIGENCE AGENT: Book me a plane south on the next wait-listing. Even the British weren't as efficient as this.

LIBRARIAN: Well, that looks a lot tidier. There's nothing like a university without students.

COFFEE-MAN: Haus buk lusim ol man bilong ritim buk![13]

LIBRARIAN: Yes, now perhaps we can get on with our work.

COFFEE-MAN: Misis, yu laikim wanpela . . .?

LIBRARIAN: Yes, please. Bringim mi wanpela waitpela kap kopi! Em i swit moa![14]

END

13. "There are no readers left in the library."
14. "Bring me a cup of white coffee. It's really sweet."

2 THE LIBRARY OF LOCKS

CHARACTERS AND ORIGINAL CAST

GAOLER	Jeffrey Awai
SOCIAL WORKER	Anne Lavender
PRISONER	David Haro
PSYCHIATRIST	David Fopp
MISSIONARY	Rosemary Wright

A corrective institution. Long cement corridors. Small barred cells. A smell of efficiency and organization. Down the corridor comes an intense lady wheeling a trolley loaded with rather tattered books.

GAOLER: Good morning, Miss Social Worker. You're on the job early.

SOCIAL WORKER: Oh yes, warder. Library trolley coming round. Anybody like a good read? Please get lastweek's borrowed books ready and pass them through the bars as I come round. Mr Mass-Murderer, I've got you those copies of *All Creatures Great and Small* you wanted to read. Yes, very uplifting. Now, who was it wanted *Great Forgeries*? Oh, you, Mr False-Pretences? Well, I can't understand that sort of thing myself, but no doubt it's all crystal clear to you. Ah me; busy with my little trolley; but we mustn't be depressed, must we? Only another ninety-nine years and we'll all be out again. And here's the *Kung fu Annual* for you as you requested, Mr Katatechop. And what for you, 764763? A comic?

PRISONER: For me?

SOCIAL WORKER: Yes, my dear man, any time you want a new book, just send for me.

PRISONER: I don't read.

GAOLER: Don't read? Are you trying to upset correctional service discipline?

PRISONER: I don't read about it. I do it.

GAOLER: Oh, don't boast now. You're only in here for stealing a loaf of bread.

PRISONER: Yes, but as soon as I get out of here I intend to do exactly the same thing again.

SOCIAL WORKER: Perhaps you'd like this little volume on the Bread of Life?

PRISONER: I don't read that religious rubbish.

GAOLER: Mmmm. He's a hard case, madam. A case for the psychiatrist, I fear. He should be along soon.

SOCIAL WORKER: *Captain Marvel*? *Requiem for a Nun*? Anyone for *The Great Escape*? Oh, good morning, Mr Psychiatrist. We just mentioned you. [*Calling*] Mr Warder, the psychiatrist is here.

PSYCHIATRIST: Yes, warder. There was someone you wanted me to see?

GAOLER: There is someone I want you to see, doctor. [*To* PRISONER] Prisoner 764763, the brain-mechanic's here to see you. Open your bonnet and give him a tinker.

PRISONER: Why don't you open my cell door so he can come in and lie down on my couch here and tell me all about it.

SOCIAL WORKER: Any men like some lovely old copies of *Women's Weekly*?

PRISONER: I'd like a woman nightly and not an old one either.

PSYCHIATRIST: Some kind of pervert, I suspect, gaoler; there's no need to open the door. Now my man . . . .

PRISONER: I'm not your man. You're not a possessive case, are you?

PSYCHIATRIST: Ah, paranoid, I see. Why did you do it?

PRISONER: I haven't had a chance to do it since I first got arrested.

PSYCHIATRIST: No; I mean, why did you steal the bread?

GAOLER: Perhaps — ha ha — perhaps he felt like a good loaf.

PSYCHIATRIST: Yes — ha ha — he didn't know which side his bread was buttered.

SOCIAL WORKER: Oh, doctor, you are a wit. Here's Enid Blyton's *Noddy* for some lucky man.

PRISONER: Hey! I'm over here.

PSYCHIATRIST: Eh? What?

PRISONER: This is me on the outside of the bars looking in at you monkeys. I stole the bread because I was 'ungry. Get it? U-N-G-R-Y, 'ungry.

GAOLER: I thought you couldn't read.

PRISONER: I didn't say I couldn't read; I said I didn't read. You deaf or what?

PSYCHIATRIST: There's no need to be offensive. How long did he get, gaoler?

GAOLER: Three weeks with hard, sir. I'll leave you alone with him.

PRISONER: Yes, Doc — a lousy three weeks; not nearly hard enough. When I left my village I was carrying a letter from my *wantoks* telling me that Moresby was a place of girls, jobs, money, beer, and tall buildings. Well, I saw a couple of tall buildings but nothing much else. My *wantok* had lost his job, and as I already told you, we were as hungry as pigs. When I get out of here I'll be hungry again. That's why I'm going to steal another loaf of bread. That letter I got at home was the worst invitation I ever received. So that's why I've made up my mind never to read anything again. Get it?

PSYCHIATRIST: What did you feel like just before you — er — — yielded to temptation and — er — purloined the baked offering? Any hallucinations, fixed ideas, anal compulsions, melancholia?

PRISONER: Hungry. I felt hungry.

PSYCHIATRIST: Illogical fanaticism, I'm afraid. Probably religious in origin. I fear his sentence was too light for such a serious criminality.

SOCIAL WORKER: How about some election brochures? They're quite gay. They should cheer you up.

PRISONER: No thanks. It's a gaol, not a nut-house.

PSYCHIATRIST: Hum. Logical. Logical. I'll see about getting your sentence reduced.

PRISONER: What for? I only got three weeks.

GAOLER: Visiting time! Number 764763, here's your sister to see you.

PRISONER: What? They allow torture in here as well?

MISSIONARY: Hallo, my brother.

PRISONER: Oh, don't be ridiculous. You think they don't know you're the missionary I left behind me? Sister? What other lies did you tell them to get in here?

MISSIONARY: Well, I am your siter-in-Christ, who is our help and our
    —
PRISONER: Yeah, yeah. I know all that. Did you bring any bread?
MISSIONARY: Bread? What did you want bread for?
PRISONER: Well, of course I wanted bread. That's why I'm in here,
    isn't it?
SOCIAL WORKER: Perhaps you'd like to read these interesting prison
    regulations.
MISSIONARY: No, thank you, I never read catalogues, especially of
    misery.
SOCIAL WORKER: Haven't we clashed somewhere before?
MISSIONARY: Oh? Not as far as I know.
PRISONER: Would you two mind having your little chat some other
    time? And look, missus, go and hawk your material
    elsewhere, please; try the women's block.
SOCIAL WORKER: It's empty at the moment, so I'm giving the men a
    double visit.
PRISONER: Well, go and talk to that rapist there, he'll tell you some
    things you won't find in books.
SOCIAL WORKER: Oh, what a good idea. That would be interesting.
PRISONER: Yeah. Leave me alone to talk with my grandmother here.
GAOLER: I thought she was your sister.
PRISONER: Are you blokes blind or what? Does she look like she
    could be any relation of mine?
PSYCHIATRIST: Refuses to acknowledge family relationships. Very
    interesting case. Two weeks would be a sufficient sentence
    surely. Anyway, don't let me interrupt your conversation.
MISSIONARY: Thank you so much. I haven't seen my dear brother
    since . . . well, since he left the catechists' school and ran away
    with my purse in order to buy his aeroplane fare.
PRISONER: Just ask her what I was doing in her room that night.
GAOLER: What were you doing in the mission house that night?
PRISONER: I was looking for something.
PSYCHIATRIST: Oh really, what?
PRISONER: Bread, of course. I told you I was hungry, didn't I?
MISSIONARY: Mr Warder, is there any chance of arranging for him to
    stay in here for a longer period?
GAOLER: You want him to stay in here longer?
MISSIONARY: Well, yes. This is the first time I've known where I can
    find him if I want him. Oh! Here's that woman again.
SOCIAL WORKER: I would always be happy to visit him for you. I've all
    sorts of interesting things for him to read after he's been out in

the sun planting pineapples. I've books of Shakespeare's sonnets and a tome on how to cook, a travel book of Hungary?

MISSIONARY: No, I shouldn't think he'd like anything like that. You don't have draughts or games?

SOCIAL WORKER: What you all need is a good read. You missionaries tend to think you're doing good by praying, but mostly souls achieve their goals by reading, not by saying. The written word, or so I've heard, is far superior teaching, then those who win the "Saved from Sin" by more emotional preaching.

MISSIONARY: Not very original.

PRISONER: Hey! what about my case?

PSYCHIATRIST: What case? Your position's quite clear, isn't it? You are destitute down here, the court has no money to send you back up there, so you are accommodated here for three weeks, after which time you'll be let out again so you can be arrested once more for being without means of support.

What could be clearer? Surely you don't think of yourself as someone special, do you? Frankly, your trivial crime is hardly deserving of a gaol sentence. A loaf of bread? Most unambitious, in my opinion.

GAOLER: That's the way, sir. Put him in his place. He's hardly fit to consort with murderers and rapists.

SOCIAL WORKER: Well, talking of murders, I've some lovely Agatha Christies here.

PRISONER: Any books by Papuans or New Guineans?

SOCIAL WORKER: Oh no; nothing seditious allowed in. What about a nice Phantom comic? They always point a good moral. The good Phantom always succeeds in defeating the devil criminals.

GAOLER: Oh, is that the lesson of Phantom?

PRISONER: I always thought the moral was that if a white man romps round the jungle in a black plastic suit, he'll smell so badly that a blind wolf will follow him slavishly around.

MISSIONARY: Ah, there you have it. I'd often wondered what that Indian wolf was doing up an African river? But the clue is the plastic, of course. Plastic is universal. Like "The Word".

SOCIAL WORKER: Oh, there she goes again.

GAOLER: Now, no quarrelling please. Your crime, by dear librarian, is literature purveying, and yours, I fear, psychiatrist, is others' minds surveying. My lady here, I really fear, would make a first-class madam, if only she had not forgot her role in tempting Adam. There should be cells for such as you who persecute convicted. You might fit in this cell yourselves, the prisoner evicted. In fact, I wouldn't mind being locked up, myself.

PSYCHIATRIST: But why? You're not going to commit . . . .

MISSIONARY: Rape?

SOCIAL WORKER: Murder?

PSYCHIATRIST: Embezzlement?

SOCIAL WORKER: Perjury?

GAOLER: No, I'm going to steal a loaf of bread.

MISSIONARY: Whatever for?

GAOLER: Because I'm hungry, hungry.

MISSIONARY: Hungry for love?

SOCIAL WORKER: Hungry for companionship?

GAOLER: No, sorry ladies, I'm hungry for escape from a boring job on only forty kina a week.

PRISONER: Hey! You're really going to let me out? What makes you think I won't rejoin the rascal gang?

MISSIONARY: The rascals always give us someone to save.

GAOLER: Well, they're more honest than you, so *you* can go in the cell.

MISSIONARY: Oh, what a comfortable-looking bunk! Much softer than at the mission.

GAOLER: In you go! Now my friend, we'll go up to Murray Barracks and help the kung fu man conduct the traffic lights.

PRISONER: We'll go down to Bulubulu and ask the all-night store for everything they haven't got in stock.

PSYCHIATRIST: Mmmm. Suppressed criminalistic tendencies brought out by the prisoner's enviable bravado.

GAOLER: In you go, too. The last person in your profession who had an original thought was Job.

PSYCHIATRIST: Oh, what a symbolically individual toilet! Quite anal compulsive.

PRISONER: We'll go and sleep in a rusty jeep at one of the scenic dumps where unhoused men can breathe again and never catch the mumps.

SOCIAL WORKER: Well, that's true, as a matter of fact. It says here in this housing report that most of the carefully constructed slums are ideally designed to breed bed-bugs, hepatitis, and loose floorboards.

GAOLER: Really, you're not as silly as you look. What other interesting local facts have you discovered in your wide reading?

SOCIAL WORKER: Oh! We shun the prose that home-grown grows as if it were the pox. In fact the muse of native views is firmly under locks.

PRISONER: Censorship, eh?

GAOLER: Put her in the cell, too, before she escapes into the same world.

SOCIAL WORKER: Oh, what a lovely view from in here! I can see all the geometrical regularities of the other side of the corridor.

PRISONER: Let's get going while the going's good.

PSYCHIATRIST: But what will you live on?

GAOLER AND PRISONER: Bread. Nourishing, flourishing bread. Vitamin-enriched, flour-bewitched bread.

SOCIAL WORKER: I've some recipes here in a book which will tell you how to bake some with currants?

GAOLER: No thanks, we'd rather steal it plain.

MISSIONARY: But why? Stealing's a sin. The prisoner's converted the gaoler. Why?

PRISONER: Because we're hungry, of course. Hungry for something not in the Book of Regulations.

GAOLER: Hey! Do you know how to start a car by joining the wires, bro?

PRISONER: Of course I do, *tura*.

GAOLER: Let's go and steal the chief warder's car then.

MISSIONARY, SOCIAL WORKER, AND PSYCHIATRIST: Help! Let us out! This is outrageous! I want to see my lawyer! Outrage! Help! Help! Outrage!

END

Albert Toro

THE MASSACRE

CHARACTERS

MOLEN, *son*
VANE, *mother*
RATO, *father*
TOVI, *uncle*
ROBERTO, *doctor*
SHERMAN, *captain*
REYNOLD, *second mate*

Theme music up and fade in to sounds of children playing.

MOLEN: I am a very old man now, you see. I have lived a very long
life and soon it will be time for me to die. From those who
returned from the sugar plantations after our contract expired,
I am the last man alive. Mally Bulla was everyone's favourite
plantation. I want to tell you this story; and later, when you are
a father of many children, you can tell it to them. You are a

This play is the first episode of a radio serial, *Sugar Cane Days*. The serial was introduced as follows: *"Sugar Cane Days* is set in the period known throughout the Pacific
as the "blackbirding days' or the 'kanaka trade'. The forced labour was little different
from slavery but was politely described as 'labour trade'. Between 1863 and 1907 the
trade in human beings was at its height. Albert Toro based his play on the stories told
by Molen, who lived through these times and who died in 1976.

lucky man today. I see cars, trucks, and ships driven by engines. *He laughs.* Ships that come here to take your father's copra to Kieta for good money . . . good money! See that harbour? Your great-great-grandfather rests there; and many more of our kinsmen who fought and were killed mercilessly by the white man. Every afternoon, when I drag myself out here to feel the last rays of the sun, I burst into tears, I still cry when I remember those who were slaughtered here. My age — I can't remember, but I think I was your age — I was with the crowd on the beach, collecting salmon that had died in a violent storm during the night. Then I heard my mother, calling me.

[*Crowd noises.*]

VANE [*calling*]: Molen! . . . Molen! . . . Mo-o-o-len!

RATO [*irritated*]: What's all this shouting! Don't you know people are still asleep?

VANE: I do know. But *where* is he?

RATO: On the beach, collecting dead salmon, from the night's thunderstorm.

VANE: A child died this morning . . . .

RATO [*firm*]: Whose child?

VANE: Mogeva's! Lightning struck through their roof. Everyone received burns. But the child was so young, it died of shock, right under its mother's blackened eyes.

RATO [*sadly*]: Poor family . . . . It is a curse. I am certain that Rosu, the rain maker, spat that on them. [*Very angry*] Give me that paddle! I am going to rid his stupid selfish head of its body!

VANE: No don't! It can't be him.

RATO: What makes you think that? He deserves a good punishment. From our god of love. Or else he should be drowned, with a huge rock fastened to his balls.

VANE [*laughs*]: What a way to kill him!

RATO: Don't laugh. Stupid men must die stupid deaths. You saw your late husband's death. Burnt alive for committing adultery. He was a stu —

VANE [*angry*]: Don't ever mention him again! Why did you marry me, eh? You knew very well the thought of him would haunt you. Get out of my house, Rato! He built this house for me.

RATO: I am sorry . . . . I am hurt myself. Angered by the death of an innocent child.

VANE: Just leave me. My son will help me with anything I might need.

[*Sound of a wooden door slamming.*]

RATO [*angry*]: Easy with that door!

MOLEN [*off mike — anxious*]: Father, it's me! What's happening?

RATO: Oh, my son, my only son! Come. Sit next to your father . . . .
Did you get any salmon at all?

MOLEN: I did, but I threw them back into the sea. [*Happily*] Do you
want me to go and get them back again?

RATO: No son. Why dead fish? You are a good fisherman. Catch
them alive and fresh.

MOLEN: What's happened to mother? Why do you look worried?

RATO: Mogeva's child was killed this morning. Just like the salmon,
she was killed by lightning.

MOLEN: Auntie told me that mother was calling for me . . . . Is my
food ready?

RATO: Maybe so . . . . Vane, where's Molen's food?

VANE: In that big basket on the fish bed.

[*Knocking. Dogs barking outside.*]

RATO: Who's there?

TOVI [*off mike*]: It's me!

RATO: The dogs are disturbed. Molen, go and see who that
mysterious person is. Some people don't seem to understand
why they were given a name the day after their brith.

MOLEN [*off mike*]: Father, father! It's Uncle Tovi, my uncle!

RATO: Oh, my in-law, welcome back. Come up and join us.

TOVI: I arrived back this morning.

RATO: And the storms?

TOVI: Those terrible nights we sheltered under the sea-beaten cliff
along the coast. During a lull we resumed our journey home,
but last night we nearly capsized. We couldn't see a thing. We
missed the island and landed in Dios.

RATO: In Dios?

TOVI: That's right. Before dawn broke, we paddled home fast, to
avoid being seen in broad daylight. We are all dead tired. We
were close to the beach when the morning thunderstorm
broke again; but it missed us.

RATO: Mogeva's child died this morning from shock, when lightning
struck their house.

TOVI: True?

RATO: Yes indeed.

TOVI: Poor child.

RATO: Even the fish died. Salmon, especially. The villagers were
picking them up on the shore, washed up by last night's high
tide.

TOVI: I'll have to catch up on my sleep today . . . . Where is your mother, Molen? . . . Molen!

MOLEN [*taken unawares*]: Ah? Ah? Yes I did.

TOVI [*laughs*]: What did you do? Where's your mother?

MOLEN: Heh! She went out awhile, before you came. She's gone for firewood. [*yawns.*] She'll be back soon.

TOVI: You need some sleep too, boy . . . . Yes, we did very well, all the pots were sold.

RATO: And how much did you make?

TOVI: We got miles of shell money, and baskets full of fat taros. But during that terrible storm we had to dump it all in the sea, to lighten the canoe! I don't know what Vane will say.

RATO: Women talk a lot, but she'll be so delighted to see you returned safely that there won't be time to think about what you brought.

TOVI: Anyway, remember the last trip we went on together?

RATO: Yes.

TOVI: You saw yourself that there were many young men in that village . . . . Now it's a place for old people; all the young have died.

RATO: But how?

TOVI: A type of sickness wiped out the main village. Rashes on the skin. Every boy that was preparing for initiation — dead!

RATO: It's those *beche-de-mer* traders who bring the white man's sickness with them!

TOVI: Exactly. That's what they now believe. Kita, the trader there, was killed and eaten. But three weeks later, his friends, who came from way down south, attacked the village and killed more people. Your friend Vanomo captured one of them. He was a clansmen of the mighty king of Saio island.

RATO: I thought so . . . that skull collector. The "devil of the sea". The chief known for his courageous warriors.

TOVI: That's him. The young warrior was later murdered, and his skull, blackened by smoke, dangles above the sacred war stone in the village. Those raiders carried some new kind of weapon: they weren't armed with spears, clubs and war shields. They had muskets, which they had received from the white *mastas* in return for young girls.

RATO: Young girls?

TOVI: Yes. The white man doesn't have beautiful women. He steals them from the islands.

[*A hard, heavy thump is heard outside, as Vane drops a load of firewood on the ground.*]

RATO: That must be your mother, Molen. Go and see!

MOLEN [*delighted*]: Mama! Uncle Tovi has returned! He's here in the house with Papa!

VANE [*happy*]: Oh really?... My long-gone brother. Oh, my brother. What did you bring for me?

TOVI [*sighs*]: I am sorry, my dear sister. We were caught unawares by a big storm, and we had to dump all our loads in the middle of the ocean.

VANE: Well, never mind, as long as you're alive. You look very tired, too. Have you eaten anything?

TOVI: I am not hungry. Just tired.

RATO: Sleep, Tovi. You need at least two days of good sleep.... Vane.

VANE: Yes?

RATO: Roast some taros; and when they're ready, wake us up. I'm tired.

VANE: *You* are tired now? Molen, are you tried as well? I might as well go to sleep too.

[*Laughter. Fading into bridge music. Cross fade into strong wind. Door opens.*]

ROBERTO [*shouting against the wind*]: Everything under control, captain?

SHERMAN: Fine, sir. Very strong wind today, eh?

ROBERTO: My word!

[*Door closes.*]

ROBERTO: This is where I always wanted to be. Life was dangerous for me as a doctor. Death was always close. Jealousy. In my profession, people are jealous. But I had more brains in my head than any of them.... You reckon cotton would be a good business?

SHERMAN: Everything depends on the owner of the ship. If you want cotton, it's you who must decide. I am only here to decide which way to turn the wheel.

ROBERTO [*laughs*]: Blackbirding is still the best. That's why I sacked my partners. You know they opposed that idea. I know the rest of you are all committed. But they were too much influenced by the government. I feared they might betray us. Anyway, how far are we from Malekula?

SHERMAN: Be there in the afternoon, if the wind stays in like this.... Where are all the boys?

ROBERTO: Playing poker in the cabin. Do you want a glass of wine?

SHERMAN: Thank you, sir.

ROBERTO: Here you are. Cheers.

SHERMAN: Cheers, doctor. I hope our first attempt at kidnapping will work out.

ROBERTO: By heavens it will! I've thought of everything. We'll attract them with coloured cloth. These natives are greedy. I've heard that you can even acquire a girl with a piece of copper.

SHERMAN: I heard that too. But I don't think I —

ROBERTO: Well, you trust your boss and do what you're told. That's why I promoted you to be the captain of this ship. Otherwise you would still be an ordinary officer . . . .

[*Wind sounds up and hold. Cross fade into distant crowd noises.*]

ROBERTO: Beautiful! See how eager those kanakas are? Maleluka natives. Reynold, organize a party and go down to the beach in a dinghy. Be armed.

REYNOLD: Yes sir.

ROBERTO: Captain, alert all the rest. These natives may be friendly one moment, but . . . .

[*Crowd noise up.*]

VOICE: They're shooting arrows at the boat! Look!

ROBERTO [*shouting*]: Get them! Shoot them! Kill them, Reynold!

[*Staccato gunfire. Screams of pain.*]

ROBERTO [*shouts*]: Bring in all the able-bodied men. And round up the wounded ones in the water. Stupid kanakas. [*Laughs.*] Their little bows and arrows are no match for our muskets. [*Laughs again.*]

[*Crowd noise. Cries of the wounded. Wailing of mourners.*]

ROBERTO [*softly*]: One, two, four, six, seven, eight, ten, eleven . . . twelve. Very good, mate. I'll promote you. Haul them up, boys. If anyone resists, shoot.

[*Crowd noise up and fade.*]

MOLEN: In that one week the ship had a load of fifty-six natives from Maleluka, Malaita, Isabel, and Guadalcanal. She als visited the most feared headhunter areas of the Rubiana Lagoon, where another twenty natives were captured. But the blackbirders sailed on, searchaing for prey.

[*Wind up. Splashes of waves against the hull.*]

REYNOLD: Captain, the wind is dropping.

SHERMAN: Open up the mainsails. And check on the hatches. If there are any dead ones down there, dump them in the sea.

REYNOLD: Yes sir.

[*Door opens and closes. Footsteps on hard planks on deck. Wind.*]

Raise the mainsail!

[*Flapping of heavy cloth.*]
Pull hard, you fellows. Hey you up there: any sign of land?
VOICE: No sir. Only rough seas and clouds.
REYNOLD: Keep looking.
[*Footsteps on deck. Sound of wooden plank being removed from hatch.*]
VOICES: Water! Water!
REYNOLD [*muttering in disgust*]: Bloody animals.
[*Steps descending ladder. Crowd noise up, almost deafening. More cried for water.*]
REYNOLD: Quiet! [*slaps.*] That will shut you up a bit . . . . Hm, hm, bloody rotten in here. I guess I better bring some water.
[*Steps. Closing of hatch. An old sea shanty faintly coming from crew. Door opens and closes.*]
SHERMAN: What's it like down there, Reynold?
REYNOLD: Pretty good. Nice and tidy, sir.
ROBERTO: Peace be with you. [*Laughs coarsely.*] All the natives behaving themselves?
REYNOLD: Perfectly, doctor. Just had a routine check on them. Seventy-six.
ROBERTO: Does that include the twenty captured at Rubiana?
REYNOLD: Yes sir.
ROBERTO: Good. I'll give them a little prayer before dark. Give me the map, captain . . . . Thank you . . . . Now, let me see, where is Buka on here?
SHERMAN: On the northern tip of the island of Bougainville. Look up.
ROBERTO: Ah, here it is . . . . Well, captain, see this cove. It looks a good harbour. Would you be able to get her in there?
SHERMAN: No trouble, sir.
ROBERTO: Very good, how long would it take to get there.
SHERMAN: Two more days, if the wind keeps up.
ROBERTO: Mate, find me a text in the Bible that I could read to the pigs in the hold.
REYNOLD: It was a dreadful failure when we tried that in Epi and Paama. Do you think it's worth trying again? [*Laughs.*]
[*Bridge music. Cross fade into children playing. Faint waves on the shore.*]
RATO: Those children playing remind me of a dream I had last night.
VANE: A dream? What about?
RATO: There was a man who came to me and said: "I am taking your son away to the depths of the forest." He is now a man, old enough to be initiated into the ancestral tribe.

VANE: What could that mean? You frighten me.

RATO: And I had a vision of seeing Molen, dressed in white men's clothes. I asked him what happened. But he crossed his lips with his finger and said: I've returned from my grandfather's land. A land full of uncountable wealth. I am going back there tomorrow, and shall return during the next mango season.

VANE: Oh no! My son must have been cursed.

RATO: If this was Rosu again, death shall be his for ever. I'll surely kill him . . . .

[*Knocking sound.*]

RATO: Come in.

TOVI: Did I hear you talk of killing?

RATO: Tovi, sit down . . . . I had a dream, and my wife thinks that Rosu has cursed Molen.

TOVI: It was only a dream. Forget it.

RATO: That's what you think.

TOVI: I've come to tell you that Molen is ready for initiation. By next month he should be handed over to the elders to prepare him for the ceremony.

RATO: Yes, you are right. But that's exactly what I dreamt. Poor Rosy. I've killed him with words, for the second time. [*Laughs.*] Anyway, Vane, you have to go to the garden and bring the fat taros only. Molen must be delivered within a month.

[*Commotion outside.*]

RATO: What's all that noise about?

[*Door opens.*]

MOLEN [*panting*]: Father, father, a schooner is coming into the harbour!

RATO: Strange. A schooner? That must be Masta Claka's.

MOLEN [*still out of breath*]: No. This one has only two masts — and plenty of coloured cloths on its railings.

RATO: That sounds interesting. Let's go and see!

[*Commotion fades. Bridge music.*]

ROBERTO [*laughs*]: Move over to starboard, captain. Give me my . . . haaa! Beauuuuutiful blacks. [*Sinister*] All guns loaded! Pig irons and cannons ready . . . boats lowered . . . . You all know your routine . . . . Don't hesitate or you'll be killed.

SHERMAN: We did it at Malaita and Robiana . . . we can do it again.

[*Sounds of wood and metal objects being moved.*]

ROBERTO [*glad*]: A good crowd all right . . . . How much space do we have?

REYNOLD: Enough space to dump the lot of them in. The aft and forward hatches are full, but the main hatch is theirs.

ROBERTO: Fine . . . . They're pulling their canoes down into the water. You see? They'll get the shock of their lives.

[*Crowd noise fading up.*]

ROBERTO: Let them come closer. Be ready for my signal.

[*Crowd noises. Paddles splashing.*]

ROBERTO: As soon as they come up to the side of the ship, drop everything on them . . . . Boats ready yet?

REYNOLD [*off mike*]: They're all down, sir.

ROBERTO: Very good. Ready? Go! Move it! Get the boats around them, quick!

[*Commotion. Splashing water. Gunfire. Confusion.*]

ROBERTO: Haul them up, boys!

VOICES: U-u-u-p! U-u-up! U-u-up!

ROBERTO [*shouting on top of the noise*]: Open the hatch!

[*Heavy planks removed. Faint cries.*]

ROBERTO: Everyone out of the water?

REYNOLD [*off mike*]: Yes sir!

ROBERTO: Right. Up the boats!

SHERMAN: There are many wounded, sir.

ROBERTO: Just dump them all into the hatch.

[*Crowd noise fades. Cross fade into bridge music.*]

MOLEN: In the third boat, a young boy, no older than myself, was instantly killed when a heavy piece of iron crashed on his head. His skull was split open . . . . The crew fished us out of the water like tunas; my father was clubbed to death with an oar. He sank like a rock, and I saw him no more.

We were herded like fish in a pond. The deck soon lost its brown surface; blood was all over it. Everything was red, like a pig feast. Cruelly, we were pushed into the hatch, which was wide open, ready to swallow us.

END OF EPISODE I

John Kasaipwalova

THE NAKED JAZZ

A play about a strange Melanesian marriage

INTRODUCTION

Since 1972 the formation and development of the Kabisawali movement on the Trobriand Islands depicts in many ways the love affair
and courting towards a very strange Melanesian marriage.

The marriage is between the female Trobriand traditionanl
culture and the male culture of the Western civilization.

The courting, the marriage, and the bearing of offspring are part
of the total progression and development of the Kabiswali
movement.

Like any marriage, the Kabiswali movement involves people and
philosophies: parents reluctant to commit themselves to new
relationships, lovers, too eager to wed, and society taking sides in
the social debate and rumours. But out of all this emerges a creative
relationship, from which a new generation is born. The Kabisawali
movement is like a marriage, and marriage involves people who
learn to *kabisawali.*

This play was first performed on the first anniversary of independence in 1976,
produced by John Kasaipwalova. Reprinted from *Gigibori* 4, no. 1 (February 1978):
40-48.

The naked eye does not make sense of and fails to see consistency in the confused actions of the people throughout Papua New Guinea. Yet out of these actions emerges the naked jazz whose music and rhythm awaits orchestration.

On the eve of the first birthday of Papua New Guinea as a nation, I voice the hopes that we, as a Melanesian nation, can bring forth this orchestra out of the discordant and divided tunes of the naked jazz.

John Kasaipwalova
Saturday, 11th September, 1976
At Tokarara

CHARACTERS AND ORIGINAL CAST

CHIEF, *traditional chief and chairman of Kabisawali; also a pastor*	John Kasaipwalova
TOULATILA, *young educated man who returns home to work for his village as manager of Sopi*	Valogusa
VALU GABENA, *village governor of Kabisawali People's Government*	Norbert Tuyega
ASSISTANT DISTRICT COMMISSIONER (ADC), *the central government's representative in rural areas*	Charles Paluwa
PUBLIC SERVANT, *administrative officer for the minister*	Martin Molosi
MINISTER, *a minister at Waigani offices*	Jerry Tokilivila
SECRETARY, *personal staff of the minister*	Bwasilou
MANAGING DIRECTOR, *chief executive officer of Kabisawali*	Thomas Gumilabai
BODA KOMITI 1, *village officers of Kabisawali*	Paul Mwaliu
BODA KOMITI 2, *People's Government*	William Kolaleu
TOULATILA'S FATHER	Paul Mwaliu
NAKAPUGULA'S FATHER	Gumakawai
DRUNKARD	Kasigabwita
NAKAPUGULA, *young village girl who is in love with Toulatila*	Albert Tokulayeya
Kabisawali members	Tohwatuplyava
	Samugwa
	Gumilabai
	Lawrence

Tohwemai
Naduhu
Kuyowesa
Clement
Mosubia

SCENE I

A Trobriand Island village at night. Darkness — suddenly the conch shell breaks the silence, people talking and exchanging betel-nut and tobacco, all waiting for a film show to commence. The film is Trobriand Experiment — *A BBC production about Kabisawali. The chief walks to the front to address Kabisawali members.*

CHIEF: Ladies and gentlemen, tonight we meet to begin the celebrations for the independence of Papua New Guinea. Already you know from the radios that big, big, things sometimes are going on in Port Moresby. Our leaders in Port Moresby are fighting very, very hard to stay on their feet so that Papua New Guinea will become independent from Australia.
We here in the Trobriand Islands are very, very far away, but *maski!* We can make independence here too. The picture you will see is about ourselves made jointly by our friends in the BBC and Sopi Arts School. Not much, but a small contribution for Papua New Guinea independence. OK. I have no more words, but maybe the manager of Sopi Arts wants to say something. [*Pauses and then calls out*] Manager!
[*Spotlight focuses on* TOULATILA, *who is busily trying to seduce a young girl in the background. He does not hear the call.*]
Manager!
[*This time he starts, dropping his lover basket and jumps to his feet.*]
TOULATILA: Yes sir! That's me! Yes, I'm coming!
CHIEF: Well, hurry up! You are keeping everybody waiting.
TOULATILA: Sorry sir. I was just trying to screw the generator for the projector.
CHIEF: Oh, I see. Everything ready for pictures?
TOULATILA: Yes sir, everything is OK.
CHIEF: All right, say your words.
TOULATILA: Sorry everybody, I have nothing much to say. I am not good at talking, because I like doing other things. But we want

you to know that sometimes me and my students work better in the dark. Sopi is like water; you see us, you drink us every day, and only when we get inside you we turn into blood. Thank you, and that's all.

[*Members clap and continue to make comments about rumours they know about him.*]

CHIEF [*rises and indicates to* TOULATILA *to return*]: Thank you, Sopi manager. Now we will start the picture, but before we start I want to remind all of you young boys and girls to keep your hands to yourselves. [*Calling to* VALU GABENA, *who is seated nearby*] Hey, Valu Gabena! Here, give these tobacco sticks to the people and tell them to behave themselves while picture is going on. This is not the proper time and place for boys and girls to *kabisawali!*

VALU GABENA: Yes sir! [*Calling out in very loud voice*] You already hear what our chief said. No *kabisawali* please when lights go out. And that means you married men too. Think of your families first. Also I'm sick of hearing your court cases with your wives and no time for my garden!

[*Conch shell blows again and the chief and the* VALU GABENA *return to their seats. Lights fade and the projector begins the film. The film runs for ten to fifteen minutes.*
Suddenly shrill policemen's whistles disrupt the film showing. Everybody jumps up in confusion asking what's going on. Projector is switched off and sound of heavy boots can be heard. Abruptly the ADC., *the* PUBLIC SERVANT *and two policemen march to the front of the white screen. The* CHIEF *and Kabisawali members look amazed and confused.*]

ADC [*shouting confidently while the two policemen have their guns ready to protect him and the* PUBLIC SERVANT]: Silence! Silence everybody! And when I speak I don't want anybody answering back. Is that clear.

[*No response from the people as he strolls up and down in front of them with his hands on his hips.*]

Now listen very carefully. We the government see you Kabisawali people as cargo cultists. You have no respect for the law. People like you and Bougainville and Mataungans and Highlanders always fight and break the laws. You should be ashamed of yourselves, because people like you give a bad name to Papua New Guinea.

[*Pauses for response — but no response from the people.*]

Now! The government in Port Moresby is doing many good

things for you. Tomorrow they will win independence for you. That independence is very, very, very big thing for all people of Papua New Guinea. Because of this, the government has sent a very important person here today. The government has already spent many thousands of kina to bring this important person here to give you a big present for independence day. I want you to listen carefully and accept the gift. This is the important person I am telling you about. [*Pushing the* PUBLIC SERVANT *forward*] Everybody clap now! Come on, clap!

[*No one claps, and the people remain silent and annoyed.*]

PUBLIC SERVANT [*starting in a hesitant tone*]: I — er — er — I thank you for your kind attention. I have come from the very big and important office at Waigani to bring you a present for Independence Day.

[*He opens his briefcase ceremoniously and brings out printed leaflets. He gives copies to the* ADC *who in turn hands them to the Kabisawali members. The members, believing it is a paper gift for rolling their tobacco, immediately start tearing up the papers for their smokes.*]

However, before I start I want somebody to translate what I say to your *tok ples,* because my boss wants you to understand everything correctly. Can anybody speak English among you?

[*A slight pause and murmurs from the crowd; finally the* VALU GABENA *steps forward.*]

VALU GABENA: I can some good English, sir.

PUBLIS SERVANT: Where did you learn to speak English?

VALU GABENA: From Hanuabada.

PUBLIC SERVANT: How long ago?

VALU GABENA: Oh, long time ago. ANGAU times before.

PUBLIC SERVANT: Thank you. You are very clever. I want you to listen and turn my talk around for people to understand, OK?

VALU GABENA: OK! [*He stands rigidly ready for the job.*]

PUBLIC SERVANT [*produces the master leaflet and starts reading from it*]: This is your present from the Waigani government. It is called the Eight Point Plan, so listen very carefully. Point One. A rapid increase in the proportion of the economy under the control of Papua New Guinean individuals and groups and in the proportion of personal and property income that goes to Papua New Guineans. OK, translate that one first.

VALU GABENA: People, I don't know what this man is talking about, but I will do my duty as your elected Valu Gabena to get rid of him as quickly as possible. Do not laugh or ask any questions or else he will waste our time more. OK!

PUBLIC SERVANT: OK. Point Two. More equal distribution of economic benefits, including movement towards equalizing of incomes among people and towards equalization of services among different areas of the country. OK, translate now.

VALU GABENA: This one too, I don't know what he is talking about but he is a stinking bastard. OK, I finish.

PUBLIC SERVANT: OK. Point Three. Decentralization of economic activity, planning and government spending with emphasis on agricultural development, village industry, better internal trade, and more spending channelled to local and area bodies. OK, turn it now.

VALU GABENA: I told you already, this man is like a bullmacow. OK, I finish.

PUBLIC SERVANT [*suspicious*]: Are you sure you turned everything I said?

VALU GABENA: Oh yes sir! Very short and very clever. Everythings you say.

PUBLIC SERVANT: OK. You better make sure. I don't want to get the sack when I get back to Waigani.

VALU GABENA: OK, sir, OK.

PUBLIC SERVANT: OK. Point Four. An emphasis on small-scale artisan, service, and business activity, relying where possible on typically Papua New Guinean forms of business activity. OK, translate now.

VALU GABENA: And the government says . . . . . I hope they cut his throat. OK, finish.

PUBLIS SERVANT: Point Five. A more self-reliant economy, less dependent for its needs on imported goods and services and better able to meet the needs of its people through local production. OK, turn.

VALU GABENA: The government says . . . and my garden is already full of weeds but nobody helps me, you dogs! OK, I finish.

PUBLIC SERVANT: OK. Point Six. An increasing capacity for meeting government spending needs from locally raised revenue. OK, translate now.

VALU GABENA: The government says . . . and before I forget, has anybody seen the lost bush knife of our *boda komiti*. OK, I finish.

PUBLIC SERVANT: Thank you. Point Seven. A rapid increase in the equal active participation of women in all forms of economic and social activity. OK, translate that much, but make sure you don't raise too much hope for these village women. Understand OK?

VALU GABENA: Yes, yes, I understand OK, and the government says . . . and I say to you our chief, remain seated and chew your betel-nut while I handle this unmannered pig. OK, I finish.

PUBLIC SERVANT: And finally, Point Eight. Government control and involvement in those sectors of the economy where control is necessary to achieve the desired kind of development. Tell them also that these eight new laws will be the laws of the Waigani government. I am leaving you copies of the Eight Points, and I want you to meet and make something from them. OK, tell them.

VALU GABENA: And the government says . . . I remind you all people, do not ask questions so he can go away quickly. OK, I finish.

PUBLIC SERVANT [*hastily closing his briefcase*]: Thank you and goodbye.
[*The police blow their whistles and they march out, leaving the people fuming in controlled amazement.*]

SCENE II

Minister's office at Waigani. The minister sits with open collar and loose tie, sweating profusely. The secretary holds a large fan and is trying her best to cool him down. In front of him a large stack of files. The central air-conditioning system in the entire office block has broken down.

MINISTER [*thumping his desk and twitching in his leather chair*]: Damn! Damn! And bloody damn! Why does this air-conditioning system have to break down at this time. Just because it is after independence, the bloody system wants its independence too. Secretary, give me a glass of iced water. I feel like a burning snake.

SECRETARY: Yes, Mr Minister, right away. [*He walks to the refrigerator at the corner.*]

THE MINISTER [*opens up a ledger report. He reads some figures and explodes to his feet, shaking in astonishment.*]

MINISTER: Holy bird of paradise! My god in heaven! Impossible! How come it is so much!

SECRETARY [*coming back with iced water*]: So much what, Mr Minister?

MINISTER: How come we have already spent two million kina in telling the people only about the Eight Points. We haven't got past the talking stage and already two bloody million kina gone.

Hell, I hope the village people enjoy what we tell them. [*Gulps down the water.*] Four months already gone and not one of my officers back from the rural areas to bring back information about the people's wishes.

[*Loud knocking on the office door.*]

Yes, come in and leave the door open for some fresh air.

[*Door opens. Enter* PUBLIC SERVANT *with a file of photographs.*]

PUBLIC SERVANT: Good morning, Mr Minister. I wish to present you personally with the results of my assignment. I am happy to inform you that my job was a tremendous success and —

MINISTER: Never mind all that. Just tell me how the village people reacted to the Eight Points?

PUBLIC SERVANT: Excellent, Mr Minister, just excellent.

MINISTER: Are you sure?

PUBLIC SERVANT: Absolutely sure, Mr Minister. They liked you so much and admired your policies so much that no one even wanted to object or interrupt when I was reading out your Eight Points. O man! To these people your charisma is really something.

MINISTER: Is that really true?

PUBLIC SERVANT: Absolutely, Mr Minister. I have all the facts and the data to prove it, sir.

MINISTER: Never mind, never mind. I have faith in you. You have done a wonderful job, officer. Papua New Guinea is really proud of you.

PUBLIC SERVANT: Thank you, Mr Minister, I am highly honoured by your wisdom.

MINISTER: How long will it take before I get a report for parliament?

PUBLIC SERVANT: Mr Minister, I intend working twenty-four hours a day on getting it ready. At that rate it should be ready for you in four months.

MINISTER: Is that the earliest you can make it?

PUBLIC SERVANT: Absolutely, Mr Minister. Normally such a report takes eight months, but I will work on it in my own time to have it ready for you.

MINISTER: Excellent, excellent, that's the kind of public servant I want in the government. By the way, how many photographs did you take in the execution of your job?

PUBLIC SERVANT: Only four hundred, Mr Minister. I lost the other five rolls in the rain.

MINISTER: Excellent, excellent. Make the report full of pictures. My brothers in the House are bored with reports that have only facts and figures. I want this report to have impact, you know what I mean.

PUBLIC SERVANT: Certainly, Mr Minister, I understand.

MINISTER: Yes, make it full of pictures like a comic book.

PUBLIC SERVANT: Most certainly, Mr Minister. This can be done quite easily. I will make sure the frontispiece is a fully blown up colour portrait of you. The village people will like that very much.

MINISTER: Brilliant! A bloody brilliant idea! [*Gets up and walks around his desk towards the public servant.*] I am impressed by your diligence, initiative, and sense of responsibility. I want you to know that commencing next week, I am promoting you to the position of departmental head. Do you have any objections?

PUBLIC SERVANT: Mr Minister, decision-making is entirely your prerogative. My only concern is my responsibility and service to the public.

MINISTER: Well, you know I am very happy to localize this white man and put you in his place because you understand our village people very well. You are an invaluable link between the government and our people.

PUBLIC SERVANT [*shaking the* MINISTER *'s hands joyously*]: Thank you sir. Thank you very much indeed!

SCENE III

Kabisawali general meeting in one of the villages. As is the pattern of these meetings, the village string band opens the protocol, followed by the short prayer led by the CHIEF.

CHIEF: Let us pray. Lord God, you who know all the inner-most secrets of all men and things, by now you have seen how every month we have meetings like this one, to find out our ideas of what to do for the good of our people. You know that this is not an easy task, because our enemies are always calling us fools and cargo cultists. Many times we work and try to do many things for our people, but the government always finds ways to destroy what we do. God, we ask you to look at their jealous hearts and to destroy their jealousness so that they can know what the people want and fill their hearts with the desires to help their own people. O Lord God, you know that because of these difficulties, our hearts sometimes have doubts and fears. We are tempted like Peter when he walked on water towards your son Jesus. But we know from the Bible how Jesus came angrily to Peter and grabbed him by the ears and said, "Simon Peter, you are a bloody fool for having doubts in your heart." In the same way, O Lord, take hold of the ears of those of our members who have doubts in their hearts and curse them and shout "bloody fools" in their ears until they are fully ashamed of themselves. Lord, we pray that you give us wisdom, give us courage, give us determination so that from our humble and few belongings we may achieve the Eight Point Plan as sent down from the Waigani government. In your name, O Lord, may all creatures of this earth sing your praises for ever and ever!

CROWD [*in unison*]: Amen!

[CHIEF *closes his Bible and solemnly sits down, thoroughly pleased with himself. The crowd begin to talk to themselves, while* VALU GABENA *walks ceremoniously to the table to conduct the meeting.*]

VALU GABENA: Chiefs, Valu Gabena, Boda Komiti, Valu Komiti and members, first I want to thank Kabwaku people for the food we have just eaten. I can see that all of you are going to carry the surplus to your villages. Agenda for today's meeting is two things. The first is about our business in Port Moresby and second one is a very serious marriage complaint. But first of all, please *boda komitis,* do your jobs.

[*He walks over to the* MANAGING DIRECTOR *and together they call up the various boda komitis to bring up their cash shares for recording. After that both of them count the total and have it ready to be announced.*]

MANAGING DIRECTOR: Chiefs, Valu Gabena, Boda Komiti and Valu Komiti, the total for today's meetings is two hundred kina!

[*People clap as he walks over to the chief and hands him the money.*]

VALU GABENA: It is now eight months since we sent our children to Port Moresby to start businesses for us. Today we are happy to have the managing director of our company to tell us what is going on.

MANAGING DIRECTOR [*walks to the centre with a report file*]: Chiefs, Valu Gabena, Boda Komiti, Valu Komiti and members, before I start I want first of all to pass to you greetings from all the corporation staff working for you in Port Moresby. They say that they are tired of eating tin fish and rice and are homesick for yams. But yams in the market are very expensive.

Anyway, I want you to know that since we started six months ago, the number of corporation staff in Port Moresby has grown from four to forty-four. While this satisfies the resolution you passed for employing our own people first, this has caused many other problems for our business. Today the corporation is facing three main problems: management working capital, and high overheads. Management problem means that as yet we do not have the practical skills to run successful business.

BODA KOMITI 1: But how come we gave you our children and all of them already finish high school and some from university?

MANAGING DIRECTOR: Sir, that's correct, my staff have the best intentions; unfortunately there is a very big difference between having a university education and having the practical skills to run a business. Sir, it's like you teaching your son how to make a garden by talking only, but he will never really know how to make a garden until he has made a garden himself.

BODA KOMITI 1: Yes, I understand, because to be a man, you must start making gardens when you are young. [*Sits down.*]

MANAGING DIRECTOR: The second problem is working capital. That means it is very hard to get loans or overdraft from banks, and also most of the businesses in Port Moresby are owned by white men and Chinese. They have a *wantok* system among themselves. To get terms and finance, it is very important to have contacts and connections. That's why the white men and Chinese don't want to see us succeed in business, especially with new contracts and connections. It will upset their *wantok* system and they will lose money.

BODA KOMITI 2: Yes, but what about the government's Eight Points we always hear on the radios?

MANAGING DIRECTOR: I don't know much about that, but I think the government is still planning about it. Anyway, our third problem is high overhead costs. That means housing, food, wages, electricity, water, and other things are very expensive in town, and we have to look after forty-four staff. So, my dear people, you know the main problems of our business. It is not easy but at the same time it is not impossible. It means we have to work harder and most important, we must not give up.

CROWD [*clapping in agreement*]: No, we will not give up.

[MANAGING DIRECTOR *walks back to his chair and the* CHIEF *rises to close discussion on the first agenda item.*]

CHIEF: Thank you, Managing Director. Tell all your staff that you are in Port Moresby because we want you to be there to make business for us. I know we cannot help you in the problems you must carry for us, because we do not know how to use the pen and the foreigners' tongues. But remember the great traditions of *kula.* You are not a man until you have braved the waves and the gales in search of new friends and contacts. Your arms have no strength if they do not learn to carry heavy loads. This is our help we give you and your staff. [*He sits down.*]

VALU GABENA: Agenda two for our meeting is the complaint of our two *boda komitis* for the marriage of their children. Already there is too much talk, and if we do not do something about it, soon our villages will be fighting against one another.

[*He beckons the two parties to stand up and explain their grievances. On one side* TOULATILA'S FATHER *with his son looking downwards all the while. On the opposite stand* NAKAPUGULA *with her father, also very indignant.*]

OK, explain.

TOULATILA'S FATHER: Chiefs and everybody, I have no quarrels except that my son has big education and I don't want him to marry village girl. I want one *dimdim* or Chinese or half-caste for my son's wife.

NAKAPUGULA'S FATHER: Ei! Shame on you, and who wants your son's big education. Education is nothing. He cannot make money, iron for houses, guns, steamers or trucks. Education only for tricking young girls!

TOULATILA'S FATHER: I want my son to marry somebody from town, so they can make big business for me.

NAKAPUGULA'S FATHER: Lying dog! They come here and look like important people but in town they are nobody. My daughter can stay and help us all in the gardens.

CHIEF [*very impatient with the proceedings*]: Listen, you two, you are wasting our time. I have only one short question to ask both of you. Are you two getting married or these young people?

[*The two fathers shake their heads in unison.*]

Well then, stop wasting our time. Before you fight, just remember, tomorrow you may have to eat in the young couple's house. Let them decide. [*Signals* VALU GABENA.] Close the meeting. Some of our members have a long way to walk back to their villages.

VALU GABENA: All right, that's the end for today. Remember next month meeting at Okaikoda village. And before you go, I ask you all to start walking so that corporation bus can pick you up on the way. No good all of you sit and wait for trucks and waste too much benzene.

SCENE IV

Two a.m. at Bulubulu Trade Store 24 Hours Service — Hohola. Two members of Kabisawali Corporation staff are serving at the counter. The record player is playing to keep them awake. Three drunkards walk into the store, making a lot of noise.

DRUNKARD: Yahoo! Next time rascals, bai mi gibem kung fu! [*Slapping onto the counter*] Large Cambridge, please.

SHOP ASSISTANT: Sorry, *wantok,* no Cambridge.

DRUNKARD: Ah, Yu tok wanem. No gat kambriss. Bloody sit!²

SHOP ASSISTANT: Sorry, we ran out of Cambridge since twelve o'clock. You know government fortnight. We won't get stock till tomorrow.

DRUNKARD: Bloody sit! What for twenty-four hour service, Yu rabis!³ [*Thumps the table.*]

SHOP ASSISTANT: Ei, be careful, will you. You might break the glass.

DRUNKARD: Small boy, yu no ken tok laik dat. Bloody basket. Mi no dok nor pik!⁴ [*The* DRUNKARD *grabs the* SHOP ASSISTANT *by the arm and roughly pulls him from behind the counter. They argue and start fighting. Soon other staff members run to join the fight in the stores. The drunkards are soon thrown out of the store.*] Yu wait, Bulubulu! Mi save yu. Bai tomorrow mi kam bek. Bloody sit! [MANAGING DIRECTOR *is woken up by the commotion and rushes to the store, but the fight is over.*]

MANAGING DIRECTOR: What the hell is going on! [*Surveying for damages*] How many times do I have to tell you not to fight with our customers.

SHOP ASSISTANT: Sir, but he started it first. He nearly broke the glass counter.

MANAGING DIRECTOR: That's not good enough. I told you already,

1. Next time, rascals, I'll Kungfu you!
2. Ah, what do you say? No Cambridge? Bloody shit!
3. You are rubbish!
4. Small boy, you can't talk to me like that! Bloody bastard. I'm not a dog or a pig!

rascals or drunkards, I don't care, but you must give them service first. Our customers are always right, so don't argue with them. Is that clear.

SHOP ASSISTANT: Yes sir.

MANAGING DIRECTOR: OK, all of you get back to sleep. We have a lot of work to do at Gerehu tomorrow. And you two, sweep up the rubbish and get back to your duty. [*He walks out of the store.*]

SCENE V

A marriage in church for Toulatila and Nakapugula. The 1CHIEF *and the* MANAGING DIRECTOR *stand at the pulpit waiting for the marriage, and the bride and groom enter singing a hymn. The bride is dressed in a grass skirt with a white veil on her head, signifying her basic traditional attitudes, with a reluctant acceptance of modern ways. The groom is smartly dressed in long trousers, necktie, shoes, and long sleeves. On his head he wears three traditional feathers, signifying that even though he appears a modern man, he is still traditionalist in his thinking. When they arrive inside the church, the* VALU GABENA *positions everybody, including the band with their instruments. When the hymn stops, the* VALU GABENA *addresses the two leaders.*

VALU GABENA: O leaders, we bring to you today two of our children who wish to be bonded in holy matrimony. Both have made mockery of their elders' expectations. They refuse to follow the ways of our ancestors and also they refuse to follow the ways of the *dimdims*. Our children here want to marry under the Eight Commandments of Waigani government. So today we bring them to you to make a blessing for their matrimony. [*The* VALU GABENA *takes his position beside the* CHIEF *and the* MANAGING DIRECTOR. *The* MANAGING DIRECTOR *hands over to the* CHIEF *a hard-cover copy of* Sand *by Michael Somare. He addresses the young groom first.*]

CHIEF: Young man, before I pray to God to bless your marriage, I want you to understand the Eight Commandments first. [*Flips to the first page ceremoniously.*] It is written in the book of Sana thus: Darkness begat light. Light begat the moon. The moon begat the sun. The sun begat the earth. The earth begat Kiriwina. Kiriwina begat Port Moresby.

Moresby begat Lae. Lae begat Goroka. Goroka begat Wewak.
Wewak begat Manus.
Manus begat Rabaul. Rabaul begat Panguna.
Panguna begat copper. Copper begat North Solomons.
North Solomans begat independence and then independence
begat you and me.
Do you understand this?

TOULATILIA: Yes, I do.

CHIEF: Then, young man, remember that you came from darkness
and unto darkness you must trace your ancestry. Do you
understand the meaning of this?

TOULATILA: Yes, I do.

CHIEF: As to you, my daughter, do you know the meaning of
independence?

NAKAPUGULA: No, never before.

CHIEF: That is good to hear, for you are still a virgin. It is also written
in the book. Your husband will teach you about independence
and help you bring forth many children.
You must learn to use the typewriter.
You must learn to drive a car.
You must learn to fly an aeroplane.
You must learn to make houses.
You must learn different kinds of cooking.
You must learn to decorate yourself in new ways.
And you must keep your house clean.
All these things you must do, so that your children can grow
up knowing these things from your womb. But above all you
must learn to love your husband. Do you understand these
things?

NAKAPUGULA: Yes, I do.

CHIEF: That being so, I want the congregation to sing a hymn first
before I pray to the Lord our God to bless their matrimony.
Somebody start the hymn, please.
[*The string band strikes up the latest Kabisawali song, and all
follow the singing. When it ends, the chief beckons the bride and
the groom to come forth and join their hands over the book.*]

CHIEF: Lord Almighty God, we your humble people gather today to
witness the holy union of your two children. We pray that what
they unite, let no man put asunder. Enlighten them, O Lord,
to see that from today every act and every speech will be part
of a long road for the new family.
Lord, we pray that you make them see that whatever they do

now is the naked jazz on which their children will form their poetry and their music in your name. May all creatures of this earth likewise sing your praises forever and ever.

CROWD: Amen.

END

Essays

Kundapen Talyaga

SHOULD WE REVIVE INITIATION RITES IN ENGA SOCIETY?

This may be the first paper of its kind. It discusses the survival chances of youth initiations, initiations of newlyweds, and related ceremonies that were of crucial importance in traditional Papua New Guinean society.

Towards the end of the Second House of Assembly our politicians started to tell us that we must revive our culture, and they have continued to do so throughout the first three years of the Third House. Abandoning cultural traits — either through force or voluntarily — is now seen as a sign of acceptance of colonial rule and foreign Christian values. The rapid move towards self-government and full independence and the vigorous localization policy of the government have imposed an anti-colonial attitude on the minds of Papua New Guineans, who therefore wish to look with fresh eyes at the neglected traditions of their forefathers.

Many of us today, of whatever creed, class or intellectual ability, stand up and say: "Yes, we must revive our culture." But how can that be done in the face of so many changes that have already happened? The whole Third World seems to have accepted Western culture.

In our own country, the family structure is changing rapidly. We are losing our links with our lineage and attaching more importance to the smaller family units. Women cry out for equal rights, and our

Reprinted from *Gigibori* 2, no. 2 (October 1975): 37-41.

government is committed to give women a say in government, even though women would have had little influence on such matters in traditional society. Children roam like free birds of the sky, seeking knowledge when and where they can and not waiting for specific initiation rites before acquiring the knowledge and habits of adults. The adults have lost their formerly accepted role of controllers, superiors and advisers, and in this transitional age we young ones often have to advise the old.

In this paper I would like to ask some questions for which I have certain answers. Should we receive our culture? How should we do it? Would it have any relevance to a changing Papua New Guinea? If we receive it, can it last? And finally, is there a danger that regional cultural revivals will promote separatism? I am sure that these same questions have been asked before in Africa and South-East Asia, perhaps as long as twenty years ago. And yet, nowhere have solutions been easily found.

For Papua New Guinea, 1973 will remain a memorable year. We could call it "the year of culture", for in that year our infant government recognized the value of culture and established the National Cultural Council under a new ministry. Since then, we have organized cultural festivals, built regional cultural centres and local museums, and have introduced cultural activities into our schools.

What does it all mean? Are we merely afraid of change? Or are we simply following the lead of other Third World countries? Are we blindly following instructions from our own government? In this paper I want to argue as an individual. And I want to look only at one aspect of culture among a single group of people, the Engas of the Central Highlands.

Before we decide whether initiation rites can be revived or should be continued in changing times, we must first look at the meaning of initiation in traditional society. What was initiation, and when was it practised in traditional Enga Society? There are 164,000 Engas, and they live in an area of 6,400 square kilometres. Among them, youth initiation was perhaps the most important period in life. It was a time when young boys first learned how they should live the life of adults. It was a time of meditation. It was a time for confession and for the interpretation of dreams. In initiation, young boys were being prepared to face the future as adults: they interpreted dreams warning of the likely death of a clansman; they were prepared for tribal fighting and possible victory and defeat, for land disputes and for trade exchanges. For each situation, the young boys' responses had to be prepared.

Initiation was also a time for purification, as this chant, "The Purification of the Eyes", shows:

This lad
Confesses and says:
I stood on Yalu ridge
And saw the thing erect,
I heard her bones crack,
I witnessed the spreading of thighs,
I heard the sound of thrusts.

Oh my poor eyes,
Splash off the evil!
Go!
What are you! O go!
Wipe it off my eyes like *ama* sap!
Cast it off my eyes as *kyangali* sap!
Get set, poor eyes,
Rotate,
My poor eyes rotate,
Halt in your position.
I shout from here.

This song is both a confession and an incantation. The initiate had to cleanse his eyes and his mind of all the things he should never have seen and never have heard. Only with a mind thus prepared was the boy ready to be taught and finally led out into the adult community. For the climax of the ceremony was the leading out from the forest and the presentation of the youths to the community. That was the occasion when young girls would reveal publicly their affection for particular young men. It was the introduction to manhood, and from then on new lights and new duties began in the man's life.

Another important initiation was held for newly married couples. For five days the groom and the bride were separately prepared by older men and women respectively, and they were told about sex. At the end of each day the groom and bride were allowed to practise what they had learned earlier. At night they could explain the difficulties they had experienced and they would be advised again.

The first question we must ask ourselves now is this: To what extent do the functions of traditional initiation rites remain important in a society formed by Western education?

Although Enga society was brought into contact with Western culture only forty years ago, a lot of changes have happened in this short time. The initiation of newlyweds has completely disappeared.

The initiation of youths has only just survived, though no longer in the same form. It is common for us to put the blame for our cultural loss on the missions, but it would be more correct to attribute it to the total impact of Western civilization and all its bearers: missionaries, government officials, teachers, doctors, medical orderlies, anthropologists, interpreters, shopkeepers, managers, crane operators — you name them.

Nowadays, youth initiations tend to be coupled with other important events in community life, such as the opening of a new school, a council chamber or a church. Youngsters take part in an initiation ceremony and then present themselves to the public during the other social function. It is hardly likely that in such circumstances the mood is the same as it was in the old days. The ceremony has degenerated into a mere display of traditional costume. The young boys hardly go through the same state of anxiety, for the ceremony does not have the same decisive influence on their lives. An initiation ceremony linked with, for example, National Day is not evidence of the survival of an important cultural feature of Enga life. It is merely a public demonstration of what the culture was like in the past. A demonstration, moverover, that is not spontaneous but suggested from the outside.

Some missions now allow youth initiations, but what the youths learn in these initiations is not what they learned in the past. Social changes have made many functions of initiation irrelevant. Children now learn about sex at a very early age. By the time they reach the age of initiation, there is little left to tell them. Many schools have lessons on reproduction, usurping an important function of the initiation rite.

Why, then, the need for a revival? This question will be answered in different ways by different people. Here are some of the reasons people have given: we must bridge the generation gap between the old and the young; we must preserve the identity of Enga society; we need to preserve our cultural identity. But what is meant by bridging the generation gap? Surely the young people know more than the old about the non-Enga world and its problems. And when we have obtained some education and we go home on a political education tour, is that not bridging the generation gap?

Most Enga want to preserve the cohesion of Enga society, but we must think twice even about this. To promote Enga values too anxiously could mean that separatism is encouraged indirectly. Now that we have accepted the idea of national unity and are crying, "Unite, *bung wantaim, ahebou!*" the tribe must be integrated into the larger national framework. And we must remember that national unity is one of the good things that Western civilization has imposed on us.

All over Papua New Guinea now, the cultural identities of different communities are being blurred. We live together with people from other communities in the big towns, and mixed marriages between different tribal groups are becoming more and more common. Perhaps this process of cultural exchange that is occurring throughout the country is helping us to understand better how many things we have in common, and perhaps each group should strengthen these common elements as a means of creating more and deeper understanding between us.

To be able to share common cultural elements, an Enga must be identifiable as an Enga. To maintain the variety in Papua New Guinean culture each group should practise what is unique to it. For example, the *te* (pig exchange), the *yupini* house, and the dance to the water spirits are some of the things that must be kept by the Enga. Then we can identify as Enga although we are Papua New Guineans.

One may ask if the world view embodied in initiation rites is compatible with the modern life of, for instance, a university graduate. The chief minister of Papua New Guinea has demonstrated in a practical way that the modern and traditional worlds can be bridged. In 1972, after being sworn in as chief minister, Michael Somare went to Murik Lakes to complete his third initiation, which made him head of his clan. Though the ritual was slightly modified for him (the normal time had to be considerably shortened because of his many other commitments) the chief carried out a real, not a sham, ceremony. Michael Somare was, of course, from the chief's hereditary line, and as a child he had been earmarked for the title. He demonstrated that most of us could accept the blending of old and new in this country. I did not see a single letter in either the local or the foreign press querying the wisdom of his decision. In a practical way the chief demonstrated respect for our culture and for the elders of his village in particular. I think that by doing this he gained in status not only in his own village but in Papua New Guinea as a whole.

Another interesting example is John Kasaipwalova, a university student who returned to his village to create a village government that would embody both the wisdom of the old people and the forward-looking energy of the young. He constantly seeks advice from the old leaders and chiefs. In his movement it is apparent that many of the values and principles of the past can still serve as guides in the present.

It is important that we ask ourselves whether the beliefs expressed in initiation rites are compatible with Christianity. Most of the educated people in Enga are still very young. We are not firm Christians, but we are what I call "feeble believers". On the other hand, our fathers, who were the first converts to Christianity, are very firm in their belief. They were given the new ideas by strangers who seemed superior. My father became opposed to any traditional ceremony, including initiation rites and funeral feasts.

When I discussed in detail the functions of initiation rites with my father and other elders, I found that the functions are in some ways similar to the functions of baptism and communion in the Christian community. In both cases young people are being prepared to become full members of society.

The early missionaries could not see parallels between Christianity and Enga culture. Consequently they condemned all Enga practices as evil. But now many churches are promoting the revival of some customs. This is due to the greater understanding they have gained of Enga traditions as a result of detailed studies undertaken by missionaries. Some churches, for example, Lutheran and Catholic, have given encouragement for initiation rites to precede baptism. However, these initiations are not traditional. Also, the churches use the initiation grounds as a Bible study camp.

There is no reason why the content of initiation should not change when the life-style of the society has changed. However, there is no need to change the traditional elements of initiation, even though they may include magic chants, when they are compatible with the new life-style. To my mind, the traditional content of initiation ceremonies is not incompatible with Christianity, and the more the churches understand about our customs, the more they will be able to accept them.

Similar blendings of old and new can be seen in other situations. In the 1974 graduation ceremony at Goroka Teachers College a graduate appeared in traditional initiation costume. The vice-chancellor of the University of Papua New Guinea stated that he was both surprised and delighted. This student clearly saw some links between the old initiation into manhood and his modern initiation into Western life.

Such identifications and compromises may help us to infuse the modern institutions with some added meaning, even if they do not genuinely revive the old. The possibility of combining high school graduations with traditional rites could be explored. This would ensure that the student would not feel he had been educated completely away from his society but that he had been educated to be a member of both worlds. Such combinations of old and new would lead old rituals to gradually adapt their content to more modern conditions.

There are many people who feel that, as more and more Enga become educated and accept jobs in the towns, Enga culture is going to shrink and die. However, moving away from the home district does not mean that we must lose our identity. There are Enga student associations and Enga welfare societies in many urban centres in Papua New Guinea. These should be used, and up to a point they are already being used, to pass on cultural knowledge. There is no reason why such associations should not organize *meri singsings* or other cultural activities in the towns.

There is really no reason why urban Enga communities should not create an initiation ceremony of their own. For what is it we learn in initiations back home? Is it not to interpret dreams, to fight and defend, to look after a family, to speak in public, to discuss and plan wars, and to settle disputes and arrange compensation? Are these not basic skills we still need in an urban environment? Adaptations of initiation in an urban environment could still be meaningful.

But we must also remember that the majority of students who attend primary school do not pass on to high school. They are not qualified to take jobs in towns and must return to their villages sooner or later. It is a tragedy, indeed, if these young people have been cut off from their culture during their brief period of schooling. There is no worse fate than being a misfit in one's own home. For these young people, it would be of immense benefit if, at primary school, they went through a proper, uncompromised, traditional initiation ceremony that would give them real status in their own society.

When discussing our own cultural problems in Enga we must not forget the impact our activities will have on the nation. We must beware lest too much emphasis on local culture should conflict with Papua New Guinean nationalism. We must preserve our own identity within the larger national setting. We must promote local culture as a means of contributing to the national culture. In the towns, we must arrange cultural exchanges with other groups. In this way we will promote understanding between and sympathy for different groups. All our local cultural endeavours must be seen in the light of the larger national aim.

I feel that initiation rites can and should be revived. But if we are to do this we must be flexible. For those who will continue to live in our villages as subsistence farmers, fairly orthodox rites may be most appropriate. But for those of us who have to live in the fast-changing environment of the cities, it is necessary to modify the rites.In many cases, initiation rituals can be identified with graduation or communion ceremonies and fused into a new cultural expression of our complex, changing times. But we should never ignore these traditions or regard them as evil customs of the past for which we should feel shame.

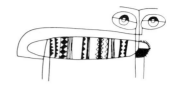

Jacob Simet

FROM A LETTER TO THE EDITOR OF "GIGIBORI"

After a few weeks of my stay here [at the Institute of Papua New Guinea studies], it became very clear to me what I wanted to do. As I briefly stated in my proposition, much about the Tubuan society has already been recorded in books. But the problem is that the Tubuan society described in these books (Brown's, Powell's, Parkinson's) no longer represents the society as it is today. Many of the rules have since been modified or simply neglected. This modification or neglect is what I am trying to look at very closely at the moment. These changes that have taken place are causing problems for the welfare of the society and they endanger its survival. Since I have been here, concern about these matters had been expressed by members of the society itself. They are questioning whether the society will survive with these modifications and these forms of neglect. They are afraid of the printing of Tubuan images on laplaps and T-shirts and of the playing of Tubuan longs on the radio. They are worried about the deliberate attempts by the various churches here (mainly Catholic) to destroy the society. It has just dawned on them that they are the only ones who can decide whether the society dies or survives.

Why are these men concerned over the printing of Tubuan designs on shirts or the playing of sacred flutes on the radio? I personally agree with them that these things strip the Tubuan

Reprinted from *Gigibori* 3, no. 1 (April 1976): 1-2.

society of its force and will eventually murder it. The big men here see that this is the way to destroy the society.

From information I have collected, the Tubuan (you can call it an art form or the basis of Tolai social organization) is made up of five parts, none of which can function by itself. For the Tubuan to have any meaning, they have to be together. Any one of the elements existing by itself has no meaning whatsoever. These elements are: the mask, the society, the rules, the songs, and the setting. I have deliberately left out the sixth element, which is magic. Though I know it exists, I cannot yet talk about it confidently, for reasons that I shall elaborate later.

If one considers the Tubuan as an art form (and that is what it is, amongst other things), I have noticed that very little or no Tolai art was ever intended to be preserved materially or removed from its setting. After every artistic performance most of the material is burnt and the rest is stored away, never to be used again. Also, I have noticed many new compositions and innovations in the songs and dances. I don't believe for a moment that this has only come about since the European contact. I think that Tolai art is a living thing, responding to each new situation. I fear that preservation by whatever means, if not very carefully thought out, may produce a Tolai art that will have lots its profundity. Like many other artistic cultures, Tolai art is made up of many interlocking elements, and none of these elements can be a meaningful art form by itslef. I think the biggest and most important element in any art form is the setting. I do not think it is right for anybody, whoever he may be, to help disintegrate an art form like the Tubuan, in order to please and entertain people who don't even appreciate it fully. Some people believe this is a way to "preserve" the art. Maybe these strangers receive some gratification out of marvelling at these fragments — but what price does the society that owns them have to pay? Has it ever occurred to these organizers and preservationists they they are turning artists into performing clowns? Do we need to tear masks and instruments out of their setting and stick them on to walls? Do we need to take a Tubuan mask and place it in a glass case, do we have to print and duplicate its image, do we have to play its secret songs in public?

To encase a Tubuan mask in a glass case is an act that would call for a heavy fine according to the rules of the society. Is this really what we have to do to preserve the art? Has anyone ever tried to find out what effect museums have in this country? What is the purpose of a museum? And what is this culture that our politicians talk so much about — the culture they want to preserve so that it can give an identity to this country? Has it occurred to them that these things we call art have social, economic, and spiritual functions? And if they see that, why do they still choose to treat it as a mere entertainment for visitors, or a curious object for people to stare at and maybe admire? Where is this Western attitude to art leading us at this moment?

These are the kinds of questions that worry me while on this research project. Some may be answered in my write-up; others may just remain questions forever to be asked and brooded on by the intellectual mind. I want to discuss these matters with others and learn of their experiences.

Earlier on I mentioned that I cannot yet talk about the magic aspect of Tubuan. This is because I am not yet a full initiate of the society. I went through the first stage as a boy, and the second stage only a few weeks ago. I still have to go through the third stage and then I can see the essence of the Tubuan society. The earliest time a third-stage initiation will take place will be next year, between April and June. It will last for a whole month.

Bernard M. Narokobi

ART AND NATIONALISM

From the earliest times of exploration by the wandering men of the
Western world, the peoples of the Pacific have been imbued with
romance and fascination. The early explorers who sailed the world's
oceans believed there was an island, rich in gold, to the east. That
island was New Guinea. But, because the navigators made a number
of stupid mistakes, New Guinea was not actually explored until
relatively late. The early maps show Papua as a separate land mass.
A study of Mr Quinlivan's independence display of the old maps
gives a fascinating account of these mistakes by the world's greatest
navigators of the time. Alan Moorehead's "Fatal Impact" that took
the lives of many Pacific peoples did not take its toll in Papua New
Guinea until some time later.

In one of the reports of these early explorers, this rich island of
gold was believed to have four kingdoms. The kings lived inland and
were very powerful. It is possible that the very early explorers who
went to the Philippines, to the Spice Islands, and later to the
Americas, might have heard the story and been afraid of the
powerful kings.

Whatever it was, the present country of Papua New Guinea was
left untouched. Other South Pacific islands, — Hawaii, Tonga,

A paper read at the seminar on art in the Third World organized by the Institute of
Papua New Guinea Studies in conjunction with the External Service of UPNG in
October 1975. Reprinted from *Gigibori* 3, no. 1 (April 1976): 12-15.

Samoa, and Fiji — were visited more frequently. Luckily, much of our art and culture remains intact, even today.

There developed a fantasy that on these sweet and enchanted islands lived simple, primitive, and uncultured natives. We fell into that same romance when we were eventually uncovered. Even today our full humanity, and our view of the universe, is understood in terms of anthropology and not in terms of beings with a valid view of the cosmos.

Today, some people continue to cherish this myth. Not only do these people hold this belief, but they go further and say that our people lived by hunting each other. They say this as if hunting humankind has never been a trait of all men everywhere. They judge our people primitive, pagan, uncivilized, and needful of all the great and sophisticated techniques and values of Western civilization.

This philosophy has resulted in mass murder of the Pacific peoples. This death is now firmly established in Papua New Guinea and is spreading like fire on Waigani grass lands. Living was an art or a skill our people learned well, long before contact. Our people knew well that living in small interdependent communities offered the best security. But this is not the art, the subject for this talk.

More and more people are now realizing that in fact the natives of these dreamed-of lands inhabit a world of complex human relationships, complex trade partnerships, and a vast wealth of knowledge and experience sufficient for their needs. Some of this wealth is manifested through the myths, symbolism and legends of our people. The supernatural symbolism, and legends of our people. The supernatural powers and the forces prevailing upon life are not only mystical and divine, but also very real and as earthly as the human beings, the animals, the fish, and the plants.

The finest art of our people symbolizes the best man can do to merge his humanity with the divine. It expresses the mystical reality of our people, who live and die and still live on the one plane. Some art is believed to be divine in origin, while other arts could not be traced to a source. The study of the art of Papua New Guinea is central to the discovery and the proper understanding of the richness of our souls. In the past, our art was seen in the context of simple carvings or intricate weavings of the primitive peoples. Hence we find static museums in the Western world, storing the primitive art objects.

Today, no true student of our art would deny that a glimpse into the enchantment of our lives can be got by an awareness of the life and the power of even a single work of art. A finely carved piece of wood becomes a being, the guardian spirit of an entire clan. A mask becomes the power behind all the great deeds of a tribe. A figure with varying colours from the mother earth becomes the centre place for meditation and serenity.

Papua New Guinea is a land of rich originality in art. It is also a complex mixture of rich variety in art. No one who has lived in a village for even a week will come out unconvinced that Papua New Guineans live in a world of two or three dimensions at once. Through their fine art they can, and do, communicate with the divine. Through their art they realize their humanity.

Recently, during the independence celebrations week, the Creative Arts Centre put on a display of what they called the "seized collections". While I was there, watching every piece of fine work of art of our people, I became deeply moved. There in that display room the atmosphere vibrated and became alive with the life of these living figures. They seemed to be saying to me, "We are your souls. Take care of us."

Those figures, whether they were hanging down on nylon strings or standing up on cement blocks, vividly conveyed messages to me. They were saying, "We are on trial. We are so very heavily dependent on the Western man now for our survival. Take us to your hearts and protect us." And yet I felt they had enough power within themselves to protect themselves, and that, whatever happens, they will survive the trial of time.

There is nothing more devastating in a nation's life than having its finest works of art on trial. There is nothing more harmful to a nation and its people than having its men and women of creative talent condemned by ignorance and omission, or not recognized for the spirit they inject into their nation.

We, Papua New Guineans of today, inherit one of the richest artistic heritages of all people. Our people had, through difficult terrain, developed distinct stylistic expressions, peculiar to their communities. They went further than that. Each family, and in some cases each person, was the heir or the proprietor of a particular style or motif. It is important to know that, while technical knowledge of the art of creating a human figure, a snake, a bird, or a fly was individualized, our art forms were still open to exchange, either internally or between different communities. Contrary to what many people believe, our art forms were distinct and personal, but at the same time they were quite open to movement among different groups. Even before the Western influence our artists were already at work uniting our people, not as a mass of human numbers, but in recognition of what each artist and his people enhancing the power and the quality of their own lives. It was an individualized unity that recognized the distinct quality of the artist in his community.

It would be a mistake to believe that art in Papua New Guinea was entirely the expression of the supernatural entities of life. Art was functional too, in that various objects were often carved for no other reason than to do a job or for decoration. In other words, there was popular as well as sacred art. Sacred art is often translated into popular art, but not all of it can be. Likewise, certain popular art is never an art for the sacred objects, although some can be.

To my knowledge, no careful studies have yet been made of the scope of our art. The records we have come from foreign explorers, foreign missionaries, and foreign anthropologists. One thing that stands out in all of these reocrds is the generalizations they give. Virtually no one has tried to study or even record art in the context of individual artists, their sensitivities, their visions of life, and their hopes and fears.

With the establishment of our political independence, our first task is to restore our self-respect, pride, and dignity. There is no better way to do this than to recognize our living and our dead artists whose works symbolize our true selves. That, then, is our first task: to recognize our artists in their own right as men and women of creativity. These people should be resurrected and studied in schools and universities. To this extent, but not beyond, we should popularize our artists and their works.

Our second task is to establish shrines and monuments dedicated to these men and women of art. Our nation is a nation of divided unity. In other words, there is a remarkable sense of the oneness of man and the universe, revealed by individualistic carvings and paintings. We have to make a history out of that reality. There is no greater way of doing this than to recognize that the Trobriand artist, the New Ireland artist, the Orokolo painter, the Sepik mask maker, to mention but a few, are equally relevant and valid to their communities and to all of us, both today and tomorrow.

Today we have little to be proud of and much to be ashamed of when we realize that we know more about foreign artists than we know about our own. True, the appreciation of art is universal quality and we should be free to appreciate other art. But our art must be, at the very least, as meaningful to us as the foreign art. It should mean more to us. And we should do everything possible to protect what we have and promote it without debasing its quality. The point is that our art is often presented to us as the grotesque markings of a primitive people, which the passing of time will exterminate.

At this historical vantage point, I can see all our forms of art converted into cheap, popular, and bare artistic styles. There is a danger that in our desperate search for political and constitutional unity we might create cheap theories, base paperbacks, and dramatic expressions as true representations of our rich, varied, and unique art forms. Nothing could hasten our spiritual death more than to embark upon a popular cowboy-and-Indian or the more recent kung fu culture.

The movies, liquor, and the shotgun have been introduced into our country. In other communities these items have killed off millions. These instruments have resulted in the gradual death of our lives. The Western cloth, the camera, the pen, and the art of writing are now part of our lives. Either we use them to give recognition to our art or we use them to debase and eventually destroy our art.

Our people are slowly becoming awake to the death of their true culture with the introduction of liquor and other items. Will it be too late to salvage our sinking souls?

Art can be a basis for pride in our rich heritage. But it should not be a cheap and popular art that tries to say that all artists are the same anyway. True art should be enjoyed by all. But it is not true art that copies people's masterpieces on to cheap cloth or poor paper. Our art must recognize the uniqueness of each artist. New political or religious movements create an incentive for new art forms. But that art has to be genuine and non-commerical if it is to be worthwhile. Papua New Guinea's political unity has offered, as it will continue to offer, an inspiration for new forms of art. But again it is my hope that this kind of art will be counted for its quality and not for its ready response to political demands.

We have a lot to do. There is still time to do it, but I am afraid too many of us give lip service to this burning cry. We are yet to build our national museum, let alone provincial or communal museums. But we must not rely on the museum to be the caretaker of our art. Ours should be a living and mobile museum.

The Creative Arts Centre needs greater support. It should become the true centre for learning, where old and young artists can meet and communicate through art. It should be the living centre for all the artists of different communities of our country to meet and teach us all about our past. We can no longer be content simply with the idea that the old man will hand down his skills to his sons and daughters. The fact is that the old men and women are dying. The young have other priorities.

Today's generations, today's government, and today's people have an obligation to support genuine efforts to preserve and promote the true art of our people.

The Institute of Papua New Guinea Studies also needs support. There is a burning need to record the dying sounds of our people. There is a great need to photograph and record our architectural styles. Stories, myths, histories, the views of the cosmos, and the entire mystery or knowledge of our lives as our people knew them should be carefully recorded.

In the long run we will be remembered as a people not for how well we mastered the Western or the foreign institutions; nor will we be remembered for how well we consume the seasonal art the Western man is producing and promoting everywhere through radio, television, books, and other printed material.

Our myths, legends, and histories are enough to provide material for millions of novels, comic strips, and cheap films that will make cowboy-and-Indian and kung fu films look unimportant.

However, in my view, the future generations of this country, and of the world, will remember our people for the genuine art they produced and for how well the succeeding generations cared for it and tried to use new forms of expression to give life and meaning to it.

John Waiko

KOMGE ORO: LAND AND CULTURE OR NOTHING

It was exactly eighty years ago in July this year that Binandere, Aega, and other riverine tribes took a political stand to defend their land and forest, water and fish, village and people, and above all the independence of their subsistance life, against the white man and his exploitation in the Northern District of Papua New Guinea. In July 1895 some clans on the central Mamba River killed George Clark, who led a party of miners to the area to exploit gold. Before the year ended other clans had killed three miners on the same river. These killings culminated in January 1896 with a massacre of a Resident Magistrate, John Green, and his entire police detachment.

Within a decade of contact with Europeans, Binandere and others had realized some important implications of the coming of the white man, his rule and his religion. One of these was that the coming of colonialism would undermine the basis of the subsistence way of life with all its ceremonial activities, especially the exchange of vegetables and pigs. It became evident during the second decade following contact that it was futile to fight against colonialism on an individual clan basis. The *Ba* or *Taro* movement started, its leadership across village and clan boundaries. *Ba*, being the main vegetable for living and ceremonial exchange, provided the symbolic basis and the ideology for the people to fight against colonial rule and domination. The main activities of the movement were related

Reprinted from *Gigibori* 3, no. 1 (April 1976): 16-19.

to the planting and harvesting of taro and other vegetables; gardening was to be carried out with the greatest care and attention, and with the genuine application of rituals and magic concerning taro growing. As early as the 1890s Sir William MacGregor had introduced a law stating that the villagers should grow coconut trees for copra. This was intended to push the villagers into a cash economy by establishing coconut plantations. This meant that the basis of living on gardening would have to be distorted or replaced by cash earning. Coconut plantations would also take up land that would have been used for the rotation of gardening within a decade. The *Ba* movement was a direct response to the introduction of a cash economy, where the long-term aim was to replace the subsistence way of life. *Ba* was a political organization whose ideology was based on the traditional society; its members expressed concern over the crops and continued to defend the continuity of subsistence living. The struggle for continuity and maintenance of subsistence independence stemmed from the fact that, without such a basis, cultural and other activities were at the mercy of colonialism. *Ba* provided a political organization on the tribal level, which allowed the people to make a determined effort to fight for their way of life based on the land.

However, the independent and widespread organization of the *Ba* movement threatened the colonial administration. The latter responded with violence against the leaders and the followers of the movement. Binandere lacked an articulate political leadership as a vehicle to make a political protest against the colonial regime and its suppression. There was no concerted effort to unite the people across clan and tribal boundaries, to define the enemy, to advocate militant action and mobilize support to fight for a way of life subsisting off the land. This lack of leadership was partly because of the lack of a central political institution large enough to enlist support from other tribes, and partly because there was no attempt, on the part of the colonial administration, to alienate large tracts of land for plantations, except for acquiring some land for police, port, and mission stations. This meant that the political resistance, as evident at the time of contact and during the *Ba* movement, remained latent for six decades.

The warriors had defended the land with spears, clubs, sticks, and stones. But they fought to protect the land on which the gardens were made to grow taro, bananas, sugar-cane, and various other vegetables; they fought to protect the forest in which animals were abundant and the fish were plentiful in the water — our irreplaceable sources of livelihood. As pointed out, they fought for an independent subsistence way of life. This was the basis on which other cultural and ceremonial activities had to depend for survival, and without which dance drama, feast making, and the idea of communal ownership would fall apart. Once the basis was displaced by other means of living, most cultural activities that were possible as a result of living on the land would inevitably disintegrate, because the land and the forest provided irereplaceable sources of food and meat for livelihood and ceremonial activities.

The ideology of *Komge Oro* is to recognize the basis of independent subsistence with the goal of attaining an improved subsistence society. It is evident from history that *Ba* and other related movements were suppressed, if not destroyed, by the forces of colonialism, and it is likely that neo-colonialists would follow a similar path.

Komge, then, stands for Kunusi, Ope, Mamba. Girs, and Eia rivers and represents those who live along them. *Oro* is a Binandere word for a men's house; it also means a form of welcome in the same language. *Komge Oro* was formed in 1969 but was not registered as a progress association until December 1974. The membership of *Komge Oro* mainly consists of people belonging to the Binandere, Aega, Chiriwa, and Biage tribes. These tribes form the basis of the association.

Komge Oro accepts the subsistence means of living as a basis on which to improve living conditions in the villages. Therefore *Komge Oro* and its members are committed to pursuing cultural, social, and economic activities based on village community initiative, and to developing resources with village leadership. This means that at least the concept of progress as a process of change, and the incorporation of such progress and change, are within the range of control of the people and their lives in the villages.

This concept of progress is far from the intentions of the foreign companies that have tried to exploit human labour and land resources in the Komge area. During 1970-71 a subsidiary of South Pacific Timbers Pty Ltd bought timber rights over a part of the land in the Binandere area. The methods adopted to acquire timber rights were immoral and ill-considered, but it was through the colonial administration that the purchase was made. A helicopter was hired in which officials of the administration and the company flew with three men from only three villages. The flight was organized for the three villagers to mark the traditional land boundaries and for the officials to map the area. Within the same week the officials returned to distribute the cash to those who they thought were the owners of the land. The intention, of course, was to stop the people from raising any objection. This malicious intention aroused a strong suspicion that foreign companies were beginning to alienate land from the people. This alerted the people to be on guard against outside companies. Moreover, many people had asked the educated young men and women to be aware of the intention to alienate land and, if necessary, to organize a campaign against any company, because if the land rights were removed it would be inevitable that the subsistence way of living would disintegrate.

It was to avoid such disintegration, and the possible replacement of independent subsistence, that *Komge Oro* leaders mobilized the owners of land and trees to reject the proposals of a foreign exploitative company during the first half of 1974. Parsons and Whitmore Pty. Ltd was determined to establish a pulp mill in the Toma area to exploit human and timber resources. The total cost of the project was estimated at about $120 million. *Komge Oro* provided the organization and the leadership in leading the people to reject the proposals, and the company withdrew its interest.

The alternative concept of progress of the people in the village differs quite markedly from that of the foreign exploiters. The latter view "development" as creating cash dependence on the part of the people. The villagers regard progress as accepting the subsistence living as a basis and seeking ways and means to earn limited cash to meet a specific need as it arises. The cash earned must not contribute towards destroying that basis, but must support and improve it. Moreover, this concept of progress *does* take into consideration other interrelationships of subsistence living, such as cultural activities in the villages.

There are certain criteria for ceremonial activities in the villages. Feast-making depends upon two of them. One is the number of pigs that one possesses and the other is the amount of vegetables in the garden. When people in the villages achieve the criteria set, they can make feasts and perform dance dramas where pig meat and vegetables are exchanged between one village and another, and between one clan and another clan. This is an important basis for cultural activities in the villages. However, the numbers of pigs raised and the amounts of vegetables grown in the gardens are only sufficient for several villages and a clan; they are not enough for big feasts involving many villages and several clans or even tribes. Therefore *Komge Oro* has started a centre for breeding pigs and poultry, using intensive methods adapted to the village situation. Two men have already graduated from Makana Vocational School near Port Moresby. They have returned to the village to build and run the centre. The aim is to produce animals partly for killing and eating during feasts, partly to make available extra stocks of pigs and poultry to the villge people, and partly for slaughter and sale if there is a big enough surplus.

The other component of feast-making is the growing of vegetables in the gardens. With the absence of able-bodied men there is a lack of labour force in the villages, which results in shortage of food. *Komge Oro* has started organizing village youth clubs whose main purpose is to help in the clearing and planting of gardens. This is to provide labour to make enough large gardens to hold ceremonies not only within a village or a clan but beyond the tribal and indeed the regional level. The purpose is to grow enough food for human beings and animals and still obtain surplus vegetables for feasts and sale.

Komge Oro is committed to supporting subsistence living so that it can be improved to make it self-sufficient as far as possible. This is to aim at an improved subsistence society and not to create a situation that produces impoverished rural peasants without land. Certainly there is a need to experiment, and to develop stocks and crops and indeed techniques that suit the village situation. We realize that there is some value in introducing new techniques to the villages. But more often than not the forms in which such techniques are available to the villager are unpalatable, and in consequence have some undesirable, and in many instances unpredictable, side-effects.

The centre was created because it will have the latitude to experiment with new animals and crops and introduce the successful ones to the villagers. The fact is that the village people are not in a position to experiment, and some even refuse to, on principle. This is because they have suffered much disillusionment with such innovations as cash crops.

The emphasis is placed upon subsistence living as a basis for self-reliance, and the acceptance of cultural activities that are bound up with that way of life. Any other innovation, be it in the form of technology, crops or techniques, must be geared towards supporting and improving the subsistence basis rather than distorting or replacing it with a cash economy. *Komge Oro* intends to promote appropriate technology relating to village situations and requirements, with the aim of training people within the communities in the use and maintenance of such technology, and to set up small village industries. In this context it is necessary to set up village forges and a tool-making centre as a pilot project. *Komge Oro* anticipates that this project will be attached to the centre for breeding pigs and poultry. This would provide a good opportunity to learn various skills related to the making of tools and to try out various small-scale techniques that may suit village needs.

Two of the techniques that are available for self-help schemes in the villages are sugar and soap making. Mr C. Gardener of the Anglican Church has succeeded in developing the manufacture of these products in the Orokaiva and Managalasi areas in the Northern District. Sugar, soap, and tobacco making will be tried for village consumption and sale. Moreover, there is a lot of clay near the proposed centre. It is hoped that the centre will encourage pot making and introduce a pottery wheel and possibly a kiln for the purpose. Other possibilities include growing coconut trees in the villages, rice growing, and fish and eel breeding. These are small-scale ventures arimed at supporting the independence of subsistence and making the villages more self-reliant.

Subsistence living as the backbone of a society would include the concept of encouraging a village barter system, which would pave the way for local markets and the traditional exchange outlets or village ceremonial exchange systems. This would in turn help to develop local markets and contribute towards establishing a network of regional and national trade. Self-help schemes are the basis and the only hope for replacing imported items on the village level. Let it be emphasized that the concern with the issue of some cash markets is, in the main, to make the ventures viable and able to support a limited cash need to improve subsistence living and encourage trade; it is not aimed at the accumulation of profit. *Komge Oro* does not want to push the people into the money economy. Future plans of *Komge Oro* must be geared towards consolidating the independence of subsistence living and at the same time introducing other techniques that will contribute towards improving village conditions. On this basis cultural activities would have a fair chance of survival at the village level.

Bernard M. Narokobi

TOWARDS A MELANESIAN CHURCH

Is it unreal to hold the view that in Papua New Guinea we should work towards a truly indigenous Church? Is it un-Christian to claim that Papua New Guinea does have a view about life that is special, unique, and particularly ours, which the Church should accept in its work of redemption? Is it irrelevant for Papua New Guinea to now claim that some of our cultural practices should become acceptable practices of the Church? And what of theology, that awareness of the Infinite Being? Haven't we Papua New Guineans a view of God that should be preserved and promoted together with the revealed messages of God through Jesus Christ and the prophets?

These are questions I have thought about for many years. My ideas are always growing and developing. In some areas my ideas are always changing. In this article I want to talk about the Christian Church; its past, its present and its future. What has the Church done to our people? What has it done for our people? What have we done for the Church, and what can we do for the Church?

I must make this point very clear. When I talk of the Church in the past I am referring to the priests, brothers, sisters, bishops and the pope in the Catholic Church, and the pastors or ministers in the other Christian churches. Even today, in spite of much propaganda, I still do not feel I am part of the Catholic Church, though I profess all its major doctrines. I will never feel part of the Christian

Reprinted from *Gigibori* 2, no. 1 (April 1975): 37-39.

community of believers until there is more honesty and democracy in the Church.

I feel a personal relationship with God and with Christ. But when it comes to feeling part of the bishops' college or part of the papal parish. I am afraid I feel very far away from them all. At times I feel the priests and the bishops are obstacles to my relationship with God and Christ. I feel they often worry more about building roads, schools, airstrips and hospitals than they worry about the humanity and the dignity of my culture.

I feel they often worry more about the number of persons who attend mass and church than they worry about the quality of Christians and Christian communities. I believe the missionaries worry more about words and sounds than they worry about whether these have any relevance or meaning to my people. With some notable exceptions, bishops appear to me to be more concerned with authority and diplomacy than with actually taking risks supporting those who struggle for peace and justice.

I am always praying to God and to Jesus that nothing will happen to change my faith in his infinite love, mercy and good judgement. However, I am coming more and more to believe that at least the Catholic Church is more legalistic than it is fair to its faithful followers. I am coming more and more to believe that the Catholic Church is more concerned with its universality in the exterior than it is with the universality of the brotherhood and sisterhood of all people.

I am prepared to say that there was a time in history when the Catholic Church was legitimately worried about its survival. I believe that era is gone forever. We must more and more trust in the infinite power of God and Jesus. We must more and more be willing to put on new shirts, different shirts, for different times and different people.

In Papua New Guinea we are burdened with the decisions that were made in Europe. I see no useful purpose in our accepting these decisions. I see the need for diversity in the forms of worship, but I see no need for too many Christian churches in Papua New Guinea.

The Catholic Church throughout the ages has promoted uniformity in forms of worship. In my view this undue emphasis on the external symbolism has resulted in outright subjugation of our traditional forms of worship. It further prevents us from exploring new methods of worship. Today, for example, many Catholics in the East Sepik area feel it's a great shame to sing hymns in the style of their traditional chants.

Far too much is being assumed by the Christian churches. Many of these assumptions have little, if any, relevance to the cultural background of our times. Some, for example, assume Christianity is a culture that is universal and equally applicable in China, New York, England, or Papua New Guinea. I believe this is an erroneous assumption leading to arrogance, imposition, and lack of the necessary dialogue that must exist between all persons, especially the missioners and the "missionized".

Many missionaries assume they are wanted. Some set up parishes and administer them as if they are not living on foreign land. The courage of Christ is being used to spread the good news, but very often it is done with the least possible awareness of the changing needs of our people. It is no wonder that some priests are amazed at the lack of initiative and spontaneity of the people.

The Church, and in particular the Catholic Church, has arrived at a point where no foreign missionary should stay on in a community or parish unless the parish requests his stay. This will necessitate structural changes in some places. No longer should the bishop have all the control. The parish should have a council that takes an active interest in the pastors.

The pastor must, to some extent, depend on the people he or she is serving. The bishop should help believers find new ministers. He should offer counsel and guidance in spiritual matters to ensure that these communities do not depart substantially from the basic doctrines of the faith. Some parishioners should be involved in the recruitment of missionaries from lands that can still supply us with missionaries. Parishes should be organized to enable parishioners to plan how funds are to be raised, to plan priorities, and to spend according to these plans. Our people will not feel the structural Church is their Church until they share in its anxieties, its difficulties, its hopes, and finally its vision for all mankind.

Unless the missionaries readjust their thinking they will find themselves continually in conflict with Papua New Guineans and their changing needs, real or apparent. The missionaries must be able to enter into dialogue with the thinkers, not merely by offering blanket answers such as, "Call in and have a chat with me", but by going out to meet the thinkers, thinking ideas through and being prepared to admit that certain practices of the churches are not essential for human growth.

Papua New Guinea is not a desert without people with cultural beliefs. Papua New Guinea has people who are deeply committed to their own cultural ethics. It follows that, as the Christian Church presses on with its eternal mission of bringing all people to God, it must develop a body of rules enabling it to accept the traditional social behaviour of the local people.

Some examples should highlight my point. When we are baptized at infancy most of us take on a European name. I was given the name of Bernard. Among some people this has resulted in the rejection of traditional names. I see no reason why people should not use their traditional names as baptismal names. It should also be possible for confirmation or baptism to take place at the age of twelve, thirteen, or fourteen to coincide with the traditional age of initiation.

Polygamy and polyandry are acceptable social practices. The practice of having two wives is contrary to Christian ethics. But it should not, in my view, be a basis for preventing people from attending church services or receiving some sacraments such as baptism, extreme unction, and confirmation. I would even go so far as to permit Holy Communion and confession for some people.

The Church could teach one-man-one-wife as the ideal for a perfect Christian in the same way that it teaches that one should not steal. But we know many people do steal. The Church teaches that murder is wrong. But the Church condones killing in a justified war. The Church should accept its progressive role. It is dealing with weak human beings.

We Papua New Guineans traditionally believe in man's totality. Man is body and spirit. Man and woman have spirits. Trees, rocks, animals all have spirits. In some communities there are hierarchies of deities or gods. In my village each clan has a spirit deity, or *Waren*. The whole village also owns a *Waren*. There is a feminine creator called the *Chokek* and the "Above All" called the *Irunin*.

I see no conflict in my professing the divinity of Christ, his sonship to God, and his equality with the Holy Spirit and at the same time believing in my ancestral link with the spirits of the old through *all* times. I do not think that it is in any way less Christian if I offer a sacrifice of, for example, a hen to my ancestral deity, the *Kravan,* in the hope that he might take it and give it to the Lord Jesus, than if I ask St Bernard or the Blessed Virgin to intercede for me.

Sanctity cannot be exclusive to one race of people alone or to one age or era alone. Among God's saints must be some of our ancestors. It follows that if we do not even concede their presence we are killing our ancestral spirits. In this way we kill our earth.

Christianity is two thousand years old. Its divine origin is acknowledged. Christ's guarantee that he will be with the Church until the end of time is recognized. The time has arrived for the Church in Papua New Guinea and elsewhere to concentrate less on legalistic structures and more on democratic approaches. Above all, it must be fully engaged in humanizing and divinizing the earth and its people.

The church and its servants must recapture the vision of its founder. It must outgrow its European historical backgrounds. Certainly for us in Papua New Guinea the Church has no justification in hiding behind the results of the power struggles that went on in Europe and elsewhere.

The present Melanesian Council of Churches (MCC) should develop into the most important national body for Church matters. For the member churches that do not depend on any other outside body for their ultimate authority the MCC should be the final authority. Those churches that surrender decision-making to another authority outside Papua New Guinea should still refer decisions that affect our country to the MCC. The accompanying plan shows the structure.

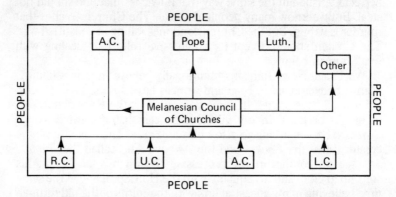

If the Christian Church is to be a living symbol of human unity then it must begin to live that unity. At the moment it presents itself as an instrument of contradition and conflict. Those who profess faith in Christ must organize themselves and offer hope through the way they live their lives. Today's world is suffering from the schisms, divisions and materialism that were a legacy of the eighteenth and nineteenth centuries. There is no reason to accept these as inevitable.

Papua New Guinea offers a hope, perhaps the last hope, that we can do something new, build something new out of the collection of errors and achievements of all the earth since history was recorded. Unless Christianity is able to offer a new hope, man is doomed to place his hope in little men and women who promise, for political gain, to bring peace, justice, and humanity to all men and women already troubled by the released energy on earth.

The future of man should not be placed too much in the hands of a few pious bishops and popes. The future of man must be in the hands of men and women everywhere. Leaders of men and women should first and foremost be men and women of practical vision. They should lead by living with the people, working with them, and slowly leading them to total freedom.

Whilst I am hopeful, I believe God must be getting impatient with men and women on whom He is relying for his radical revolution.

John Kasaipwalova

SOPI

The Adaptation of a Traditional Aesthetic Concept for the Creation of a Modern Art School on Kiriwina

Because our process of Kabisawali is a total movement involving our politics, our economy, our villages, our families, and our persons, we are as a matter of consequence engaged in changing our given historical reality and at the same time attempting to create a cultural environment that is relevant to our present needs. In brief, our movement cuts through the breadth and depth of our society, exploring and harnessing the inevitability of change and forcing upon that change the historical necessity of choice as to which way our actions are to be directed and what kind of a society we are to create. Our Kabisawali therefore includes our movement for cultural development.

By this we do not mean that there is a perfect cultural state already given and towards that we must develop, nor are we saying that our past and present are non-perfect states out of which we must develop. By development we do say, however, that the force of our eyes being opened and understanding our given present prompts us to dig deep into the essences of our past and give them the forms both contemporary and meaningful for us. Take a blind

Discussion paper no. 5, presented at the Institute of Papua New Guinea Studies in 1975.

man and teach him his world by his four other senses then after thirty years give him his sight. By doing so we are saying what we are.

The wider implications of the Kabisawali movement since 1972 have been a revival of traditional ties and simultaneously an accelerated acceptance of change and the inflow of new ideas and non-Kiriwina values. These found expression quite spontaneously in the eighty-five villages of the Trobriand Islands. These cultural resurgences, while all having a tremendous force of enthusiasm, had common weaknesses resulting from the overwhelming pressures of parochial isolation coupled with very limited access to materials and a wider stream of external ideas through which new art forms and self-knowledge could be explored. Artists like Valaosi, Beona, Mawawa, Meyakasa, and Sebwagau sought the assistance, limited though it was, of the Kabisawali Village Development Corporation Ltd. However, that was not enough. The corporation had neither the resources nor the access to the facilities outside the Trobriands. At best it was able to introduce only two artists into the national Centre for Creative Arts at Port Moresby.

Chief Nalubutau, a consultant to us, recognized our problems and kindly made available an area of approximately ten acres around the natural caves of Bweka as land on which to build our own art school, to encourage and assist creative artists from our villages. At the same time our ideas had begun to take shape and expression as we undertook to teach and learn from each other. It is proposed that the name of our art school be Sopi Arts Centre. The following brief notes which are the first articulation of some of our ideas, comprise (*a*) a statement of our general aims, and (*b*) a proposal of a means by which we can contribute towards the general cultural development of Papua New Guinea as well as learn from other people.

Kiriwina traditional culture has its base in subsistence gardening and fishing, the surpluses of both activities being the prime mover of trade and exchange both between the villages and between Kiriwina and the mainland and other islands. Our customs, our architecture, our oral literature, our beliefs, and our value systems are directly rooted in this subsistence agriculture.

The recent pressures of Westernization exerted by missionaries, traders, and administrators have had a shocking effect on our societal cultural expressions. Many of our traditional cultural practices have been forcibly modified or even declared wrong and consequently outlawed. However, while these influences have generally been parasitic, they have not totally uprooted our culture.

Most of our people even now depend on the gardens and fishing for their primary source of livelihood. Consequently, many of our traditional art forms are still perpetuated. But they are being further challenged by newer technological forms of communications and by an educational system that takes more and more of the younger generation away from the villages and places them in wage-earning jobs.

Our cultural development project is not concerned with preserving that traditional cultural base, although we do preserve some aspects of it for the purposes of clarifying and understanding what has been *dimdimed*. While we deny that we are trying to retain our traditional culture at all costs, we affirm at the same time our belonging to this cultural base. We reflect and are part of the contemporary tensions between our traditional cultural base and the force stemming from a completely different cultural base.

Many of our younger artists have been exposed to these new forces through education, and after standard two or three they have returned to their villages to be gardeners and fishermen. A brief look at the historical backgrounds of two of them will reveal that their failure to make the grades and to continue with their education stems from their stronger links with their traditional cultural base. Valaosi, for instance, was penalized for participating in customary rituals regarded as evil by the missionary. Meyakasa survived as far as standard three at Gusaweta but quit because of too much praying.

In a sense, it is natural that a system unsympathetic to our traditional cultural base should cull out those who have strong ties to that base. Those who have survived and maybe "succeeded" have done so at the expense of denying their cultural base. It is not uncommon to see teachers and other public servants wearing sunglasses as big as crocodile eyes and smart socks and shoes looking down on the village drop-outs. Yet the village drop-outs are potentially a very creative force if given the encouragement and the opportunity to express themselves. It would be fruitful for institutions like the national Centre for Creative Arts to be aware of this potential not only in Kiriwina but in other parts of Papua New Guinea. The availability and accessibility of materials and ideas could play an important role in stimulating and fostering a cultural growth from the said traditional cultural base.

Traditional artists, magicians, and their related institutions cannot now survive without some modifications. It is very difficult for those fully immersed in the traditional culture to make these modifications. However, the newer generation, accepting change, has the historical advantage of directly learning from and giving new forms to the traditional culture in a process of growth. We find that our thirst for self-knowledge is leading us to look for tutors from amongst our traditional artists. Valaosi, Meyakasa, and myself, for instance, have begun to learn from Chief Nalubutau. Other prominent traditional artists will undoubtedly provide us with invaluable ideas and knowledge as we begin to build up and explore other fields such as music, dancing, drama, and painting. Already in the field of painting and carving the discovery of new forms of expression and the clarification and expansion of our ideas have been greatly prompted by our understanding of roots within the traditional cultural base. Accepting the challenge of growth and creativity from these roots means, however, breaking through the current over-saturation of the colonial superstructure — through the problem of our immediate colonial cultural confusion.

The recent cultural impact of colonialism has caused confusion. Historically, foreign contact is an integral aspect of Kiriwina society, in particular through the Kula. Kula facilitated a continual process of exchange, inseminating our society with fresh ideas and influences from outside and at the same time disseminating our own identity. The coming of *dimdims,* however, marked the beginning of a period of cultural confusion in which the *dimdim* culture neither enriched the host culture nor allowed itself be enriched by its newly formed contact. For a start, the colonizing *dimdims* were themselves confused. Products of an alienating culture, they reflected the one-dimensional dynamic progression of their industrializing society.

The *dimdims* came with a technology superior to that which they found, and their cultural confusion was based on an assumed sense of being equipped with a superior humanity as well. For us our confusion stems from our overwhelming fear of and amazement at their superior technology, so we mistakenly assumed our own humanity to be inferior. The colonial cultural confusion took root and began an anomalous growth of its own precisely because we failed to contribute in the belief that we had nothing to give, and the *dimdims* failed to receive, in the belief that they had everything to impart and needed nothing from us. Instead of the give-and-take relationships that characterized our foreign contacts through Kula, the colonial contact soon became a force-and-surrender relationship.

When Mesi Moteni arrived with his gang of police led by Kiwiwi and Kimai, he carried out expeditions into the villages using the rhetoric of law and order but practised instilling fear of *gabemani, polisimani,* and power of the gun. Clan obligations, village loyalties, and the prestige of the various chiefs that were the major forces of social law and order were replaced by a pervasive fear of the gun. Subsequent kiaps only reinforced this fear by various acts — summed up rather succinctly by Meyakasa in his woodcut pieces "Waitasui" and "Babadi". These events are now part of our oral history.

Tonugwana and Oada each in his confusion sought to implant a different cult as the essence of Christianity. Methodist and Catholic missionaries pursued bitter and at times open rivalries, and we were fool enough to follow them and accept their confusion as the price for tasting some of their wealth.

The educational system of schools and grades aimed at making young people reject their own cultural base so that they could be fitted into an urban culture or into institutions of the colonialists. Even the recent attempts to balance this only constitute minor tinkering with the total direction. Education provided new skills and exposure to new ideas, but it was also at the same time a major tool for manipulation for confusion — the cultural confusion that is necessary to the growth and success of foreign-interest institutions. We assisted by complying and depending on these institutions.

International cultural contacts are necessary and desirable for our growth and renovation of our society, but they must proceed without the confinement and rigidity we have experienced to date. We seek international contacts in order to gain new techniques and ideas, and these contacts must, like the Kula traditions, form a process of growth and give-and-take to and from our brothers in other communities of Papua New Guinea and beyond.

New techniques and ideas, if not taught from books, grow out of experiential exposure. Creative growth is an expression of a social reality that is original and imaginative — original in the sense that it is rooted in a tradition yet refuses confinement by that tradition, and imaginative in that the hand and the mind create simultaneously. Imagination and originality indicate a tension change and non-change.

In 1968 Yadumwalu, Samugwa, Valaosi, Digilipa, and Mokepwesi of Yalumgwa village carved out of wood their own guitars and ukuleles. They taught themselves to handle the instruments and set about composing their own songs. All of them had dropped out of the local primary school for various reasons and could not afford the instruments (then popular) sold in the trade stores. Their songs and their music were neither traditional nor imported, but their own. During the high political tensions of 1973 they composed at least forty songs all reflecting the contemporary political events.

At about the same time Bulapapa and Yobwita of Kwebwaga village had started experimenting with diverse musical instruments and song compositions. Unfortunately for these artists, their audiences were mainly village people who appreciated the words and the meanings of the songs composed but could not respond to and understand the music. Thus they could not find the necessary social response and criticism to push their skills into newer directions. This response did not come for many of them until teachers and students returning for Christmas vacations demonstrated different styles of handling the instruments.

Valaosi, Meyakasa, and Beona began to experiment with their acquired skills in carving in order to break the heavy deadening pressure of carving for the tourists. Valaosi had his first exposure to the outside world when, late in 1973, he went to the Centre for Creative Arts in Port Moresby for a stay of three months.

Molosi left Hagita High School early in 1974 and was given a scholarship at the Centre to study painting. I attempted to write but found no immediate audience at the village level, so much of my time was better used in communications in the other spheres. Traditional artists like Sebwagau, Nalubutau, and Masawa responded to our requests for tutoring and information. They soon recognized the emergence of our new thinking and began actively to criticize the contemporary expressions. Our first play was performed at Pilaluma on Saturday 18 January 1975, when we sized up our audience with *Sadada Pilaluma Kaboboda* — a group-written play/musical.

Our first attempt to establish cultural links with other communities in Papua New Guinea was with the Boera people during Milamala of 1974. With the assistance of the National Cultural Council, travelling expenses were facilitated. Return visits were made by four of our chiefs to Boera village, and the event became highly publicized among our villages. While our people on both sides were uncertain of "what next", the potential of such a contact was quickly realized by our artists. Creation of a national cultural identity will in the future depend on these direct village-to-village contacts. The rich possible diversity in cross-fertilization has yet to be recognized by our own people.

By 1974 we had begun to form ourselves into a flexible association and had learnt from each other. As we discussed techniques and ideas, we formulated our own conceptions. In

December 1974, Molosi, Meyakasa, Valaosi, and myself inspected the site at Bweka and started clearing for the first building for our art centre. At the time of writing, the first building is nearing completion. Gaiyowa and Talemwa have taken over the construction.

From spontaneous beginnings we have come together and begun formulating ideas of our own. We saw the necessity for an art centre of our own that would be a focal point for us to learn from our own environment and the outside world. We wanted an art centre that would cater for the needs of our own creative people as well as provide facilities for artists wishing to come from other parts of Papua New Guinea and overseas to teach and learn from us.

Sopi and *kwegivayelu* are two terms often used in the appreciation of art works and performances of artists and craftsmen in our society. The same classification can be applied to all fields of art, from carving to music; although different terminologies are used, the value concepts are the same.

It must be pointed out that works of art produced by artists with *sopi* and artists of *kwegivayelu* are all regarded as works of art and are of similar importance. An example that comes to mind is the carving of *luguloguva*. On first impression, comparable pieces strike one as being similar; however, upon closer inspection one can see a radical difference between the work of *sopi* and the work of *kwegivayelu*. *Kwegivayelu* more often reflects perfection of form and content in a given tradition, whereas *sopi* often takes the given tradition and gives it new form and content. Admittedly the distinction presupposes knowledge of the tradition.

The inception of the magic of *sopi* also differs from the inception of *kwegivayelu* magic. *Kwegivayelu* can be instilled into either a child or an adult, whereas *sopi* can only be implanted in a child. With *sopi* there are no subsequent rituals necessary, and the artistic growth coincides with the organic growth of the artist.

Kwegivayelu literally means "voice that follows". An artist of *kwegivayelu* magic, for instance, could see the work of another artist and then go away and after a period of time he could then reproduce what he had seen. *Kwegivayelu* combines technical skills with perception of details. A *kwegivayelu* artist could go down to the beach and listen to the voice of the sea — the sound of waves, wind, and cliff. He could come away from the beach and with his own voice reproduce the voice of the sea. Others listening will hear the voice of the sea; however, it comes from the artist rather than the waves, wind, and cliff.

An artist of *sopi* magic will use the voice of the sea to speak his love, his anger, his fears, his sexuality; in short, he uses the voices of the sea as his medium for communication either with himself or with others.

While an adult can become an artist through the magic of *kwegivayelu* very late in life, a *sopi* artist is an artist because of his reponses to the magic instilled at childhood. *Sopi* artists are often equipped with the various theories of art because a major component of their learning involves the intimate transmission of magic, history, etc., from the adult relative with that knowledge.

My grandfather once said that the biggest qualitative difference between *kwegivayelu* and *sopi* is that the artists of the former magic will only go to either the sea or the caves for inspiration while the latter will go to both and return to the midst of the village surroundings to create.

The sea with its open skies and limitless horizons has always emphasized the bigness of the outside world and consequently the lighted two main problems — the solution of which, we feel, will caves — sources of water that is cool and refreshing, the beginnings of which are mysterious — have made our traditional artists acutely aware of the almost limitless potential in any person. The influences of the sea and the caves are ineffective if not related to the village. In brief, the village is the reality of living and growing with other people.

The school for the *sopi* artists is the seas, the caves, and the village, the sea representing the outside world, the caves representing the subjective human potential, and the village representing the complex of human interrelatedness. While the physical surroundings of our *sopi* arts centre at Bweka provide a beginning point, it is our intention not to confine our practice of the arts to the centre. From our starting point we intend to develop a contemporary cultural environment which appreciates both the traditional Kiriwina base and the new influences from without.

Yolala, or painting, has in the past been closely related to two specific areas, Kula canoes and the houses of chiefs. Technically *yolala* is applied after the carvings have been completed. The three traditional colours used in *yolala* are red, black, and white. While custom restricted popular use of *yolala*, the more common form lies in the *soba*, or body painting.

Both Nalubutau and Kekwabuguyau have contributed much to the development of our ideas in this field, while Martin Molosi quickly adapted new ideas and techniques during his stay at the

Centre for Creative Arts. A student following has begun to build around these three artists and in the future will contribute greatly to the spread of ideas. Already with a wider range of colours and the requirements of new social functions, *yolala* is finding new expressions. For instance, paintings on trucks and buildings have begun to emerge, and with this increasing ability to utilize new materials, the arts of *yolala* and *soba* will undoubtedly extend into the field of textile design and dresswear fashioning.

As stated, he *yowage* arts were practised by a few artists and were limited to the Kula canoes, the yam houses and the *ligisa* of chiefs. Recently, however, carving has become the most popular skill in the Trobriands. It has grown its own anomolous momentum through the demand of tourists for artefacts. The traditional artists have often expressed disgust at the recent trends. Nevertheless, the skills acquired have certainly developed in many directions, but the frustrating pressures of carving for the tourists has meant the removal of much content from carving. The uncritical crassness of the tourists, who either look for "authentic" pieces or fine handiwork, only has caused much confusion.

To counterbalance this trend, Kabisawali embarked on the purchasing of these artefacts with the intention of enforcing some quality control and directing these skills towards a meaningful expression. The degrading pressures of haggling with the tourists over prices has also been the concern of the Kabisawali government.

A rethinking of the role of carving is beginning to develop, and already Meyakasa and Valaosi have expanded upon new ideas through their works. Meanwhile, the Sopi Arts Centre has begun to sponsor our traditional artists to allow them exposure to the outside world. We hope to combine their traditional skills with new ideas to create new forms of *yowaga*. We are considering an exhibition for Valaosi and Meyakasa some time in 1975.

Oral literature has been the most popular art form for passing on legends, history, morals, and social values. As the number of educated people increases, reading and writing will become a major medium of communication. As it stands now, much of the content of reading and writing is from another culture, which seems to be rather sterile and technical.

Our objectives in the field are to communicate with local requirements in Kiriwina and other languages for communicating with the outside. Our literary ideas are being developed and it is hoped that some of our works will be published.

At present literary ideas from *yosokana, kwanebu,* and *wosi* are being explored, and the current activities involve mainly two areas — one dealing with the collection and translation of our given tradition and the other the involvement of development of individual writers.

In the field of music, our experiments with theatre and general discussions on music as a communications medium have highlighted two main problems — the solution of which, we feel, will give expansion to our ideas on music of our own. Traditional musical instruments included *kesosau* (drums) and *pegolela* (flute). The forms of music that have evolved with the traditional usage of these instruments spoke and reflected a cultural reality that is no longer the same today. That traditional form has therefore a rigidity of its own which constrains responsiveness to our present. There is no reason why this rigidity cannot be broken to allow the imprisoned musical potential to flourish outwards freely. This enclosed rigidity, being the first of the two problems immediately confronting us, is further compounded by the pervasiveness and intensity of radio music.

Radio music makes most of the educated young people want to play guitars and ukuleles without showing them how. It also subtly projects the "Hawaiian style" and the tourist image of the "South Pacific musical style". Central District guitarists and song composers perhaps are among the first to be intensely influenced by these, and their products in turn were copied by many outside the Central District, mainly through radio broadcasts. The rigidity of the forms of the radio music is not surprising, and this makes it very difficult for a virile musical expression to flow forth. Instead, radio music has created duplications and imitations — the consequence of which is a music of depressed melancholy. It is not difficult to see this characterized by the "*lalokau*" songs. Full of self-pity and feelings of helplessness.

Our modest experiments with flutes, guitars, and drums betokens a tremendous potential. Unless Yobwita and Bulapapa receive the encouragement, the present experiment may not develop. Recently Bulapapa has suggested a combined orchestra of traditional and non-traditional instruments for a new *kesawaga*.

Glossary

ANGAU	Australian New Guinea Administrative Unit
baal	string apron
bilas	finery, ornaments, decoration
boi	labourer or servant, regardless of age
boi house (haus boi)	labourers' quarters
bosboi	overseer
buai	betel-nut
dimdim	European
gabemani	government
garamut	wooden signal drum; slit gong
haus tambaran	ancestral spirit house; men's ceremonial house
kambang	lime chewed with betel-nut
karuka, kaukau	sweet potato
kiap	patrol officer
kundu	drum
lusman, lusmeri	drifter, loose person (male and female)
Mally Bulla	Maryborough (Queensland)
mangi	usually spelt " *manki* " — child
maski	never mind, it doesn't matter, who cares?
masta	master, European
maus wara	a good talker
meri	woman, girl, wife
misinari	missionary
moka	pig exchange feast in the Western Highlands
pamuk	harlot
pasim maus	shut up!
pekpek	excrement

pekpek house (haus pekpek)	lavatory
PMV	"Public Motor Vehicle" — any commercial passenger truck
polisimani	policeman
rabis	poor, downtrodden, worthless, useless
raus!	get out!
singsing	festival with dancing; singing, song
skin diwai	back of a tree
tanget	shrub whose leaves are used for, among other things, covering the buttocks in the Highlands
tasol	that's all; only, alone, just; but, however
tok ples	local language, mother tongue
uroh	great thanks
wanpis	alone, without relatives, an orphan, without a mate
wantok	one who speaks the same language, friend, neighbour, fellow countryman

Notes on Contributors

Ulli Beier was director of the Institute of African Studies in the University of Ife, Nigeria, from 1971 to 1974 and director of the Institute of Papua New Guinea Studies from 1974 to 1978. He has founded several literary and cultural magazines: *Odu,* a journal of Yoruba studies; *Black Orpheus,* a journal of African literature; *Kovave,* a journal of New Guinea writing; and *Gigibori,* a journal of Papua New Guinea cultures. He has been associated with two Nigerian theatre groups and taught creative writing at the University of Papua New Guinea.

Nora-Vagi Brash is currently working for the Papua New Guinea Teachers' Association. She has been an actress in the National Theatre Company and has written several plays, two of which were produced by the National Theatre Company and on the National Broadcasting Commission network. She is a native of Kilakila village, near Port Moresby, and is married to Elton Brash, who teaches literature at UPNG.

Iriye Diaya is a subsistence farmer in Koali Lomba village. He has had no Western schooling and sees himself as a traditional story-teller. "A Successful Marriage at Last" is the only one of his stories that has so far been transcribed and translated.

Arthur Jawodimbari is director of the National Theatre Company. He was one of the most prolific playrights in the late sixties and early seventies, but his time has recently been taken up with administrative work and play production.

John Kasaipwalova is one of Papua New Guinea's most brilliant writers and thinkers. He gave up his university studies in order to create a grass-roots political and cultural movement (Kabisawali) in his native Trobriand Islands. Although the movement was initially highly successful, it ran into considerable opposition from more conservative groups on the island and also from the central government in Port Moresby. John Kasaipwalova was accused of misappropriating a cultural grant given to him by the National Cultural Council and was sentenced to serve two years in jail. He ultimately won his appeal, but only after spending eight months in jail. He emerged from the experience without any bitterness and is currently planning to start a fishing business in Lae.

Kama Kerpi is a graduate from the University of Papua New Guinea. He carried out an extremely interesting study of the peace-making processes employed in his native Chimbu area. He was subsequently involved in bringing hostile parties together during actual clan fights in Chimbu. He has written a play, *Voices on the Ridge,* which was performed by the National Theatre Company.

John Kolia is a naturalized citizen of Papua New Guinea. He is deputy director of the Institute of Papua New Guinea. He received his doctorate from UPNG with a thesis on the oral history of the Balawaia people of the Rigo district. Has published two novels, *The Late Mr Papua* and *A Compulsive Exhibition.* Two more novels are forthcoming. John Kolia has written numerous radio plays, fifteen of which have been performed by the National Broadcasting Commission.

Bernard Narokobi is chairman of the Law Reform Commission, chairman of the board of trustees of the Papua New Guinea Museum, and a leading member of the National Cultural Council. He has also written plays, one of which, *Cry of the Cassowary,* was performed by students of the University of Papua New Guinea. He is the leading proponent of the philosophy of the "Melanesian Way", which could be called Papua New Guinea's equivalent to Senghor's "negritude". He writes a weekly column in the *Papua New Guinea Post-Courier* on questions of cultural identity and has contributed widely to scholarly magazines.

Hengenike Riyong was trained at Teachers' College, Goroka. He worked for a while with the Raun Raun Theatre in Goroka before he became a teacher at Chuave High School.

Somu Sigob was a security officer in the UPNG library when he died in 1975. He has never written anything, and the colourful account of his life included here was spoken on tape for students of the History Department at UPNG.

Jacob Simet is a research fellow in the Institute of Papua New Guinea Studies. He is currently on leave of absence with the ANU in Canberra in order to work for a masters degree. Jacob Simet wrote poetry in the early seventies, but has recently turned his energies to scholarly work.

Russell Soaba is currently a research fellow in folklore at the Institute of Papua New Guinea Studies. He has been one of the country's most consistent writers since the late sixties. His novel *Wanpis* is to be published by the Institute of Papua New Guinea Studies. He has published numerous short stories and several plays. His plays have been performed by the National Theatre Company, by the NBC, and by students of the university.

Michael Thomas Somare is Papua New Guinea's first prime minister, currently serving his second term. He has shown great interest in all cultural matters and has given consistent support to the arts in Papua New Guinea.

Kundapen Talyaga is a research worker in the Institute of Applied Social and Economic Research in Port Moresby. He has produced excellent trnaslations of his native Enga poetry and has written articles on cultural issues.

Kumalau Tawali was the first Papua New Guinean to have a volume of poetry published (*Signs in the Sky*); A second volume of poems is forthcoming. One of his early plays was performed by the Prompt Theatre in Canberra. He is currently a teaching fellow in the Literature Department of UPNG.

Albert Toro is a member of the National Theatre Company. *The Massacre* is his first play.

John Waiko was one of the most dynamic and influential writers in the late sixties and early seventies. His play *The Unexpected Hawk* made a considerable impression when it was first performed in Port Moresby by students of UPNG. The play was also produced by Al Butavicius for the Prompt Theatre in Canberra. John Waiko is currently working for his doctorate in history at the Australian National University.